Sustainable Business Model Innovation

Inspiring the Next Game: Strategy Ideas for Forward Looking Leaders

BCG Henderson Institute

Sustainable Business Model Innovation

Edited by
David Young and Martin Reeves

DE GRUYTER

ISBN 978-3-11-129489-6
e-ISBN (PDF) 978-3-11-129526-8
e-ISBN (EPUB) 978-3-11-129595-4
ISSN 2701-8857

Library of Congress Control Number: 2023940495

Bibliographic information published by the Deutsche Nationalbibliothek
The Deutsche Nationalbibliothek lists this publication in the Deutsche Nationalbibliografie;
detailed bibliographic data are available on the internet at http://dnb.dnb.de.

© 2023 The BCG Henderson Institute
Cover image: Hybert Design
Typesetting: Integra Software Services Pvt. Ltd.
Printing and binding: CPI books GmbH, Leck

www.degruyter.com

Acknowledgments

We would like to acknowledge all of the authors whose work appears on the following pages: Douglas Beal, Simon Beck, Kilian Berz, Katherine Brown, Veronica Chau, Bryann DaSilva, Julia Dhar, Robert Eccles, Maha Eltobgy, Tian Feng, Jack Fuller, Marine Gerard, Gerardo Gutiérrez-López, Rich Hutchinson, Madeleine Michael, Benedicte Montgomery, Annelies O'Dea, Ulrich Pidun, Sana Rafiq, Martin Reeves, Massimo Russo, Vinay Shandal, Ron Soonieus, Sonia Tatar, Leonore Tauber, Konrad von Szczepanski, Judith Wallenstein, Mark Wiseman, Wendy Woods, David Young, Balázs Zoletnik.

We would also like to acknowledge the broader BCG Henderson Institute community: our Fellows, Ambassadors, and operations teams over the years, who have all made invaluable contributions to our research; our academic collaborators, who have expanded our horizons of new ideas; and our BCG practice area partners, who have collaborated with us on several of these articles.

https://doi.org/10.1515/9783111295268-202

About the BCG Henderson Institute

The BCG Henderson Institute is the Boston Consulting Group's think tank, dedicated to exploring and developing valuable new insights from business, technology, economics, and science by embracing the powerful technology of ideas. The Institute engages leaders in provocative discussion and experimentation to expand the boundaries of business theory and practice and to translate innovative ideas from within and beyond business.

https://doi.org/10.1515/9783111295268-203

Contents

Part 3.3: **Link to Value Drivers of the Business**

Part 3.4: **Enable Systems Level Strategy**

Part 4: **Conclusion**

David Young and Martin Reeves
Introduction
The Why, What, and How of Sustainable Business Model
Innovation

Introduction

This book explores the *why, what,* and *how* of sustainable business model innovation (SBM-I) —a new method by which corporations can optimize for both business and social value using their core businesses to deliver the financial returns expected by their owners and, in tandem, to help society meet its most significant challenges. At the BCG Henderson Institute we have examined hundreds of business models to develop a systematic approach for reimagining business models for economic and social sustainability, creating new modes of differentiation and advantage, embedding societal value into products and services, managing new performance measures, and reshaping business ecosystems to support these initiatives. While reimagining business models is a tall order for any management team, particularly during disruptive change, the following compilation of articles —originally published between 2019 and 2023—offers inspiration and guidance to create more competitive and sustainable companies. The company's future, our environment, and society depend on doing so.

Part 1 presents *why* SBM-I should be pursued. We explore how the wider context for business is fundamentally changing and the imperative to systematically understand the sustainability limits, vulnerabilities, opportunities, and potential of the company's current business models and ecosystems to avoid limiting its future competitiveness, license to operate, growth, and shareholder returns. We explain why few business models today deliver both competitive advantage and create positive environmental and societal value. We then discuss the implications for setting strategy, building business plans, measuring performance, and leading change.

Part 2 describes *what* SBM-I is and offers a rigorous way to assess a business model for its robustness and resilience and the footprint of its environmental and societal impact. In a sample of more than 500 corporate sustainability initiatives, we discover that only one in five qualify as SBM-Is; they explicitly connect positive environmental and societal outcomes to drivers of competitive advantage and value creation. We then identify the leaders, just one in three, those stretching the scope of business model innovation and changing the bases of competition. Fewer still create differentiated and scaled positive impacts on emissions or other externalities matching the capacities and scale of the business to do so. In-

https://doi.org/10.1515/9783111295268-001

terestingly, we find that SBM-I Is in every industry, geography, big incumbents, and new disrupters. We also identify ten specific archetypes of SBM-I, building blocks of business model innovation, with distinct implications for the robustness and resilience of the business model, the way the company competes, and the environmental and societal value it creates.

Part 3 explains *how* to execute SBM-I. We outline a four-step innovation cycle that begins with expanding the business canvass by mapping the ecosystem and its stakeholder dynamics, applying scenarios for possible futures, then using both to stress-test the current business model and gain insight into its vulnerabilities, failure points, and opportunities. We then show how the second step applies SBM-I building blocks in combinations to innovate the business model's robustness, resilience, and environmental and societal benefits footprint. The third step then evaluates the required investments and resulting economics. Steps two and three are iterative to optimize the business model for both business and societal value, which is then operationalized and scaled in step four into a fully competitive SBM-I. We also explore how a company scales its SBM-I to both accelerate the company's business advantage and shape the company's broader ecosystem to account for the scarcities in inputs or gaps in the business ecosystem needed to help achieve its SBM-I. Often collective action is necessary to ensure the infrastructure and environment required for its sustainability and that of its industry and value chain. We illustrate how a company can apply a combination of partnerships, sustainability business ecosystems, and corporate-led sustainability alliances to work around market and capability limitations, accelerate transitions, and reshape ecosystems for sustainability. We conclude Part 3 by illustrating the remarkable opportunities for innovation, advantage, value creation, and impact by winning through the great climate upheaval. Companies embracing the challenge will drive innovation throughout their business models, value chains, and ecosystems.

The decade ahead offers a historic opportunity to boldly reimagine businesses for sustainable value creation and a sustainable world. We hope that this book will provide some insight and inspiration into how to become a pioneer in doing so.

Part 1: **Why Business Needs Sustainable Business Model Innovation**

David Young, Wendy Woods, and Martin Reeves

1 Optimize for Both Social and Business Value

As we approach a new decade, we are also approaching *a tipping point for business*, with new benchmarks for what constitutes a good company, a good investment, and a good leader. The defining expectation: good companies and investments will deliver competitive financial returns while helping society meet its biggest challenges, and in so doing will enable sustainable business.

Building Resilient Businesses, Industries, and Societies

Leaders with foresight and courage will use this dynamic to create new opportunities for growth, sustained returns for shareholders, and greater societal impact. To do this, they will need to think in new ways, create new modes of competitive advantage, pursue deep and *broad business model innovation*, and engage strategically with ecosystems. They must merge the two currently disconnected uses of the "S-word" in business: sustainability and sustainable competitive advantage.

The implications for companies, capital, and capitalism are profound. Here, we share our take on the emerging era of business value, and the chief executive officer (CEO) agenda for value and the common good.

Why is Corporate Capitalism at a Tipping Point?

Stakeholders are beginning to pressure companies and investors to go beyond financial returns and take a more holistic view of their impact on society. This should not surprise us. After all, we have lived through two decades of hyper-transformation, during which *rapidly evolving digital technologies, globalization, and massive investment flows have stressed and reshaped every aspect of business and society.*

As in previous transformations, the winners created new dimensions of competition and built innovative business models that increased returns for shareholders. Many others found their businesses at risk of being disrupted, with familiar formulas no longer working. To meet the unwavering demands of Wall

https://doi.org/10.1515/9783111295268-002

Street, many companies relentlessly optimized operating models, streamlined and concentrated supply chains, and specialized their assets and teams—leaving them less resilient and less adaptable to shifting markets and trade flows. The resulting waves of corporate restructuring, consolidation, and repositioning have fractured companies' cultures and undermined their social contracts.

Furthermore, this hyper-transformation cascaded beyond individual companies and created socio-economic dynamics that left many people and communities economically disadvantaged and politically polarized. Combined with the increasing shared anxiety that Earth's climate is changing at a faster rate than the planet can adapt to, a global zeitgeist of risk and insecurity has emerged. As we enter the 2020s more citizens, investors, and leaders are convinced that the way business, capital, and government work must change—and change quickly.

We now must rethink the sustainability of the whole system in the face of extreme externalities—or risk losing social and political permission for further progress. The 2030 UN Sustainable Development Goals (SDGs) identify the moral and existential threats that we must meet head-on. While some question the breadth and timeline of the SDGs, most agree that, if achieved, they would create a more just, inclusive, and sustainable world. Goal 17 calls for new engagement by companies and capital in partnership for collective action across the public, social, and private sectors. Five years into the SDG agenda, there is ample evidence that governments, investors, and companies are beginning to exercise their capacity to create much-needed change.

Change is Underway but is Hardly Sufficient

Many institutional investors are integrating ESG (environmental, social, and governance) assessments into their decision making, and they are expecting companies to report on how they deliver on those metrics. New efforts promote radical disclosure, like the Bloomberg/Carney TCFD (Task Force on Climate-related Financial Disclosures), which encourages signatories to report on the climate risks of their financial holdings. New standards initiatives are creating a foundation for nonfinancial performance accounting, and the prospect of widespread "integrated reporting" seems realistic. Companies are investing in "purpose" and defining their contributions to society against material ESG factors and SDG goals. Corporate sustainability and CSR (corporate social responsibility) functions, historically on the sidelines, are now being integrated into line business activity, with progressive companies expanding the scope of competition to include differentiation on environmental and societal dimensions. And through industry consortia, many companies are taking collective action on issues that both threaten their right to operate and open up new opportunities for their industries.

Such examples are important early signals that the context for business is changing. However, for all the progress on commitments, agreements, metrics, and policies, there has been little aggregate progress against top-level goals, like reducing CO_2 emissions, cutting plastics waste, or narrowing social and economic inequality within nations. Without demonstrable impact and collective progress, social and political pressure will only build, further threatening the legitimacy of corporate capitalism.

A New Societal Context for Business

Companies will face escalating social activism by investors, stakeholders, social mission organizations, and policymakers on issues of climate risk, economic inequality, and societal well-being. Governments and local communities will set a higher bar for a company's right to operate, and in a connected world a company's local performance will quickly affect its global reputation and trigger social and regulatory consequences. Stakeholders will expect radical transparency on ESG performance. This will shift investors' perceptions of a company's risk and opportunity, skewing capital toward those that deliver both financial returns and positive societal impact. To satisfy a growing demographic of socially minded consumers and businesses, companies will need to demonstrate "good products doing good" and anchor their brands and identity around a credible purpose. Talent will gravitate toward companies that give employees a line-of-sight to making the world better while also providing a fulfilling career.

To win, companies will need to define competition more broadly, adding new dimensions of value through environmental sustainability, holistic well-being, economic inclusion, and ethical content. This will require radical business model innovation to enable circular economies for precious resources; to provide assets that are shared rather than owned; to broaden access and inclusion; and to multiply positive societal impact.

At this critical moment for corporate capitalism, business is more trusted than government, according to the Edelman Trust Barometer. Farsighted corporate leaders will see the opportunity for their industries to mitigate environmental and societal threats, catalyze collective action to discover new solutions, shape wider ecosystems, and expand trust with stakeholders. Such actions will be indispensable to *strengthen social permission for corporate capitalism* before it is further undermined.

Management will Need a Value and Mission Mindset

As in previous transformative eras for business, it will take a shift in managerial mindset to unlock new ways to win. We need a fundamental rewiring of managerial imagination and decision making, underpinned by an equation for corporate value that goes well beyond delivering a predictable profit and loss (P&L) and a steady dividend stream.

The starting point is to instill an inspiring purpose that captures the broader ambition of the business beyond profit and gives employees meaning in their daily work. *"Purpose" should not be a comforting and self-congratulatory statement of what the company already does,* however—that would be an impediment to progress. Rather, it should define the aspirational societal contribution of a company based on its unique attributes, and inspire awareness of the broader context and progress toward business and societal value.

Armed with purpose, leaders can promote a culture of curiosity and courage to stretch their business models in new ways, into their surrounding economic, environmental, and societal ecosystems. Knowing that such transformative thinking can be impeded by traditional metrics, which only tell us how to ascribe value, farsighted leaders will work to change what we value. They will break from the tyranny of quarterly financial reporting by engaging investors and stakeholders in the company's performance against a more balanced scorecard, demonstrating how their actions will transform the business model, better positioning the company to deliver returns and societal impact over time. They will think beyond designing their operations and organization mainly for efficiency, and thoughtfully engineer-in redundancy, diversity, and flexibility for more resilience and adaptability. And they will enrich their decision making by including staff with nontraditional business skills.

Success in the coming decade will take management teams that both know the business and envision its larger potential to compete differently, with benefits for both shareholders and the common good.

CEOS Need an Agenda for Value and the Common Good

We frame the journey to new corporate value and the common good around six imperatives. It begins with reimagining corporate strategy, then involves transforming the business model, reframing performance and scorekeeping, leading a purpose-filled organization, practicing corporate statesmanship, and elevating governance (see Figure 1.1). While challenging to execute, we argue that this agenda will be essential to create a great company, a great stock, a great impact, and a great legacy.

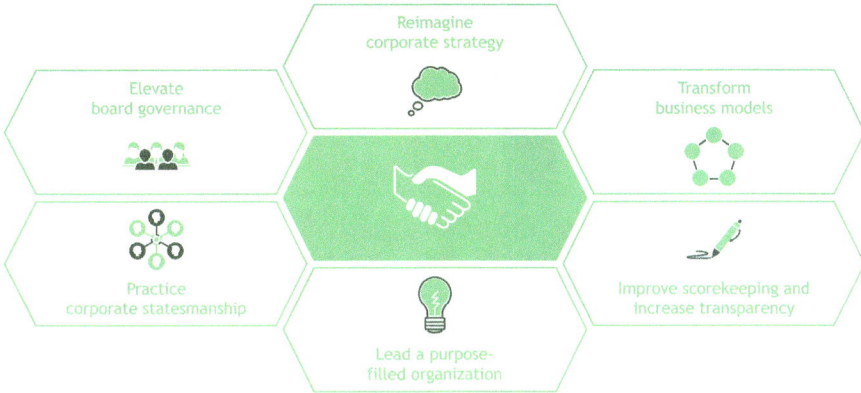

Source: BCG

Figure 1.1: An agenda for value and the common good.

Reimagine Corporate Strategy

We believe few companies have strategies for this new era of business. Figure 1.2 illustrates the ambition of such a strategy, which establishes *competitive advantage at the intersection of shareholder value, corporate longevity, and societal impact.* The "quality" of the strategy is thus judged by how it delivers both total shareholder returns and total societal impact.

Consequently, it widens the scope of competition to encompass creating rich differentiation and relative advantage in multiple areas of societal value. It embeds "social value" into new business constructs, shared value chains, and reconstructed ecosystems. It also opens, broadens, and deepens markets to enable access and inclusion. And it expands the scope of business by calling for coalitions for collective action that address existential risks to environmental and societal ecosystems (see Figure 1.3).

This new type of strategy flips leadership's perspective from "company-out" to "societal needs-in," by asking how a specific SDG target could be met by extending the company's capabilities, assets, products, services, and ecosystem—and those of its industry. Figure 1.4 lists ten questions that strategists should incorpo-

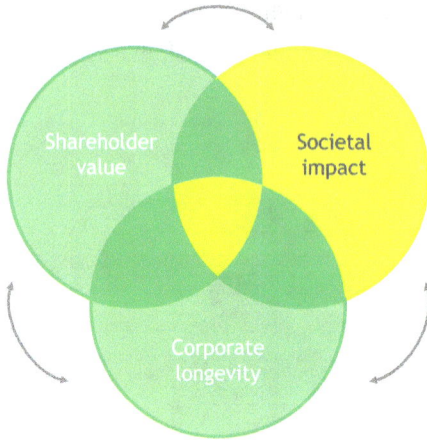

Source: BCG analysis

Figure 1.2: Corporate strategy cannot separate social impact from the business.

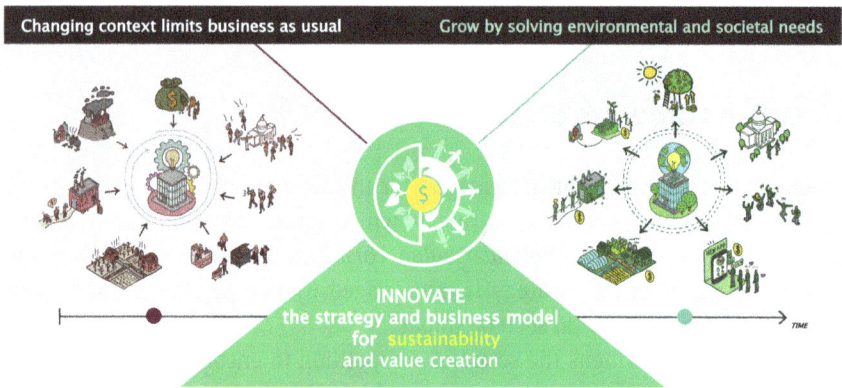

Figure 1.3: Winning in the '20s demands innovation for both business and societal value.

rate into their strategy processes to ensure that they embrace the opportunity to create both shareholder returns and societal impact.

However, these new strategies cannot simply be grafted onto existing business models. Business models themselves will need to be transformed. Sustainable business model innovation (SBM-I) takes a much wider perspective than traditional business model innovation by considering a broader set of stakeholders; the system dynamics of the socio-environmental context; longer time horizons for sustaining adaptable advantage; the limits of business model scale, viability,

1 Does our purpose lead to sustainable value creation? Is our self-interest aligned with social value?

2 Are we "on purpose" and, if not, are we taking corrective action accordingly?

3 Are those actions sufficient in impact and speed?

4 Are we defining the boundary of what we measure and manage appropriately?

5 Are other stakeholders represented in or part of our strategy process?

6 Are we measuring the long-term competitiveness of the business? Have we balanced the present and the future?

7 Where does our business model fail first as a result of ESG-related risks?

8 How will we address this weakness with sustainable business model innovation?

9 Do we have the right collective-action platforms to address pressing problems?

10 Are we exercising corporate statesmanship to effect external change?

Source: BCG

Figure 1.4: Ten questions for strategists in a new era of business.

and resilience; the cradle-to-grave production and consumption cycle; and the points of leverage for profitable and sustainable transformation.

Transform Business Models

We can already observe ten topologies for sustainable business model innovation, sometimes in combination, all with the potential to increase both financial returns and societal benefits.

– **Own the origins.** Compete on capturing and differentiating the "social value" of inputs to production processes, products, or services. For example, pursue cleaner energy, sustainable practices, preserved biodiversity, recycled content, inclusive and empowering work practices, minimized waste, digitized traceability, fair trade, and so on. Performance here will require differentially advancing the societal performance of the supplier base and its stewardship of resources, communities, and trade flows. Achieving this may require backward integration to ensure fast and complete upstream transformation and then holding and using these new capabilities for competitive advantage and differentiation.

– **Own the whole cycle.** Compete by creating societal impact through the whole product usage cycle, from creation through end of life. This competitive typology puts a wide aperture on the business and requires systems analysis to uncover business models that offer the richest competitive and financial options. For example, designing for circularity, recyclability, and waste to value; creating offerings that enable sharing rather than owning to ensure high utilization of resources and end-of-life value; constructing infrastructure to facilitate circularity and repurposing; integrating into other value chains to capture societal value; educating and enabling consumers to choose whole-cycle propositions on the basis of value to people and planet. To achieve these ends, expect to reposition operations, reinvent supply chains and distribution networks, pursue new backward or forward integration, acquire business adjacencies, or undertake unconventional strategic partnering.

– **Expand "social value."** Compete by expanding the value of products or services on six dimensions: economic gains, environmental sustainability, customer well-being, ethical content, societal enablement, and access and inclusion. Then advocate new standards, increase transparency and traceability, tune marketing and segmentation, engage customers on the product's wider value and their involvement in bigger change, and seek premium pricing. In business-to-business offerings, help customers integrate the full social value of your products, services, and business model into their own differentiation and ESG ambitions.

– **Expand the chains.** Compete by extending the company's value chain, layering onto other industries' value chains to extend the reach of your products and services and the societal impact for both parties, while changing the economics and risks of doing so. For example, use the reach of a consumer products distribution system to extend payments and financial services to small merchants; layer one company's health services onto another company's physical supply chain to benefit its workers and their families while expanding markets for health services; or use the byproducts of one company's operations as feedstock in other companies' value chains.

– **Energize the brand.** Compete by digitally encoding, promoting, and monetizing the full accumulated social value that is embedded in products and services, along the whole value chain—from origins to customer, from cradle to grave. Use such data to rethink differentiation, the brand experience, customer engagement, pricing for value, ESG reporting, investor engagement, and even potential new businesses. For example, strengthen the brand with promotions that showcase the business's performance on the open, clean, green, renewable, and inclusive attributes of its operations; and increase customer engagement and loyalty by using data on the product's environmental and societal footprint to empower customers in choosing how their lifestyle affects the planet and its people.

– **Nudge sustainable consumption.** Apply technology for behavioral insights and economics to nudge and enable consumers to make more sustainable choices in ways that propel the portfolio. Fairphone is a Dutch social enterprise, which is reimagining the consumer electronics business model to produce and sell a more ethical and durable smartphone. The Fairphone is composed of sustainable materials, including responsibly sourced and conflict-free tin and tungsten and recycled copper and plastics; it has a modular design that can be upgraded and repaired by swapping out components. When customers go to purchase, the default excludes items most customers already own like chargers and cords, and includes a "nudge" to recycle their phone. The company also has a cradle-to-grave phone leasing model to recover and reuse old devices.

– **Decarbonize for advantage**. Compete by differentially decarbonizing operations and products/services faster and deeper than competitors, and capture value in sourcing, pricing, market share, and loyalty. This requires companies to go above and beyond incremental changes, and use decarbonization as the mechanism for advantage. For example, decarbonize operations to produce a low-carbon commodity—like cement or steel—and command a green premium from conscious purchasers. Or create a new product or offering that reduces downstream emissions, helping customers lower emissions from their own operations.

– **Exploit energy flexibility**. Compete by engineering operating and ecosystem energy/power supplies to take advantage of volatility in energy source pricing and capacity for advantage in energy costs and mix. This is more than typical demand response; by treating assets like real options as an asset-backed commodity trader would, companies can harness price volatility driven by renewables penetration while also improving resilience to shocks. Find the hidden flexibility in existing assets. Invest in reconfiguring assets to make consumption of energy more flexible—for example through new technologies or equipment upgrades. Unlock flexibility in upstream and downstream processes. Design new assets to have inherent physical flexibility.

– **Relocalize and regionalize**. Compete by contracting and reconnecting global value chains to bring societal benefits closer to home markets in ways stakeholders value. For example, build local and regional brands that better express local tastes and values; source from smaller local producers to minimize logistics emissions and strengthen local economies; reimagine production networks against total environmental and societal costs; capture local waste streams as feedstocks for other activities; or reconstitute jobs for microwork to use local talent.

– **Build across sectors**. Compete by creating models that include the public and social sectors to improve the company's business and societal proposition, particularly in emerging and rapidly developing economies. For example, work alongside governmental bilateral aid institutions and non-governmental organization (NGO) development organizations to improve the agricultural capacity of small farmers so they become reliable sources of agricultural inputs to the agro-processing value chain; partner with global environmental organizations and governments to promote the reuse of ocean plastics as feedstocks to production systems; partner with governments to strengthen social safety nets and prevent corruption through digitization and electronic payments; or partner across sectors to restructure recycling systems to enable higher penetration of waste-to-value business models. Extend this into industry coalitions for collective action that reshape broader rights to operate and generate new opportunities.

These archetypes often work in combination—like building blocks—all with the potential to increase both financial returns and societal benefits. All create new sources of differentiation, operating advantage, network dynamics, and societal value—enabling more durable and resilient businesses that benefit shareholders and society. But to assess and improve the performance of these business models and communicate their value, we need to expand today's scorecards.

Improve Scorekeeping and Increase Transparency

Managers will need new scorecards for a fuller equation of business value to assess and reward performance and inform decision making. While today's ESG measures are a start, their use and the mindset they represent, as for most nonfinancial reporting, remain anchored in compliance, not business advantage. Consequently, scorecards and reporting must go beyond mapping general ESG materiality. Instead, they should focus the business and its stakeholders on insightful metrics that directly connect the company's unique purpose and business models to the way the company creates differentiated value and societal impact—its full business value (FBV).

These metrics will assess performance throughout the value chain—from procuring inputs, to owning the post-use cycle, to establishing the company's full societal footprint. As with financial performance, good companies will integrate these metrics into their managerial software—operating plans, target setting, investment decisions, executive compensation, and employee recognition. Further, the company will promote radical transparency of its FBV scorecards, fully reflecting them in investor relations and corporate communications, quarterly calls, and annual meetings, and making them integral to marketing, social media, public relations, and government affairs. As a result, stakeholders will see the company in new ways and its advantages relative to peers on new dimensions.

Lead a Purpose-Filled Organization

Talent prizes purpose. Consequently, winning and engaging the best talent depends on reinforcing a motivating purpose that captures ambitions beyond profit and gives employees meaning in their work. Research shows that companies with a motivating purpose have higher employee engagement, and that higher engagement correlates to better financial performance. So purpose is a win for recruiting employees with "mission-mindedness" and enhancing the organization's energy and performance.

But building a stronger organization will take rethinking the skills and capabilities that can truly differentiate performance on both financial and societal metrics. The organization can no longer delegate sustainability and social responsibility to individual departments; rather, those considerations need to be fully integrated into operations and decision making. That requires augmenting line businesses with nontraditional business skills—finding people capable in systems thinking, anthropology, social dynamics, behavioral economics, sustainability, and development policy.

Those workers will become part of agile teams that conceive innovative operating models optimized for both operational effectiveness and societal benefit within value chains, markets, and customer segments. That requires developing and rewarding new ways of working that are more flexible, embedding rapid cycles of learning and deployment, and reaching into the wider business and societal ecosystem to create positive change and performance. Successes in doing so create the stories that bring purpose alive for the organization and energize its culture.

Practice Corporate Statesmanship

It will take the scale and capacity of entire industries and their ecosystems to help solve society's biggest challenges, such as reducing plastic and food system waste. Thus, farsighted leaders will turn threats to their industry's right to operate into opportunities for reinvention and expansion. Rather than ignoring these risks or mobilizing their government affairs groups to block change, *they will instead practice strategic statesmanship* and build coalitions for collective action within their industry, and sometimes across industries, to find and scale new solutions.

As in their own companies, they will articulate a compelling purpose and vision for how the industry and ecosystem could expand the total value delivered to society, while ensuring the industry's longevity, profitability, and resilience. They will promote platforms that foster pre-competitive research and development (R&D), scale solutions, expand access and inclusion, accelerate industry learning and standards, and build capacity in the larger industry ecosystem. They will seek new partnerships with the public and social sectors to multiply what the industry could accomplish alone and shape new models of collective action for positive societal change.

Elevate Board Governance

Boards need to build new capacity to responsibly guide management toward setting an ambition for the full role the corporation will play in society. As with current management, most directors spent their careers focused on financial performance, with some sidelined activities in CSR and sustainability. However, to steer the company in this new era of business and hold the CEO accountable for the company's financial, environmental, and societal performance, boards will need to be educated on societal needs and the SDGs; they will need directors with different skills and life experience in the social sectors; and they will need to restructure committees, charters, and policies to provide oversight on social performance. They must challenge long-held views about the boundaries and time horizons of business, about what makes a good CEO, about new risks and rights to operate, and about measuring performance, and they will need to expand their view of managerial competence beyond the ability to hit annual business targets. And they must *assess whether management is building a more resilient and adaptable company that delivers for shareholders and society* even at the expense of short-term financial performance.

This ambitious agenda challenges us to reconceive business, commit to purpose, and pursue sustainable business model innovation. Doing so will open up new opportunities for growth, shareholder value, and benefits to society and the planet. CEOs and their boards can wait to be pushed into this agenda by competitors, customers, and regulators. Or they can embrace it proactively and use it to reinvent the company, reshape the industry, propel the stock, deliver remarkable impact, and leave a notable legacy of corporate public good.

David Young and Wendy Woods

2 Innovation is the Only Way to Win the Sustainable Development Goal (SDG) Race

As institutions around the world gauge their progress toward achieving the goals outlined in the United Nations (UN's) 2030 Agenda for Sustainable Development, one thing is clear: we are moving too slowly to keep pace with growing societal needs and are in danger of coming up woefully short of those targets.

It has been clear from the start that considerable new investment is needed to close the nearly $2.5 trillion annual gap between what is being spent today and what would suffice to meet the UN's seventeen ambitious Sustainable Development Goals (SDGs). It is also clear that filling the gap requires the public sector to work effectively with the social sector and to enlist the enormous capacity of the private sector. In response, BCG and other SDG proponents have worked to create new models designed to bring the public, private, and social sectors together in support of the SDGs—including encouraging companies to use their formidable resources and scale to address societal issues and mobilize new sources of capital.

These moves are critical, but they are not enough. In addition to looking for ways to close the investment gap, we need to rewrite the equation, focusing on how to reduce both the amount of investment necessary and the time needed to achieve results. We can improve in both areas today, but only if we leverage innovation. There are examples of proven technologies and approaches from around the world that, if adapted and deployed at scale, could meaningfully narrow the SDG investment gap. It's time to get serious about accelerating innovation on our way to meeting the SDGs.

Steps to Bridge the Investment Gap

Proponents of sustainable development have met in dozens of venues around the world to develop a game plan for achieving the SDGs. Unfortunately, all the effort and good intentions have not as yet sufficiently sped progress toward filling the SDG investment gap to meet the 2030 targets. And while the organizations that should be leading the field—multilateral and bilateral development finance institutions and national development agencies—may have the appropriate vision and rhetoric, most of them are not moving quickly enough. They continue to

https://doi.org/10.1515/9783111295268-003

struggle on various fronts: in changing the way they work and organize, in developing the necessary capabilities, and in crafting suitably large development projects quickly enough to absorb the capital that investors are ready to put to work.

Our assessment is that most of the effort to bring more energy and resources to the SDGs today focuses on three important and reinforcing strategies.

–   **Creating new cross-sector partnerships**. The UN has registered more than 4,000 partnerships in the global registry of voluntary commitments and multistakeholder partnerships, some of them targeting specific thematic areas where business can make a difference. These partnerships include Food Reform for Sustainability and Health (FReSH), a global business partnership that uses a consumer-focused, systemic approach to drive progress toward achieving healthy and sustainable global food production by 2030, and the CEO Partnership for Financial Inclusion, which brings together ten global corporations from different sectors to build private–private partnerships to advance financial inclusion.

–   **Reshaping corporate strategy.** Many progressive corporations are paying greater attention to environmental, social, and governance (ESG) measures. They are broadening their approach to building competitive advantage and new business in a way that includes thinking deeply about their activities' impact on environmental sustainability and societal needs—sometimes explicitly in connection with achieving the SDGs. Such efforts demonstrate that companies can rethink *how to factor societal issues into corporate strategy and performance* and ultimately be rewarded by investors.

–   **Mobilizing capital toward societal impact.** Capital is flowing into socially responsible investments, new ESG funds, and a range of new SDG-related bond issuances (most of which are oversubscribed), proving that it is possible to mobilize capital toward SDG outcomes. This gives development and social-mission organizations new opportunities to take advantage of private capital.

Innovation: The Big Accelerator

As important as these three strategies are for driving SDG progress, they can too easily focus on filling the SDG investment gap rather than fundamentally altering it. This is not terribly surprising. After all, most of the thinking about and discussion of the SDGs comes from a development mindset. But such conversations are trapped in a cycle of appealing for budgets and delivering on proven programs. This leads planners and decision makers to look at the same interventions and run the same math to estimate what it will take to achieve development outcomes, thus reinforcing those models and programs. It does not stimulate radical and transformative innovation.

As in business, innovation can significantly shift the economics of potential solutions and the timeline for delivering them. New technologies and approaches have the potential to fundamentally alter the cost of achieving progress. That's why innovation is critical to advancing the SDGs. It can support and advance both company strategies related to societal impact and initiatives undertaken by new cross-sector partnerships. At the same time, the increased mobilization of capital helps fuel efforts in both areas (see Figure 2.1).

Certainly, effective innovation efforts are underway today in many quarters. Most development institutions now have innovation units tasked with boosting their own capacity for innovation and funding new approaches to programming. Multiple crowdsourcing innovation efforts, such as country Innovation Labs, MIT Solve, and UNLEASH, are in operation as well. And there are efforts to systematically raise the innovation capacity of countries through processes such as science, technology, and innovation (STI) road mapping.

Most of these efforts, however, fall short of driving large-scale innovation. Of all the forces that the private sector can bring to bear in attempting to advance the 2030 SDGs, by far the most powerful is its unique capacity to innovate quickly, attract capital to innovative solutions, and drive innovations at scale. That combination is hard to find in the public sector or the social sector, but it's the private sector's lifeblood.

Each year, BCG publishes its report on the world's most innovative companies. Our research identifies what successful innovation models look like and what transformations are necessary to get there. One crucial attribute at the core of such success is a commitment to nurturing a culture that allows new thinking and approaches to emerge and flourish, coupled with an organizational capacity to rapidly scale and deploy innovation.

Numerous examples of innovations highlight the potential impact that advances in innovation could have if they were accelerated and scaled with the help of the private sector.

– **Hunger**. The United Nations World Food Programme (WFP) launched its Innovation Accelerator in 2016 to identify, support, and scale up new approaches to solving world hunger. One pilot, called Building Blocks, uses blockchain technology to offer Syrian refugees residing in the Azraq camp in Jordan a more secure and efficient way to receive electronic cash transfers. The initiative transformed a process that used to involve lines, paperwork, and manual due diligence into one that takes just seconds. In addition, by automating the cash transfer system and eliminating the need for intermediaries, WFP cut transaction fees by a stag-

Figure 2.1: Achieving the SDGs requires action in four areas.

gering 98%, freeing up funds that the organization could then redirect toward humanitarian relief. The success of the pilot prompted WFP to expand the initiative in early 2018; currently the program supports more than 100,000 refugees residing in camps across Jordan. WFP and UN Women are now partnering to use the same Building Blocks platform to provide assistance to food-insecure Syrian women in Jordan.

– **Sanitation**. Safe disposal of waste is a huge challenge in many countries. Lack of adequate sanitation spreads disease, making it a contributor to more deaths globally than measles, malaria, and acquired immune deficiency syndrome (AIDS) combined. The Bill & Melinda Gates Foundation, which is known for emphasizing innovation, has funded innovators of various new, low-cost sanitation technologies, including dry combustion, which converts waste into small blocks of fuel rather than flushing it away with water. Private companies may someday commercialize such technology and seize part of a global market that is expected to reach $6 billion by 2030.

– **Safe water.** New technologies can help address the problem of lack of access to clean water that challenges in the region of 2.1 billion people around the world. One new approach is a plasma water sanitization system developed by inventor Alfredo Zolezzi that can decontaminate water and rid it of nearly all viruses and bacteria in just two-tenths of a second.

– **Education**. In India, 2,700 childcare providers are using a mobile app to improve early childhood education. In that country, childcare providers deliver daily caregiving services for children and new mothers, and also teach children who are from three to six years old. That workload can be overwhelming, seriously limiting their ability to carve out time for actual instruction. The app expands and improves instructional time in several ways. It provides lesson plans for providers and includes videos that demonstrate how to conduct educational activities. It helps motivate providers through the use of game-like features, tracks student outcomes, and allows providers to communicate with parents through personalized messages. The app has gained an impressive level of traction with more than 70% of providers using it daily. More important, the number of childcare providers who spend more than two hours daily on actual instruction has increased by more than 60%.

– **Financial inclusion**. This area has experienced especially strong positive momentum. Banks, telecommunications players, and others have deployed mobile and digital technologies to change the economics and extend the reach of financial services—from credit to insurance—to previously excluded populations.

– **Environmental sustainability.** The conservation organization World Wide Fund for Nature (WWF) has found that the production of just eight commodities—including seafood, beef, sugar, paper, and cotton—drives most environmental degradation. To tackle this problem, WWF recently partnered with BCG Digital Ventures to launch OpenSC, a tech-enabled platform that promotes sustainable production and consumption of these commodities. Using such tools as data science, machine learning, and blockchain, the platform enables businesses and consumers to verify claims about sustainable and ethical production and trace products throughout their supply chains. Consumers using the platform can scan the Quick Response (QR) code on a product to see information about where the product came from, whether it was produced sustainably, and where its supply chain travels took it before it reached them.

Test Your Innovation Strategy for the SGDs

We need many more such efforts and at much larger scale. Public sector and so-cial-sector groups must develop strategies to rapidly incentivize and partner with the most innovative private companies and investors in order to draw on their formidable skills and resources to advance the SDGs. In that way, such groups can create and scale up innovations and support the rapid, broad deployment of new technologies to the places where they are needed most.

At the outset, however, senior management in the public, social, and private sectors should ask some critical questions to test an organization's innovation efforts on behalf of the SDGs. If the answers are unsatisfactory, it's time to rework the innovation strategy.

For government development institutions, social-mission organizations, and foundations, the following questions are worth asking:

- Have we identified the specific areas within the institution's mandate that most need breakthrough innovation to reduce investment needs and increase impact to achieve the 2030 goals?
- Have we identified the companies, institutions, and investors whose capabili-ties best position them to create the needed innovation? Have we engaged them effectively by understanding their innovation and deployment capabili-ties, inviting them into our thinking, educating them about the specific SDG needs, co-conceiving potential solutions, and presenting mechanisms to in-centivize and de-risk their participation?
- Have we understood and adopted the best practices from the private sector and from the world of venture capital to build and manage a portfolio of innovations?
- Are we working to avoid fragmentation, below-scale efforts, and duplicative pilots—and are we instead cooperating and collaborating with other players to advance high-impact ideas?
- Are we shifting budgets to make more funding available to stimulate and sup-port big bets on innovation, mitigate investment risks, and ensure that we are helping to scale innovations for maximum impact?
- Have we retooled the organization to ensure that it can perform the preced-ing tasks effectively, and have we reinforced a culture that does not constrain or kill innovation and engagement with the private sector?

Answering a different set of questions can help companies figure out how to step up innovation efforts for the SDGs:

- Does the company's growth strategy identify new business opportunities in the SDGs and consider ways that the company's capabilities can be extended to achieve new growth and greater societal impact?
- Does the company understand what parts of its innovation portfolio (new technologies, products, or services) could make a difference in achieving the SDGs?
- Has the company joined key industry consortia that have identified an area of the SDGs in which the industry can make a true difference—and is notable impact occurring?
- Is the company partnering with governments and multilateral or bilateral development agencies to achieve the SDGs through innovation and new business growth?
- Has the company tapped into development agency mechanisms and created strong partnerships with them to de-risk investment and to deploy innovations that can help achieve the SDGs?

It's time for SDG champions in the public, social, and private sectors to assess how well they are running the race to 2030. Although we have some good runners among us, we are at risk of finding ourselves far from the finish line in 2030. If, however, we unleash private-sector innovation in the SDGs' cause, we may finish strong.

Martin Reeves, Julia Dhar, David Young, and Annelies O'Dea

3 Will Net-Zero Get Us to Net-Zero Emissions?

The growing number of companies making Net-Zero carbon commitments offers a ray of hope for progress on climate change.

Currently about ~33% of world's largest companies and more than ~50% of countries have pledged to reach Net-Zero at dates varying mostly between 2030 and 2050.[1,2]

More commitments will almost certainly follow—as one company moves, others in the industry feel pressure to follow—either to avoid being seen as a sustainability laggard, to fend off regulatory requirements that might be more stringent, or to build advantage in a shifting competitive landscape. A single company with the courage to set ambitious targets[3] can ratchet up the efforts of an entire industry, while seizing early advantage. As of October 2021, virtually all of the world's airlines have pledged to reach "Net-Zero" by 2050, having previously promised only a 50% net reduction in emissions in 2009.[4]

Net-Zero has become the gold standard for government and corporate commitment on climate change. But is this increasing focus on Net-Zero sufficient to address climate change robustly? If not, what else do we need to think about and act upon?

What is Net-Zero?

Net-Zero is an *accounting mechanism* that measures a company, country, or individual's carbon footprint using an accepted standard.

---

1 The TCFD develops voluntary, consistent climate-related financial risk disclosures for use by companies in providing information to stakeholders.

2 See Principles for Responsible Investment (PRI) and CFA Institute, *Guidance and Case Studies for ESG Integration: Equities and Fixed Income*, 2018.

3 https://www.bcg.com/about/partner-ecosystem/world-economic-forum/ceo-guide-net-zero?utm_medium=Email&utm_source=esp&utm_campaign=covid-nr&utm_description=weekly&utm_topic=winning_net_zero&utm_geo=global&utm_content=20220118&utm_usertoken=CRM_348c7a5358ff9d49cc7e5fc1b688008a0b7a8c611.

4 The Sustainability Accounting Standards Board (SASB) develops sustainability accounting industry standards to help businesses communicate financially material information to investors.

https://doi.org/10.1515/9783111295268-004

In the credits column are the metric tons of carbon dioxide and carbon dioxide equivalents (for other greenhouse gases like methane and nitrous oxide) that a company produces through the direct (Scope 1) and indirect activities (Scope 2) of the company as well as its supply chain (Scope 3).

In the debits column, emissions that cannot be immediately reduced by the company can be offset by paying someone else to take an equivalent amount of carbon out of the atmosphere. Such offsets can use both nature and human-made technologies to remove greenhouse gases, although the former predominate today. Common nature-based methods include sequestering carbon in plant matter by planting new forests, protecting existing ones, or restoring previously logged ones. *Technological* approaches include capturing greenhouse gases such as methane gas at landfills, nitrous oxide at chemical plants, and direct carbon capture from of the air.

A company, country, or individual is said to be Net-Zero when the debits equal the credits—meaning the entity is not contributing additive greenhouse gases to the atmosphere. The idea is that if all countries, companies, and individuals become Net-Zero, we end up Net-Zero for the planet.

The Impact of Net-Zero

The Net-Zero concept has some strong merits in facilitating effective collective action toward the goal of taming climate change.

First and foremost, Net-Zero provides a measure of transparency and comparability in accounting for carbon emissions. Little progress will be made overall without clear accounting and accountability for environmental impact.

Second, the scheme creates an easy way for companies and countries to make both long-term decarbonization commitments and create immediate impact. Companies can plan a realistic path for decarbonization, while using offsets in the short term.

On its face, this should result in:
- progress towards climate stability and a means to track it
- a scalable mechanism for an increasing number of players to commit over time and peer pressure to encourage this
- reputational benefits for companies with consumers and procurement preference with business-to-business (B2B) customers
- consumer engagement and contribution through support for brands with Net-Zero commitments

– reduction of risk for shareholders as their investments adopt sustainable business models without abrupt disruption to short-term returns
– increased protection for nature, as most carbon offsets today are nature-based

However, a closer inspection revealed that Net-Zero also has some significant limitations that, if unaddressed, could easily misrepresent and undermine progress toward the ultimate goal of environmental sustainability.

Fifteen Important Limitations of Net-Zero

Notwithstanding the benefits mentioned, Net-Zero has some significant gaps and limitations that need to be addressed to attain sufficient impact overall.

We have captured these in a series of scenarios, all of which have examples in the present. Each captures a problem with definitions, implementation, or scope leading to emission reductions being postponed, exaggerated, or diminished. These could compound the challenge of making real progress by providing a false sense of accomplishment and mistaking activity for progress.

We represent these scenarios with simple diagrams. The circle represents the planet. Inside the circle is a *red* up arrow representing an emitter (let's assume it's in the global North where the United States and many other large emitters sit) and a *green* down arrow representing a carbon offset (let's assume it's in the global South where many nature-based offsets are located today). The numbers represent the net emissions of the planet—a 1 indicates positive emissions, and a 0 indicates Net-Zero emissions. Time flows left to right, with each circle indicating a series of snapshots in time. A dotted arrow represents an event not captured by Net-Zero accounting or implementation.

In Figure 3.1, our net-positive emissions today become Net-Zero at some point in the future through a combination of emission reductions and purchased carbon offsets. All emissions that could not be reduced are offset by compensating carbon offsets. Progress against goals can be accurately tracked and attributed to certain decisions, actions taken or not taken.

Multiple standards and implementations of Net-Zero accounting exist, potentially leading to a distorted overall picture of progress, as shown in Figure 3.2.

If pledges exclude certain activities, our view of progress is distorted, leaving some of the most intractable emissions challenges beyond public scrutiny. For example, basing a Net-Zero pledge on only direct company operations and energy inputs (Scope 1 and 2) but excluding the full supply chain and inputs required to make the

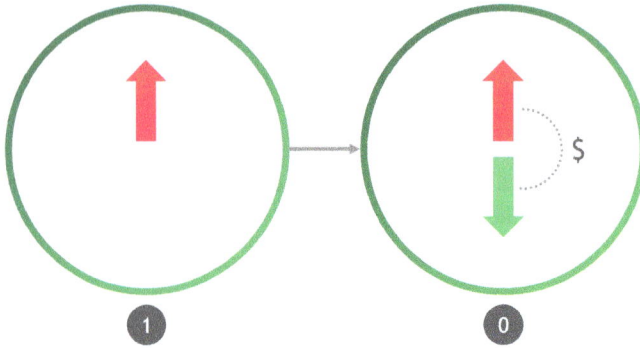

Figure 3.1: Base case/Net-zero achieved as intended.

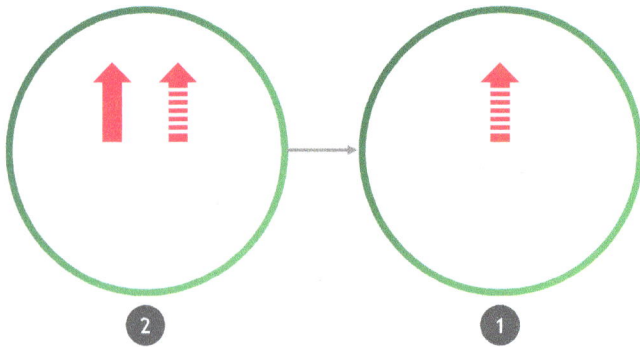

Figure 3.2: Limitation 1: Definitional consistency/completeness.

end-product (Scope 3) can make heavy-emitting industries and companies appear to be Net-Zero and obfuscate the need for more transformative change. Similar examples occur for countries that exclude the climate impact of their exports from calculations.

The ability to verify reported reductions or the execution of offset pledges represents an increasingly complex challenge as the number of efforts expand, opening the scheme to manipulation (see Figure 3.3). We have already seen that companies' promises to achieve Net-Zero are accomplished by much fanfare, with significantly less attention given to the knottier problem of how the realization of these commitments is to be confirmed. A lack of common definitions and standards makes verifiability even more challenging.

Carbon offsets that are allowed to sit simultaneously on multiple entities' balance sheets can inflate apparent impact (see Figure 3.4).

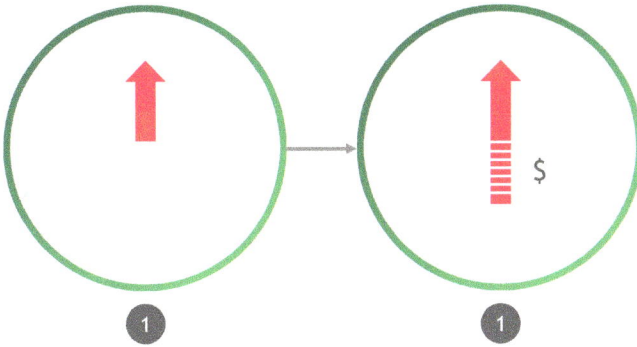

Figure 3.3: Limitation 2: Verifiability.

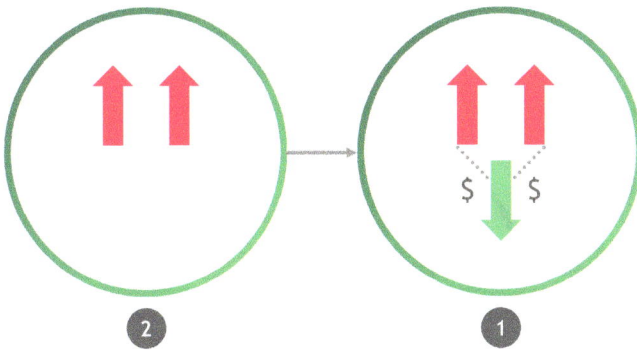

Figure 3.4: Limitation 3: Double counting.

The singular ownership of carbon offset purchase is already a significant issue.[5] When a company buys an offset in the Amazon rainforest how can they be sure that same offset isn't sold to someone else concurrently? Such lack of verifiability makes it difficult to buy carbon offsets with confidence, particularly for smaller companies and individuals who also have an ambition and need to become Net-Zero.

In Figure 3.5, nature-based offsets do not have an immediate effect—afforestation schemes take time to realize their full effect. The resulting short-term imbalance can lead to further climate deterioration.

---

5 See, for example Eccles, Robert and Svetlana Klimenko, "The Investor Revolution," *Harvard Business Review*, May–June 2019, https://hbr.org/2019/05/the-investor–revolution; Rogers, Jean and George Serafeim, "Pathways to Materiality: How Sustainability Issues Become Financially Material to Corporations and Their Investors," Harvard Business School Working Paper, No. 20-056, 2019; Kuh, Thomas, Andre Shepley, and Greg Bala, "Dynamic Materiality: Measuring What Matters," 2020.

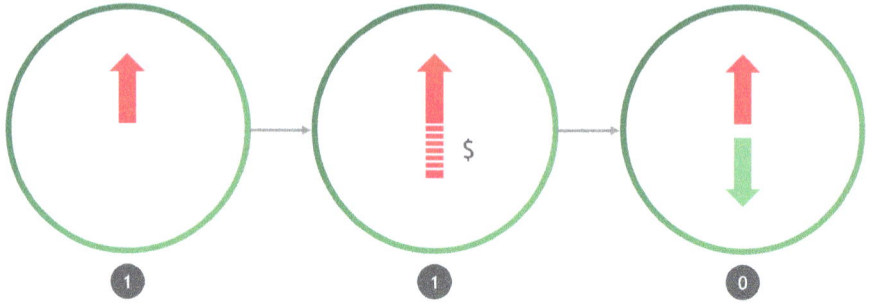

Figure 3.5: Limitation 4: Delayed impact.

Figure 3.6 shows where carbon offsets can encourage the postponement of decarbonization, best clarified by asking the counterfactual—what action would have to take place instead if buying carbon offsets weren't an option? Creating an "easy out solution" in the form of a carbon offset may distract or delay companies from the hard but more meaningful and permanent work of reducing their carbon emissions.

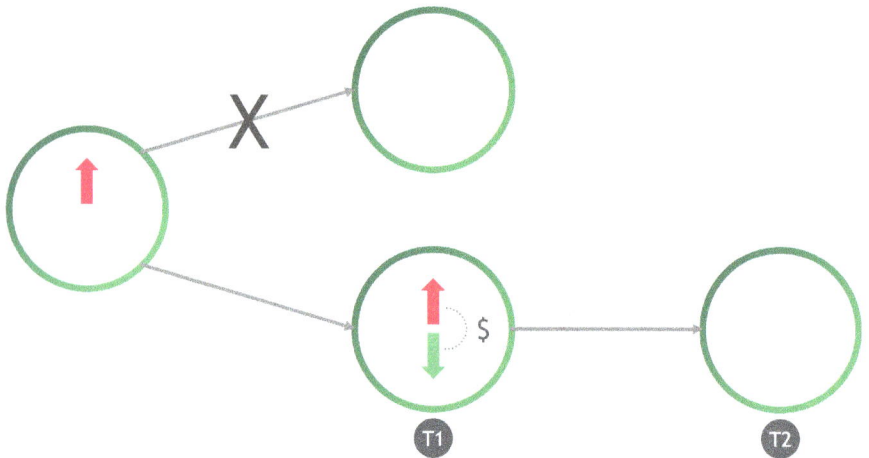

Figure 3.6: Limitation 5: Postponement of decarbonization.

History suggests that complex social mobilization efforts often require a high and shared sense of urgency, as well as a mutual feeling of interdependence. The promise of Net-Zero at a distant future date may result in increased complacency and delayed transformative actions by companies (changes in business models) and individuals (changes in consumption or lifestyle patterns)—ultimately preventing us from reaching Net-Zero in time to avert catastrophic climate impact.

In Figure 3.7, carbon offsets are bought and debited in the present, with the understanding that the resource will be maintained into the future. When a company emits a greenhouse gas it does so with 100% certainty. However, a carbon offset requires ongoing stewardship and can therefore be considered to have an increasing discount rate over time. For example, an acre of forest that is sold this year as a carbon offset may be destroyed next year due to neglect, fire, or even willful gaming on the part of the seller.

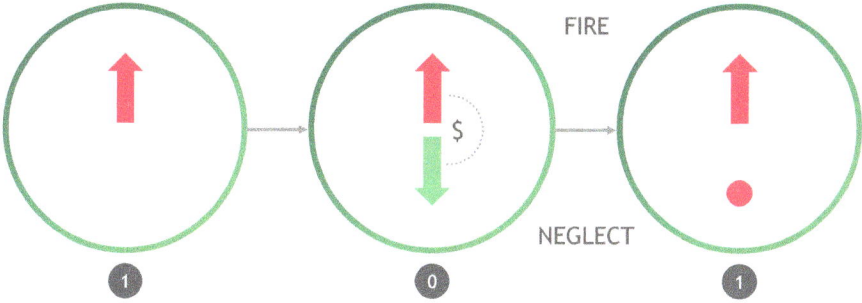

Figure 3.7: Limitation 6: Permanence.

If buying a carbon offset leads to a reduction of greenhouse gas emission that would have happened independently, then the carbon offset is non-additive (see Figure 3.8). For example, a company can pay someone to build a wind farm that will displace a coal power plant and provide cleaner energy. However, if that wind farm was going to be built either way, the net effect has been to improve the business case for the wind farm, but not to create an additive offset.

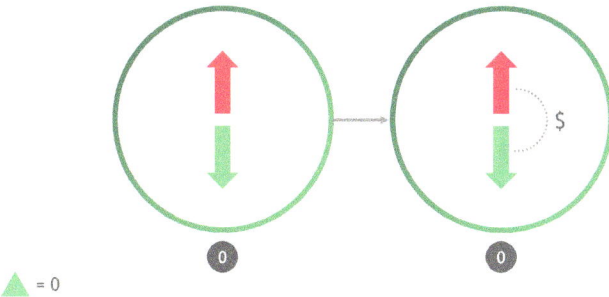

Figure 3.8: Limitation 7: Non-additivity.

In Figure 3.9, leakage occurs when efforts to reduce emissions in one place shift emissions to another place where they are uncontrolled or uncounted. For exam-

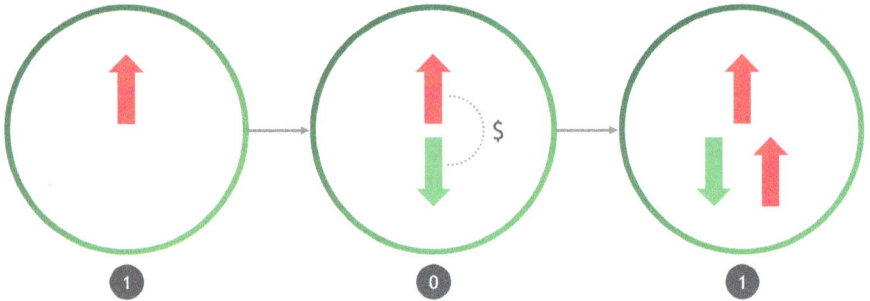

Figure 3.9: Limitation 8: Leakage/Coverage.

ple, "protecting" an acre of forest in Brazil from logging through a carbon offset program may result in the logging of an acre of forest in Borneo—particularly if there has been no reduction in demand for forest lumber and furthermore the price for forest lumber has increased due to scarcity driven by carbon offset programs. If the Net-Zero pact does not cover all regions and participants, then real progress will be reduced and apparent progress will be exaggerated.

Net-Zero pledges that depend on the use of compensation mechanisms like carbon offsets are effectively commitments to buy offsets in the future at an unspecified price (see Figure 3.10). The finite nature of verifiable, protectable carbon offsets paired with a strongly increasing demand for carbon offsets between 2030 and 2050 when companies near their pledge dates, will inevitably drive up the price of offsets. This could make planned carbon offsets economically unrealistic and thus result in pledges that cannot realistically be fulfilled.

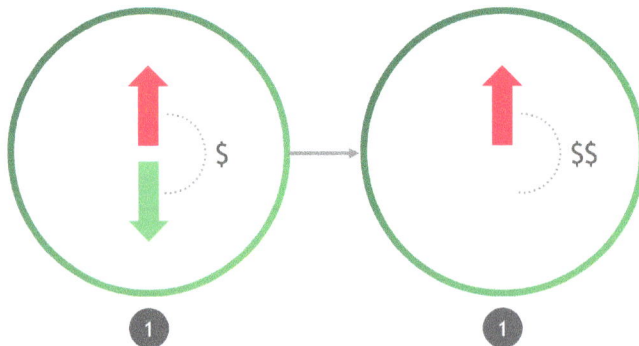

Figure 3.10: Limitation 9: Economic viability (inflation of offset prices).

The voluntary nature of the Net-Zero system will inevitably result in limits to emitter coverage (see Figure 3.11). The biggest emitters with the most intractable transformation challenges will have the least incentive to commit. Without the arrival of highly disruptive competitors or regulation, present incentives to take significant action may be insufficient. Given the necessity that all entities become Net-Zero for the planet to be Net-Zero, the voluntary scheme will not be able to attain its ultimate goal of a Net-Zero planet.

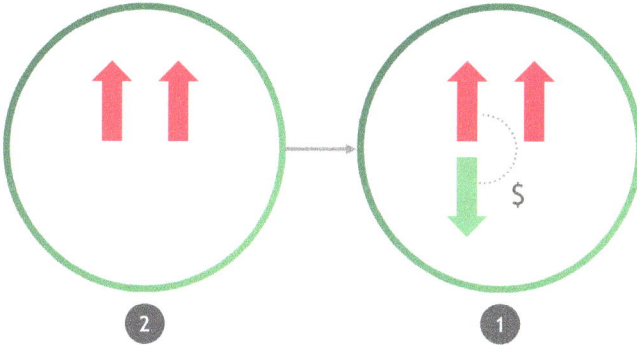

Figure 3.11: Limitation 10: Voluntarism.

The majority of carbon offset solutions available today involve paying someone to ***not*** take an action—such as paying someone to ***not*** log a virgin forest (see Figure 3.12). Such financial incentives may encourage individuals to ***project*** an action (for example, log a forest) they had previously not intended to take. This is of particular concern in developing countries where many of these natural resources sold as carbon offsets reside and alternative economic opportunities are limited, creating strong incentives for this deception to occur.

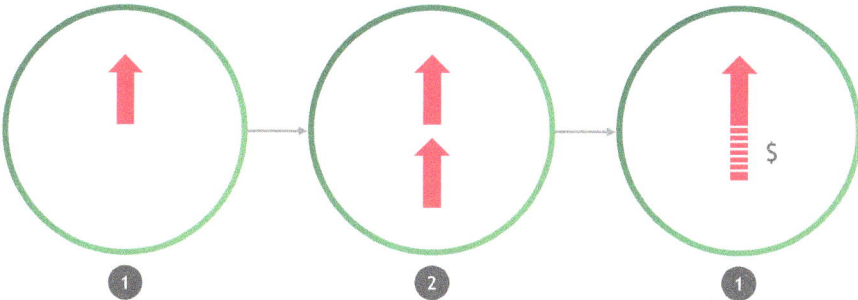

Figure 3.12: Limitation 11: Moral hazard.

As shown in Figure 3.13, developed countries emit a larger share of emissions due to their higher level of industrialization and consumption. Developing countries, by contrast, could be frozen at current relative income levels if economic development is obstructed by incentives that overly bias the use of a country's resources for providing offsets beyond its borders.

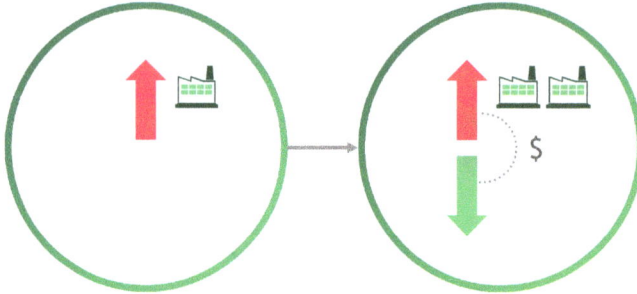

Figure 3.13: Limitation 12: Inequity in economic development.

Methane and nitrous oxide have ~30 and ~300 times the heat trapping effect of carbon dioxide respectively. Yet, many climate change pledges today focus exclusively on CO_2 reduction using words like "carbon zero" and "carbon neutral." This over-simplification of sustainability efforts to carbon neutrality undermines the ultimate goal of climate sustainability. This has created meaningful confusion about the scope of announced Net-Zero pledges, impeding individual Net-Zero pledges summing to planetary Net-Zero (see Figure 3.14).

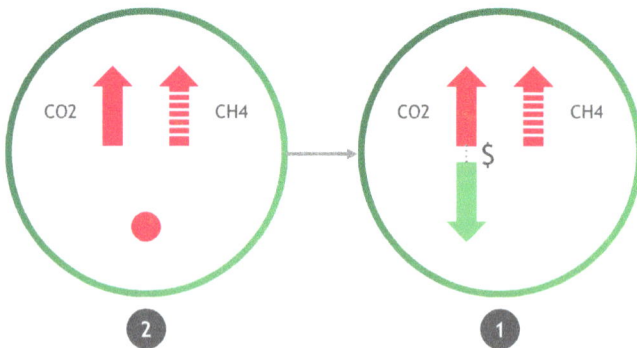

Figure 3.14: Limitation 13: Over-simplification (reduction of sustainability to carbon neutrality).

The mobilizing of attention and resources towards Net-Zero pledges is something to be celebrated. However, attending only to narrowly defined carbon reduction goals could be self-defeating. For example, if non-greenhouse gas (GHG) pollutants and other activities that lead to species depletion and the degradation of nature are not addressed, then the natural buffering capacity of the planet could be reduced, undermining carbon offsets and the ultimate goal of climate sustainability (see Figure 3.15).

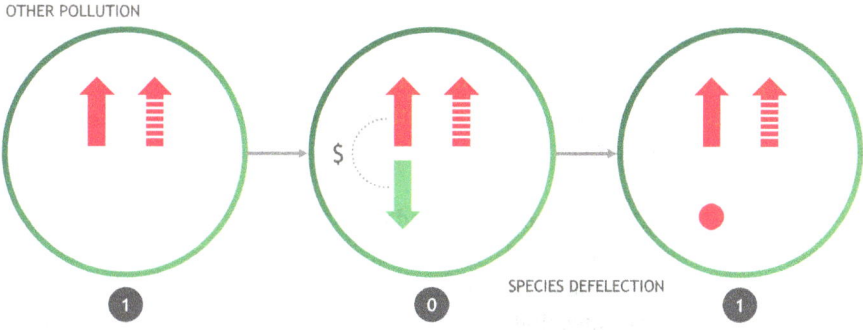

Figure 3.15: Limitation 14: Over-simplification (reduction of sustainability to decarbonization).

Net-Zero sets a goal, but not the path to reach it (see Figure 3.16). For simple problems, such an approach may be effective in leaving room to innovate and try new solutions. However, the complex, unprecedented, inter-dependent, and transformative change required to reach Net-Zero as a planet may not be achievable without a coordinated transition plan and the research, investments, policies, and regulations to support it.

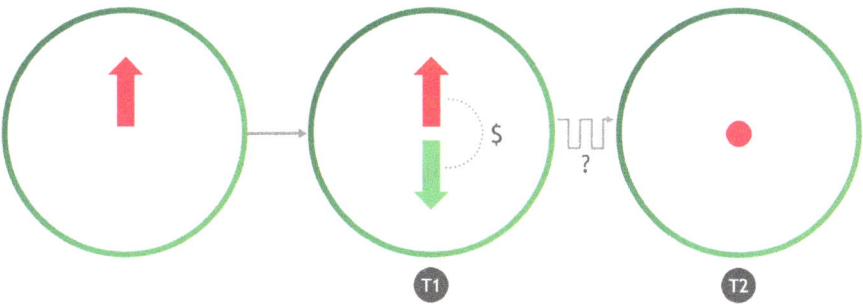

Figure 3.16: Limitation 15: A goal without a path.

Elements of a Better Path Forward

Given these limitations, how do we best leverage the momentum created by Net-Zero to evolve ever more robust solutions and pathways? We don't pretend to have the complete answer, but some elements of a better path forwarding move beyond today's Net-Zero approach might include the following.

Enhancing Net-Zero

Net-Zero provides a meaningful system of accounting and accountability and can be enhanced to remove some of these limitations. While definitions are continually being improved, sufficient attention also needs to be given to how these are applied in practice.

– **Establish consistent definitions/standards:** Net-Zero emission targets must account for all GHG emissions of companies and countries, in all aspects of operations. While methane and nitrous oxide remain harder to address, their high impact necessitates that they are included. This should address the limitations of *definitional consistency and completeness.*

– **Create mechanisms of verification:** Audited inventories of carbon offset resources can be established to provide a means of *verification*, to eliminate *double counting*, to monitor *permanence*, and to help project the inevitable *inflation in offset prices.*

– **Split out the reporting of and accelerate decarbonization:** Carbon offsets cannot be allowed to substitute for or postpone addressing emissions, the root cause of climate change. Companies and countries should be required to report separately for emissions reductions and offsets. This should help address the problem of *postponement.*

– **Accelerate commitments:** Net-Zero pledges in the distant future must be coupled with interim commitments. These are essential to increasing the sense of urgency, accelerating near-term action, and providing the ability to monitor progress and of course correct towards the ultimate target, which will help overcome the limitations of *delay* and *postponement of true reduction.*

Moving Beyond Net-Zero

In addition to enhancing Net-Zero mechanisms, we must pursue a more multidimensional view of sustainability and put in place the financial, operational, technological, behavioral, and cultural support to enable the transformative action necessary to achieve climate sustainability for the planet.

- **Multidimensional view of sustainability:** Consider sustainability beyond the single dimension of carbon emissions to include all relevant factors, including other GHG emissions, species diversity, air and water quality, and nature preservation. This multidimensionality can help to overcome the risks of *over-simplification.*
- **Develop a behavioral strategy:** While there is significant work underway to improve accounting, more work is required to understand the behavioral economics of decarbonization, so that the right nudges, sticks, and kicks can be used to direct human action in the desired direction and address the limitations of *moral hazard* and *non-additivity.* In particular, we need to harness the power of future regret to mobilize present action.
- **Ensure sustainable economics for decarbonization and offsets:** Plan for carbon economics to shift over time as demand for offsets and sustainable inputs create new scarcities and price inflation to address the limitation of *economic viability.*
- **Develop transition paths:** Reaching Net-Zero will necessarily require large-scale societal change. What are the major shifts economically, technologically, and societally that must be made? How do we act on and sequence these major shifts *collectively*, to provide the foundation for *individual agents* to meet their Net-Zero targets? This should address the limitation of *goals without paths.*
- **Accelerate innovation:** Decarbonization will require more, cheaper, and better solutions than we have today. We do not currently have the approaches to meet our commitments and we must accelerate the rate of discovery, scaling, and deployment of technological and nature-based innovations through increased funding, private and public partnership, and international cooperation.
- **Regulatory and fiscal policy:** Regulatory and fiscal policy should be put in place to make corporate and societal transformation a viable path. Like a ball rolled down the street, the regulatory policy forms the curb—channeling the direction of the ball while the fiscal policy determines the decline of the street—providing the force to overcome friction and accelerating the path of the ball to its desired direction. Together, regulations and financial policy can help overcome the problems of *volunteerism, leakage*, and *inequity of economic development* to ensure that planetary Net-Zero happens expeditiously, ubiquitously, and equitably.

Katherine Brown, Maha Eltobgy, Douglas Beal, Veronica Chau,
Robert Eccles, Vinay Shandal, Leonore Tauber, Wendy Woods,
and David Young

4 Embracing the New Age of Materiality: Harnessing the Pace of Change in ESG

Developing the Capability to Anticipate Future Material Issues

Investors are building a range of capabilities to enable them to pursue sustainable investing strategies with greater sophistication. Examples include building their own views of which environmental, social, and governance (ESG) topics are material in the sectors where they invest, rather than relying on third-party views; shifting ownership of the analysis process from generally siloed ESG teams to portfolio managers and portfolio construction teams (and deepening the level of that analysis); scrutinizing issuers' broader purpose and sustainability strategies, as opposed to relying on standard disclosures; and engaging more meaningfully with management teams on sustainability issues. All this is encouraging. More recently, early exploration of another capability has emerged: more accurately assessing which environmental and social issues will become material over time and integrating these forward-looking perspectives into investment decisions. This paper presents a framework that can help investors to further build this crucial capability.

Why Looking Ahead Matters

In an era of hyper-transparency, it is increasingly important to focus on disclosure. As the Fourth Industrial Revolution enables unprecedented transparency, pressure to disclose is mounting. For example, in January 2020, Larry Fink, Chairman and Chief Executive Officer, BlackRock, USA, wrote in his annual letter to CEOs that BlackRock would be expecting disclosures in line with the guidelines

Note: Republished with permission from World Economic Forum. Originally published at weforum. org, March 2020.

https://doi.org/10.1515/9783111295268-005

set by the Sustainability Accounting Standards Board[1] (SASB) and the Task Force on Climate-related Financial Disclosures (TCFD). While work is under way to consolidate and streamline the demands placed on companies (for example, the call to action by the World Economic Forum's (WEF's) International Business Council (IBC)), this does not lessen the amount of data companies are being asked to disclose. In fact, these demands could intensify as technology advances provide investors and others with large volumes of data about companies' operations and impact. An often-cited example is the ability of satellite imaging to provide asset-level carbon emissions data. With access to richer information about any issuer's sustainability performance, investors need to know what to factor into investment decisions—that is, ESG issues that are material today and those that are likely to become material in the future.

The rate at which issues that are currently immaterial become material is accelerating. As observed in recent works,[2] the combination of transparency and rising stakeholder influence is, in part, driving this acceleration. Stakeholders, such as non-governmental organizations (NGOs), activists, and civil society groups, are now much better equipped to have an impact on the performance of a business, often before most investors have become aware of this. In a hyperconnected world, one in which information can be disseminated widely and immediately, movements such as #MeToo can emerge and achieve scale rapidly, creating legal, branding, recruiting, retention, and other challenges for any company whose policies against harassment and discrimination are inadequate. The ability to anticipate stakeholder reactions to emerging sustainability issues and how they could affect a business and its performance is therefore critical.

> We cannot wait for corporate reporting to become perfect; we need to become more forward-looking now and push for better corporate reporting at the same time.
> —Brian Deese, global head, Sustainable Investing, BlackRock, USA

Value-creation plans must optimize performance against current and future material ESG issues. Many of today's business strategies and value-creation plans include initiatives aimed at improving performance on sustainability issues

---

1 The Sustainability Accounting Standards Board (SASB) develops sustainability accounting industry standards to help businesses communicate financially material information to investors.

2 See, for example, Eccles, Robert and Svetlana Klimenko, "The Investor Revolution," *Harvard Business Review*, May–June 2019, https://hbr.org/2019/05/the-investor–revolution; Rogers, Jean and George Serafeim, "Pathways to Materiality: How Sustainability Issues Become Financially Material to Corporations and Their Investors," Harvard Business School Working Paper, No. 20-056, 2019; Kuh, Thomas, Andre Shepley, and Greg Bala, "Dynamic Materiality: Measuring What Matters," 2020.

that are currently considered material. This is an important development and signals growing recognition of the contribution of strong sustainability performance to business value. The next stage in this evolution will be the introduction of initiatives that aim to improve performance on ESG issues that are likely to be material for a company in the future. Businesses that do this will gain a competitive advantage and investors that select companies taking this approach—or that encourage their management to do so—will benefit.

> For businesses to thrive in the 2020s, they will need to understand the forces that will shape the next 10 years and use them to their advantage. There's no doubt that sustainability and societal impact issues will be a leading force for driving value creation
> —Rich Lesser, global chief executive officer, Boston Consulting Group (BCG), USA

Materiality as a Dynamic Process: A Framework for Action

The framework outlined in Figure 4.1 provides investors with guidance on the signals to look for to better identify and manage dynamic ESG issues and to incorporate them into the process of portfolio construction, security selection, and stewardship. The framework builds on the depth of existing research in this field, and comprises four key drivers—each of which is gaining momentum—of the growing dynamism in the materiality of ESG issues.[3]

A key first step in anticipating the future materiality is to closely monitor new evidence on the environmental and social impacts of corporate practices. Three developments are driving the dynamism of materiality:

Robust and compelling evidence is emerging on the impact of environmental and social externalities. Global social movements rejecting single-use plastics, for example, have been influenced by evidence from scientists and international institutions on the volume of the world's plastic waste and its negative impacts on oceans. Similarly, the growing number of scientific publications highlighting the harmful effects of air pollution in cities has prompted public and political debates on banning combustion vehicles. The investors consulted for this paper said they were more frequently using signals, such as a rise in scientific research activities or grants for research, to anticipate where evidence will emerge that could affect asset values in key sectors or markets.

---

3 A recent analysis of historical data on sustainability issues by data provider Truvalue Labs indicates that ESG factors material to companies and industries vary over time.

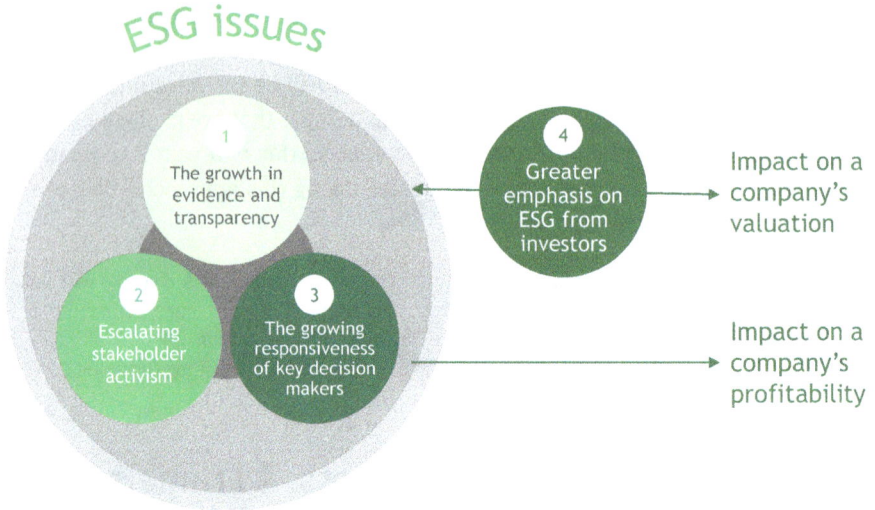

Source: World Economic Forum and BCG

Figure 4.1: Framework on how ESG issues become financially material over time.

The breadth and depth of data are expanding. The Fourth Industrial Revolution—the rise of technologies such as artificial intelligence (AI), blockchain, and virtual reality—is enabling the production of vast amounts of new information, creating inescapable levels of transparency. Blockchain, for example, enables full traceability—from source to store—and is already being used to verify products such as sustainable timber and conflict-free diamonds. Investors are now using AI to identify inaccurate reporting. Satellite technology is generating images that are being used to monitor environmental changes.[4] For example, Robeco, an asset manager, plans to pilot satellite imagery that will enable the real-time monitoring of palm plantations to verify companies' commitments to zero deforestation.[5] Armed with the transparency these tools provide, investors can rely more heavily on their own insights, making it increasingly difficult for companies to shape the narrative about what is material or to hide their externalities from the markets.

---

4 The company GHGSat, for example, pursues remote sensing of greenhouse gas (GHG), air quality gas, and other trace gas emissions from any industrial facility in the world and provides GHG emissions monitoring data.

5 See Rust, Susanna, "ESG Roundup: Robeco to Pilot Satellite Imagery Use," IPE, 13 November 2019, https://www.ipe.com/news/esg/esg-roundup-robeco-to-pilot-satellite-imagery-use/10034553.article.

The dissemination of information has reached unparalleled speed and scale. A recent petition addressed to a global company following the wildfires in Australia, reaching approximately 160,000 signatures in a week, illustrates the speed at which events can translate into the increased materiality of environmental trends, which can have an impact on a company's value. The #DeleteUber campaign resulted in more than 200,000 users deleting their accounts. This had a material impact on the company; notably, the event was referenced as a risk factor in its S-1 filing in advance of its initial public offering.[6]

Of the investors consulted, several are already tracking incidence-based information via social platforms, the media and corporate reports for negative environmental or social headlines. Furthermore, additional signals such as mounting scientific evidence of the impact of environmental or social challenges will strengthen investors' ability to detect indications that this first stage of materiality has been triggered.

> If you feel uncomfortable about your production process or supply chain, there's probably a reason why. In a time of radical transparency, look at your products, practices and your value chain.
>
> —Therése Lennehag, head, Sustainability, EQT Partners, Sweden

Matarin Capital: Incorporating a social crisis into investment and portfolio construction decisions
Citing evidence of the negative macroeconomic impacts of the opioid epidemic in the United States, Matarin Capital identified the opioid epidemic as a financial risk for investors with the potential to cause stock prices to spiral downward. Matarin Capital developed a proprietary approach to incorporate this future material risk into its investment process, recognizing that traditional financial risk models may not capture those risks. Blending qualitative and quantitative analyses (that is, opioid news events, outstanding lawsuits, business exposure to the opioid supply chain), analysts at Matarin Capital identified a list of companies bearing significant risk. They then designed a proprietary risk constraint on its portfolio exposure that set a pre-specified and constrained total limit for exposure to the opioid risk factor. With its forward-looking approach, Matarin Capital made its investment process responsive to the emerging material risks and complemented its traditional financial risk models.

---

6 See Leskin, Paige, "Uber says the #DeleteUber Movement led to 'Hundreds of Thousands' of People Quitting the App," *Business Insider*, 13 April 2019, https://www.businessinsider.com/uber-deleteuber-protest-hundreds-of-thousands-quit-app-2019-4?r=DE&IR=T.

Escalating Stakeholder Activism

Evidence of a company's positive or negative externalities does not automatically make the underlying issue financially material. For example, evidence of the impact of carbon emissions on climate change or the negative health effects of sugar has existed for several decades. The second stage in the process, when evidence triggers materiality—sometimes in a matter of days—comes when stakeholders (including, sometimes, shareholders) apply evidence in a way that causes a significant change in societal expectations. In recent years, the ability of stakeholders to use evidence to affect business value has been growing. Three key developments are behind this increase:

NGOs and activists are more frequently focusing their efforts on investors. The "Insure Our Future" campaign, representing environmental and consumer rights organizations, is pressuring the insurance industry to stop insuring coal and tar sands projects. The group creates public ratings for insurers and has called out laggards.[7] These "financially savvy eco-warriors"[8] are also providing investors with targeted information. The Global Coal Exit List, for example, was created by an NGO to provide a practical divestment tool for the finance sector.

Advocacy groups and activists are deploying highly professional campaigns and media strategies. Climate activists, with more than 300 organizations involved, are planning an unprecedented number of events ahead of the 2020 U.S. presidential election. Capitalizing on the 6 million people supporting worldwide climate strikes in September 2019, climate activists are now targeting voters with widespread voter mobilization campaigns. Following the UN climate change conference in Madrid in 2019, more than 200 climate activists organized a response called "Polluters Out," which within 20 days had established a website, a multilingual launch video, a press release in seven languages, and a list of demands. The group is active in more than 40 countries and uses online tools such as Slack, Zoom, and Google Drive to organize collective action and involve other actors, such as climate scientists.[9] Investors need to pay more attention to these efforts as they could, in the long term, lead to regulatory shifts, which would have sector-level effects on asset values.

---

7 The "Insure Our Future" campaign is demanding that US insurers end insurance for the fossil fuel sector. See "Insure our future, not climate change" at https://www.insureourfuture.us.

8 See van der Voo, Lee, "'Kids are Taking the Streets': Climate Activists Plan Avalanche of Events as 2020, Election Looms," *The Guardian*, 25 January 2020, https://www.theguardian.com/environment/2020/jan/25/climate-change-election-2020-youth-activism.

9 See van der Voo, Lee, "'Kids are Taking the Streets': Climate Activists Plan Avalanche of Events as 2020, Election Looms," *The Guardian*, 25 January 2020, https://www.theguardian.com/environment/2020/jan/25/climate-change-election-2020-youth-activism.

Large funders and the general public are giving greater support to environmental advocacy campaigns. For example, the European Climate Foundation is financing a number of environmental NGOs and initiatives, and amplifying the financial support of foundations. A recent study concluded that "environmental NGOs have never been better supported, and their concerns have never been more urgent and compelling."[10] In the past two years, new activist networks such as Extinction Rebellion have emerged, driven by growing frustration at the inadequacy of policy responses.

Several investors consulted mentioned that they regularly meet with environmental NGOs to gain an in-depth understanding of their agendas and concerns. To better anticipate what issues may become material in the future, investors can analyze the different investors and industries that advocacy groups are targeting, how successfully they are deploying media strategies, and how funding flows toward different environmental and social causes are developing as a result.

BlackRock: Gaining forward-looking insights by evaluating a company's preparedness to perform well in the future
To gain forward-looking insights into a company's performance in a future low-carbon economy, BlackRock has developed a low-carbon transition framework. The framework seeks to go beyond traditional ESG scores by evaluating companies' preparedness to minimize risks and maximize opportunities associated with a low-carbon economic transition. BlackRock has identified five "pillars" it believes to be particularly material in the future—such as energy production or carbon-efficient technology. It evaluates individual companies across these pillars using a wide range of external and proprietary ESG data. Taking the industry-specific context into account, BlackRock then calculates a transition score per company. Comparing its own assessment with ESG scores provided by third parties, BlackRock has found a low correlation and considers its proprietary framework to capture forward-looking and differentiating insights.

The Growing Responsiveness of Key Decision-Makers

Over the past three years, the developments outlined in the previous section have been having a more powerful influence on triggering the third stage in the process: influencing key decision-makers, who are able—whether through the way they shape legislation or the purchasing choices they make—to directly influence a company's profitability. Examining regulatory developments, consumer behavior, and employee expectations reveals a noticeable shift in their responsiveness.

---

10 See Berny, Nathalie and Christopher Rootes, "Environmental NGOs at a crossroads?" *Environmental Politics*, vol. 27, no. 6, 2018, p. 947.

Policy-makers are responding to mounting stakeholder pressure and evidence. In January 2020, the German government decided to gradually eliminate coal power by 2038. This is a significant political win for climate activists.[11] Another example is how the European Union (EU) and governments in the United Kingdom, the Netherlands, and Scotland are setting plastic waste reduction targets (Figure 4.2). Following public campaigns last year, the EU responded with stricter emission regulations for the car industry. And China, which is facing growing public pressure to tackle air pollution, developed a three-year action plan in 2018, including clean air and emission targets to achieve by 2020.

Estimated number of new regulations on single-use plastics entering into force at the national level worldwide

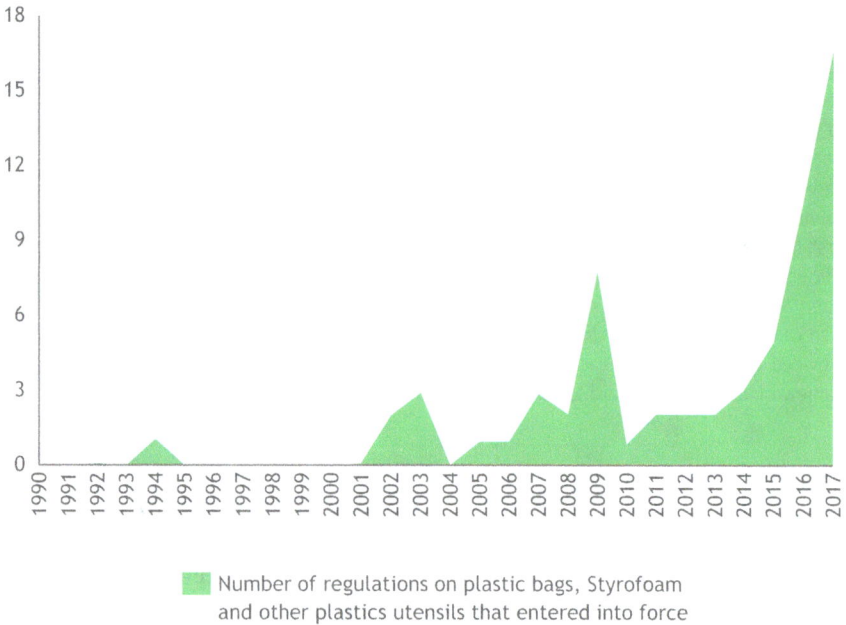

Number of regulations on plastic bags, Styrofoam and other plastics utensils that entered into force

Source: UNEP, 2018, p.24

Figure 4.2: Rise of new regulations on single-use plastics, 1990–2017.

---

11 See Buck and Chazan, 2019.

Consumer attitudes are shifting. Consumer demand for sustainable products and services is reaching new peaks. A recent analysis by Boston Consulting Group (BCG) shows that 72% of European consumers prefer to buy products with environmentally friendly packaging. Globally, 46% of consumers are willing to forgo preferred brand names in favor of eco-friendly products. Some 38% of global consumers also indicate the willingness to pay a premium for eco-friendly and sustainable materials.[12] Business leaders consulted from the food and agriculture sector confirmed that this shift in consumer demand is having an impact on the kinds of innovations they are making in their offerings. A recent study of consumer purchasing of consumer packaged goods (CPG) between 2013 and 2018 found that sustainable products were responsible for 50% of the market growth during that period[13] and accounted for a 16.6% dollar share of the market.

> Consumers are increasingly using their purchasing decisions to send companies a message about the imperative to create positive total societal impact. ESG issues are the C-suite issues of today and tomorrow.
> —Wendy Woods, managing director and senior partner; vice chairman, Social Impact, BCG

The increase in U.S. plant-based food sales and the flight shaming movement in Sweden (Figure 4.3) are seen as recent indicators of a strong shift toward eco-friendly consumer behavior in developed economies.

Talent is demanding more from employers. Employees are increasingly voting with their feet by choosing to work for employers and in sectors that have sustainable business models. A recent Boston Consulting Group analysis shows that 67% of millennials expect employers to have purpose and want their jobs to have societal impact. With millennials and Generation Z employees making up 59% of the workforce in 2020, business needs to adapt to their demands.[14] The mining industry's ability to attract talent is diminishing, for example, because of its tarnished sustainability reputation—something that business leaders in the industry consider a growing business risk.[15] The past 24 months have also seen a sharp rise

---

12 Willingness-to-pay survey of 1,000 global consumers on sustainability products using data from IRI, Nielsen, SPINS; analysis by Boston Consulting Group.

13 See Whelan, Tensie, "Sustainability-Marketed Products Are Responsible for Half the Category Growth in CPG," Corporate Eco Forum (CEF), 18 March 2019, http://www.corporateecoforum.com/sustainability-marketed-products-are-responsible-for-half-the-category-growth-in-cpg/

14 See Bailey, Allison et al., "Organizing for the Future with Tech, Talent, and Purpose," Boston Consulting Group, 16 September 2019, https://www.bcg.com/de-de/publications/2019/organizing-future-tech-talent–purpose.aspx

15 See EY, "Top 10 Business Risks Facing Mining and Metals in 2019–20," 2018, https://assets.ey.com/content/dam/ey-sites/ey-com/en_gl/topics/mining-metals/mining-metals-pdfs/ey-top-10-business-risks-facing-mining-and-metals-in-2019-20_v2.pdf

32% increase in US plant-based food sales since 2017[1]

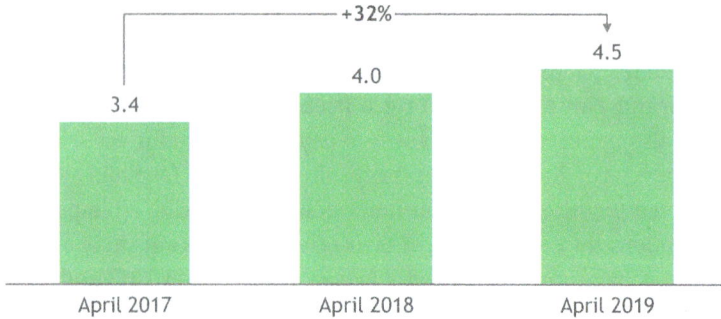

Airplane passengers declining month-on-month in Sweden

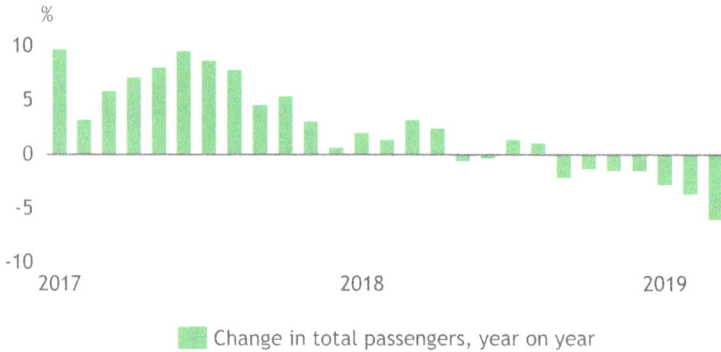

Change in total passengers, year on year

1. 52 weeks ending April 2019
Sources: Plant Based Foods Association, 2019; The Economist, 2019

Figure 4.3: Eco-friendly behaviours: A driving force behind consumer trends in more developed economies.

in employee activism, with employees publicly criticizing their employers on climate policies, forming advocacy groups or submitting shareholder proposals.[16]

---

16 See BBC News, "Amazon 'Threatens to Fire' Climate Change Activists," 3 January 2020, https://www.bbc.com/news/business-50953719.

A Greater Emphasis on ESG Issues from Investors

Investors can play a pivotal role in the process of dynamic materiality. If there is sufficient alignment among investors on how to evaluate the performance of companies on ESG issues (and that information is used to inform portfolio construction and security selection), investors can cause certain ESG issues to become material. More broadly, a sufficiently influential investor who places enough public emphasis on a certain issue can cause management teams to shift their attention to that issue. Both trends are playing out.

There are signs of convergence on how ESG performance is measured. The general lack of correlation among rating agencies' ESG scores is well documented.[17] And given the continued reliance on such scores by many investors, capital is hindered in its ability to collectively influence trading multiples of laggards and leaders. Recently, however, some signs of convergence in scores have appeared, notably on the environmental dimension.[18] Such convergence among investors gives corporate management teams more clarity on how investors will evaluate their current sustainability performance.

Some investors are using their influence to emphasize certain ESG issues more openly. In the United States alone, the percentage of shareholder resolutions that included environmental and social issues grew from 33% during the 2006 to 2010 time period to 50% in 2017.[19] Asset owners are also placing greater emphasis on investor stewardship efforts. Some large asset owners have recently awarded passive managers higher fees for stewardship activities.[20] Leading asset managers consulted confirmed that they are significantly expanding their stewardship capabilities. A few more activist investors are also making sustainability a more important part of their agendas. For example, Trian Partners, a New York based asset manager, recently encouraged DuPont and Danone to promote workplace diversity and to reduce emissions and waste.

---

17 See Berg, Florian, Julian Koelbel, and Roberto Rigobon, "Aggregate Confusion: The Divergence of ESG Ratings," MIT Sloan School of Management, 2019.

18 See Berg, Florian, Julian Koelbel, and Roberto Rigobon, "Aggregate Confusion: The Divergence of ESG Ratings," MIT Sloan School of Management, 2019.

19 See Eccles, Robert and Svetlana Klimenko, "The Investor Revolution," *Harvard Business Review*, May–June 2019, https://hbr.org/2019/05/the-investor-revolution.

20 See Riding, Siobhan, "World's Biggest Pension Fund Steps up Passive Stewardship Efforts," *Financial Times*, 16 September 2019, https://www.ft.com/content/8e5e0476-f046-3316-b01b-e5b4eac983f1.

> Some ESG issues today are not perceived as material enough. We put them on the table pro-actively to make them more material, as we know they will be long term. —Therése Lenne-hag, head, Sustainability, EQT Partners, Sweden

These developments are welcome, particularly as they mean investors are starting to give management teams better guidance on how current ESG performance is evaluated. That said, as capital becomes concentrated in fewer and fewer hands, the ability of investors themselves to influence the materiality of ESG issues (and some of the more public tactics used) will have to be watched closely.

The Children's Investment Fund (TCI): Launching a public campaign on corporate carbon disclosures

The Children's Investment Fund, a long-term activist hedge fund, launched a public campaign to pressure all companies in its portfolio to disclose their carbon emissions, reduction targets, and transition plans. In its public warning letters, which are available on the investor's website, TCI lists seven disclosure recommendations and pledges to vote against directors of those companies who do not comply with these requests. TCI seeks to influence change by remaining a holder of shares and by creating pressure via voting and "public embarrassment." Two years ago, the activist investor JANA Partners applied similar tactics—a public campaign and letter—to pressure Apple to develop solutions for children's excessive use of its products. Here, the investor addressed a social issue that could potentially impact business in the future but was not specifically related to the company's operations or disclosures.

Implications for Companies and Investors

What becomes financially material is changing faster than ever. This has clear implications for both investors and companies. Investors must build their ability to anticipate future material issues and assess corporate preparedness to address social and environmental challenges. Companies need to develop stronger processes for monitoring and proactively managing emerging issues. To be ready for this new age of materiality, investors and companies should ask themselves the following questions (see Figure 4.4):

Five Questions for Investors in the New Age of Materiality

1. Have we developed convictions about how we expect the financial materiality of ESG issues to evolve by sector or industry? Do we continuously update these based on new information?

2. Are these convictions informed by data that goes beyond the reporting and the ESG scores of companies, such as conversations with management or alternative sources of data?
3. Do we use our convictions about the outlook on the financial materiality of ESG issues to inform our security selection and portfolio construction decisions?
4. Are we, through our stewardship activities, engaging with management teams on their strategies for improving performance against the issues that we expect to become financially material in the future?
5. Are we contributing to broader efforts to understand dynamic materiality through the transparent reporting and disclosures we make about our portfolios?

There will be significant transition risks for certain industries that investors need to better understand. Moreover, ESG metrics are not particularly useful in measuring these future risks, given that they are too static and focused on today . . . hence, developing more forward-looking measurements of climate risks and opportunities is essential.

—Mark Carney, governor of the Bank of England

Five Questions for Companies in the New Age of Materiality

1. Do we have a view on which ESG issues are, and will become, material to our business?
2. Is our view informed by a sufficiently wide range of data and do we continuously update our views based on new information and environmental and social developments?
3. Do our views on current and future material issues inform our strategy-setting process at the enterprise and business unit levels? Accordingly, are we being innovative in the way we develop our products and services?
4. Are we successfully implementing the changes needed to perform well against future material issues? And is the speed and impact of our execution sufficient?
5. Are we using our forward-looking view and strategy regarding future material ESG issues to engage with investors and other stakeholders (that is, in corporate reporting)?

We are looking for companies with a clear purpose position and a forward-looking plan. A company's future vision on its transition is key and needs to be integrated in its investor proposition and used in its dialogue with stakeholders.

—Henry McLoughlin, director, Corporate Development, Capricorn Investment Group, USA

Investors

1 Have we developed convictions about how we expect the financial materiality of ESG issues to evolve by sector or industry?

2 Are these informed by the data that goes beyond the reporting and the ESG scores of companies?

3 Do we use our convictions to inform our security selection and portfolio construction decisions?

4 Are we engaging with management teams on their strategies for performing well against future issues?

5 Are we contributing to broader efforts to understand dynamic materiality through reporting and disclosure?

Companies

1 Do we have a view on which ESG issues are, and will become, material to our business?

2 Is our view informed by a sufficiently wide range of data and do we continuously update those views?

3 Do our views on current and future material issues inform our strategy-setting and innovation processes?

4 Are we successfully implementing the changes needed to perform well against future material issues?

5 Are we using our forward-looking view to engage with investors and other stakeholders?

Figure 4.4: Five questions for investors and companies in a new age of materiality.

Looking Ahead: An Action Plan for Investors

Which ESG issues become material has never been more dynamic. As the broader ESG landscape evolves, so too will how investors think about dynamic materiality. Given the expectation of continued action by regulators and other stakeholders on environmental and social issues, every industry will, to varying degrees, undergo sustainability-related transitions. As such, dynamic materiality will become increasingly important, and innovation in how investors and management teams approach this topic will be warranted and welcome. The World Economic Forum will continue to engage on this important topic as it relates to its broader goal of supporting industry transitions to a more sustainable future. As this collective conversation continues, the Forum welcomes further engagement from the community in identifying and leading opportunities for shared action, and in advancing this important dialogue on the materiality of ESG.

Part 2: **What is Sustainable Business Model Innovation?**

David Young and Martin Reeves
5 The Quest for Sustainable Business Model Innovation

Corporations are making significant progress in addressing sustainability. Most large companies now have a statement of social purpose, many are signatories to the UN Global Compact and support the Sustainable Development Goals, many report progress against material quantitative metrics, and some have joined collaborative efforts to tackle existential environmental or societal issues. Davos 2020 further added to the momentum on stakeholder capitalism, disclosure of progress on environmental, social, and governance (ESG) metrics, and climate response.

These actions are encouraging. We have argued that corporations should optimize for both social and business value,[1] using their core businesses to deliver the financial returns expected by their owners and, in tandem, to help society meet its most significant challenges. To do so, we suggest that leaders reimagine corporate strategy[2] by creating new modes of differentiation, embedding societal value into products and services, reimagining business models for sustainability, managing to new measures of performance, and reshaping business ecosystems to support these initiatives. While this is a tall order for any management team, the future of the company, our environment, and society depends on doing so.

Limitations of Current Mainstream Approaches

Beyond this progress, few companies have tried to systematically understand the sustainability limits, vulnerabilities, and potential of their current business models and ecosystems. As a result, they risk diminishing their future competitiveness, license to operate, and shareholder returns. This oversight is not entirely surprising. Over the last few decades, managers have relaxed their ambitions regarding sustainable competitive advantage and have focused instead on shareholder returns. The result has been a greater reliance on financial strategies and mergers and acquisitions (M&A) and a relentless optimization of processes and organization for efficiencies. While such priorities can create shareholder value in the near term, they can also hide weaknesses in the business model and work

---

1 https://www.bcg.com/publications/2019/optimize-social-business-value.
2 https://www.bcg.com/capabilities/corporate-finance-strategy/corporate-strategy.

https://doi.org/10.1515/9783111295268-006

against the building of sustainable advantage. And when it comes to issues of sustainability and societal challenges, managers have often treated these separately from core business operations.

We have a long way to go before the two main uses of the S-word in business — sustainability and sustainable competitive advantage—fuse coherently in a way that can guide management thinking and corporate action in the decade ahead. This disconnect is both a wasted opportunity and an urgent social priority. For all the effort to date, we are making little or even negative aggregate progress in essential areas like carbon emissions, even as the societal effects and business impacts are increasingly apparent.

Current approaches have three critical limits: an overemphasis on compliance and reporting, a bifurcation of intent, and a primary focus on the company level.

There has been notable progress in defining metrics for materiality and sustainability and supporting them with increasingly relevant and better quality data, but this has inadvertently created an overemphasis on reporting and compliance per se, rather than on strategy, action, and advantage. Instead of measuring action and progress against a strategic plan, ESG metrics have become an end in themselves.

This emphasis on sustainability as compliance gives rise to the second issue, the separation of strategy and sustainability considerations. Hence, progress on sustainability metrics is often (and ironically) not closely connected with progress in building sustainable advantage and performance. Quarterly calls and annual reporting emphasize financial returns. Material sustainability issues are considered separately, often in a separate organization with separate reporting and little connection to what drives value in the business.

Generic ESG metrics across industries are too coarse-grained to be closely aligned with any particular firm's capabilities and strategy. Materiality metrics attempt to address this by identifying the critical issues by industry. However, industry boundaries are blurring (seven of the ten largest firms in the world are industry-spanning platform businesses), and companies sharing a common end product exhibit increasingly divergent strategies and business models. The emphasis is therefore on reporting at the level of the individual company, sometimes including parts of the supply chain but rarely including the full business ecosystem, the industry, or the broader network of stakeholders—all of which have a role in constraining or enabling advantage and sustainability. This is a critical flaw, since many sustainability issues, like plastic waste or global warming, require collective action. They require the integration and amplification of other participants in an industry's value chains and ecosystem for impact at scale, the adoption of agreed-upon norms and goals to prevent free-riding, and the trust and cooperation of nonbusiness stakeholders.

Figure 5.1 shows the spectrum of company maturity from corporate social responsibility (CSR) to sustainable business model innovation (SBM-I), the focus of this article. CSR often does little for either competitiveness or societal benefits at scale. More mature stages include driving compliance through incremental improvement of business processes, undertaking single-point innovations for sustainability in response to new compliance or stakeholder pressures, and, ultimately, pursuing sustainable business model innovation. Few companies are positioned on the far right of the spectrum, a requirement for them to win through the 2020s.

A New Approach: SBM-I

SBM-I addresses the limitations of current approaches. It builds on traditional business model innovation[3] but applies it to a much expanded context. The basic idea is first to test the company's current business model for sustainability against a broader temporal, societal, and spatial context so that its vulnerability to externalities, its sustainability limits, and its potential to create new environmental and societal value all become apparent. Second, it explores business model innovations by applying a combination of modular "transformations" to address limits and leverage potentials. Next, it connects business model innovations back to the core drivers of business advantage and financial performance in order to assess how they can deliver both value and sustainability. New models are piloted and tuned to capture advantage in the market and with investors and stakeholders, and to understand what changes are needed in the business ecosystem or at the industry level to create the right context for success.

---

3 https://www.bcg.com/capabilities/innovation-strategy-delivery/business-model-innovation.

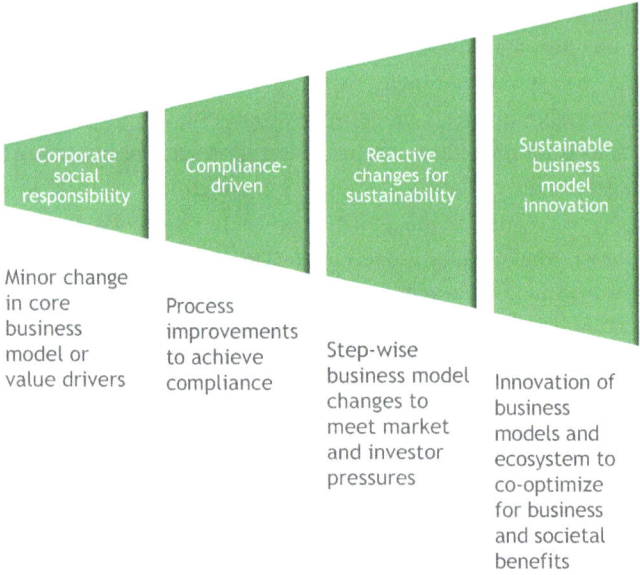

The four panels read left to right:

Corporate social responsibility
Minor change in core business model or value drivers

Compliance-driven
Process improvements to achieve compliance

Reactive changes for sustainability
Step-wise business model changes to meet market and investor pressures

Sustainable business model innovation
Innovation of business models and ecosystem to co-optimize for business and societal benefits

Source: BCG analysis

Figure 5.1: From compliance to sustainable competitive advantage.

David Young, Martin Reeves, and Marine Gerard

6 The Secrets of Sustainability Front Runners

Every enterprise is finding that its space for business as usual is increasingly constrained by the planet's environmental limits, by broader social and economic needs, and by rising stakeholder demands. Consequently, in addition to addressing all the traditional factors defining competition, company strategies now need to explicitly confront the dynamic socio-environmental externalities of the business. From their impacts on climate to the communities where they operate, the growing challenge for business leaders is to navigate through wider sustainability constraints while still delivering the financial results on which its employees and shareholders depend. But new opportunity can be found in creating innovative business models that integrate growth and value creation with the generation of broader environmental and societal benefits. And we've seen that some leading companies are fundamentally reimagining their businesses to turn sustainability into core business advantage.

Take the example of Schneider Electric, a digital energy management firm based in Rueil-Malmaison, France. Driven by a vision to be a leader in sustainability, the company has reimagined its business model over time, evolving from initially being a French-based, traditional electric installations player to becoming a truly global leader in digital sustainability solutions. Today, much of this company's business model relies on the EcoStruxure platform. Introduced in 2007 and enabled with sophisticated digital tools, analytics, and the Internet of Things (IoT), EcoStruxure manages the data and controls for buildings, infrastructure, data centers, power grids, and industries. By shaping the way its customers manage their energy consumption and sustainability footprint across almost half a million sites, EcoStruxure has helped them collectively save 90 million metric tons of CO_2 per year (equivalent to taking almost 20 million cars off the road for an entire year).

Schneider Electric also actively works on improving environmental and societal impact in other ways. For instance, it has worked on a ground-breaking collaboration with Walmart to provide increased access to renewable energy across the retailer's United States-based supply chain. The initiative, called the Gigaton Power Purchase Agreement (GPPA) Program, is designed to educate Walmart suppliers about renewable energy purchases and facilitate adoption through aggregate purchase agreements.

https://doi.org/10.1515/9783111295268-007

The company also worked with countries around the world to develop fast-track health-care facilities throughout the COVID-19 pandemic. In China and Turkey, Schneider helped get new hospitals operational. In the UK and Italy, it helped convert exhibition centers into temporary hospitals. In France, India, and Spain, it helped manufacture respirators, and on a global scale, it worked on rapid deployment of solutions to enable intensive care units to better manage the challenges of the pandemic.

These efforts are emblematic of Schneider Electric's reimagination of its business model, from being a traditional B2B electrical distribution equipment manufacturer to becoming a recognized global leader in environmental sustainability solutions. Its annual revenues have grown accordingly, from €15 billion ($18 billion) in 2007 to €27 billion ($33 billion) in 2019. In January 2021, the prominent Canadian "clean capitalism" magazine *Corporate Knights* named Schneider Electric the most sustainable corporation in the world.

Companies face increasing constraints on conducting business as usual. Stakeholder expectations from all sides are demanding accountability to address negative impacts and increasingly demanding that companies go beyond mitigation and demonstrate positive environmental and societal benefits.

And in recent years, businesses have invested in significant initiatives to demonstrate their commitment to creating environmental and societal benefits—or at the very least, mitigating their harmful practices. Many companies have developed sustainability initiatives that aim to reduce greenhouse gas emissions, improve general quality of life, reduce vulnerability to diseases, or lift people out of poverty. But too often these efforts remain fragmented, lacking scale and impact. And too often they are disconnected from underlying drivers of business value. In interviews, executives say their greatest challenge with these initiatives is integrating them into their core business. These initiatives have limited ability to release the tightening constraints on a company's opportunity space. To break through, companies must make sustainability a source of business advantage, and that requires taking a new approach that seeks out innovative ways to address environmental and societal needs through their core business models.

Sustainable business model innovation (SBM-I) brings these two ideas together, addressing the main challenge executives face in making sustainability a source of advantage. Figure 6.1 depicts competitive advantage and business value on the left, environmental and societal benefits on the right, and in the center, the place to focus attention: continued development and improvement of a sustainable business model. Companies like Schneider Electric solve for their business objectives and their environmental and societal commitments together, widening their opportunity space in the process.

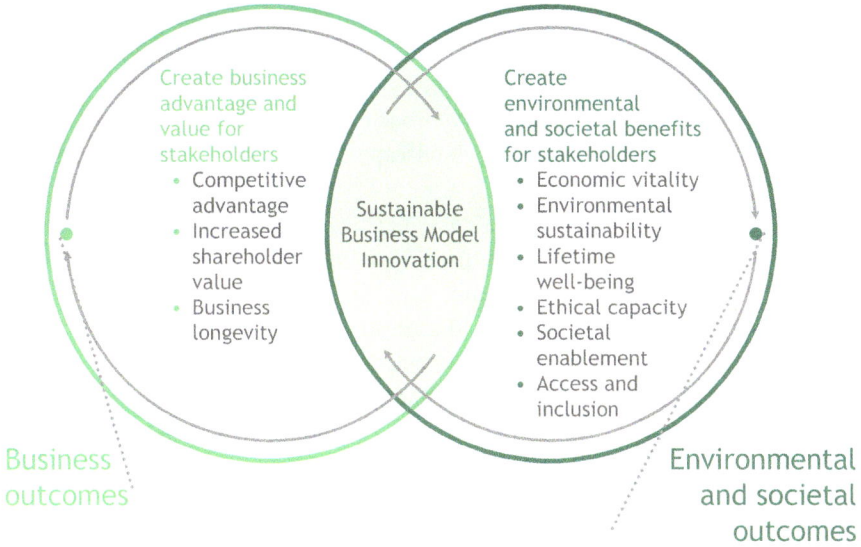

Source: BCG analysis

Figure 6.1: The two engines of Sustainable Business Model Innovation.

The Landscape of Sustainable Business Model Innovation

As part of our BCG Henderson Institute research on SBM-I, we sought to understand how far companies have moved in building out sustainable business models. In a sample of more than 500 sustainability initiatives around the world, we found just one in five cases where companies changed some part or all of their core business model to generate environmental and societal benefits and business value. Even among these companies, few have captured the full potential possible through SBM-I. There are two main reasons for this shortfall.

First, most companies have only begun their SBM-I journey. They still regard corporate social responsibility as a matter of compliance and securing a "license to operate" from regulators and public opinion. They limit themselves by thinking of their environmental and societal benefits primarily in the narrow terms of ESG performance. It takes time and concerted executive attention to develop the necessary attitudes, mental models, strategies, and practices that can leverage the core business and turn sustainability into an advantage.

Second, there has not yet been a holistic, structured approach for designing sustainable business model innovations that generate full value. The intersection of business value and environmental and societal benefits does not occur by chance; it takes a rigorous innovation approach and a set of organizational design choices. In this article, we look at the landscape using SBM-I to build competitive advantage.

To understand the state of sustainable business model innovation, we plotted more than 100 case studies against three dimensions to depict the landscape of sustainable business model innovation:

– the scale and scope on which SBM-I changes the business model
– the extent to which SBM-I is creating business advantage
– the magnitude of the environmental and societal benefits SBM-I creates

Expanding the Scale and Scope of Innovation

This dimension represents the scale and scope of the company's SBM-I initiatives. It includes how ambitious the effort is—for instance, the extent of its reach across the company's value chain, or how many businesses and product and service lines it involves. How willing are they to use sustainability to reimagine business-as-usual? Could it lead them to a fundamental reimagining of their business model?

Companies tend to fall into one of three stages of maturity on this dimension. In initial stages of SBM-I development, the focus is generally on improving the environmental and societal benefits of a product or process. For instance, the Swedish fintech Doconomy launched "DO," a mobile banking platform and credit card that helps consumers track, limit, and offset the CO_2 emissions associated with their purchases. This offering directs consumption toward more environmentally friendly products and services.

In the next stage, the SBM-I initiatives focus on enriching the company's value chain—upstream with its suppliers, downstream with distributors and customers. The Brazilian cosmetics company Natura, for example, developed its very popular line of EKOS nature-friendly cosmetics by sourcing products in ways that empower indigenous communities and preserve and replenish biodiversity in the Amazon rainforest. Similarly, PepsiCo's well-established sustainable farming program helps more than 40,000 farmers across 38 countries adopt precision technologies and regenerative agriculture and soil health management techniques. As a result of this program, the potatoes used to make Frito-Lay products sold in the United States and Canada are sustainably sourced.

Downstream, Samsung's large-scale e-waste recycling program was active in 54 countries as of 2018; it had collected more than 3.55 million tons of products since 2009. The apparel brand C&A made a similar commitment to "circular fashion," launching a program to take back and donate or recycle garments from consumers. Since 2012, the program has collected in the region of 1,000 tons of used garments in Europe, Brazil, and Mexico. In addition to managing waste responsibly, the Samsung and C&A programs are also poised to improve resource use as they gain scale. They can potentially serve as a valuable source of input materials to develop more circular models—for example, providing precious metals for electronics manufacture or textile fibers for garments.

Some companies go still further, *reimagining the business model* to deliver environmental and societal benefits. They unlock new growth opportunities by solving for environmental and societal needs heads-on, often transforming their core business model. Schneider Electric, with its EcoStruxure platform, falls into this category. So does Yara, a pioneering Norwegian agricultural products company, which diversified beyond its traditional fertilizers business to launch a digital "smart" agriculture arm. Using satellite imagery and connected sensors and dispensers, Yara's solutions enhance customers' farming yields while reducing the amount of water and fertilizer dispensed and providing optimal support for crops. A third example is the Dutch social enterprise Fairphone, which is reimagining the consumer electronics business model to produce and sell a more ethical and durable smartphone. The Fairphone is composed of sustainable materials, including responsibly sourced and conflict-free tin and tungsten and recycled copper and plastics; it has a modular design that can be upgraded and repaired by swapping out components.

Gaining Business Advantage

The second dimension has to do with the level of business advantage derived from sustainable business model innovation. Here, too, there are three stages of maturity, depending on the way each company builds its brand and competes in the marketplace—or, better yet, changes the nature of competition.

In the initial stages of business advantage, SBM-I *enhances and amplifies the brand.* Its environmental and societal benefits increase differentiation, competitiveness, and stakeholder value. Natura's sustainable EKOS cosmetics line and Fairphone's ethical phone appeal to consumers who value sustainability and wholeness, attracting their loyalty and willingness to pay premium prices.

In further stages of advantage, SBM-I *shapes the business ecosystem and its stakeholders' values and dynamics.* On the basis of its capacity for business model innovation, the company influences industry norms, standards, and regulations, along with supplier and consumer demands and behaviors. For example, Dell's Digital LifeCare platform enables early screening of non-communicable diseases and care delivery for hard-to-reach populations in rural India. To deploy the platform, the company works with stakeholders across the ecosystem, including the Government of India and a diverse ecosystem of partners. Digital LifeCare's enrolled population has grown from 58,000 in late 2018 to nearly 60 million as of mid-2020, positioning the company as a critical player in the country's digital health infrastructure. Similarly, the Dutch company Royal DSM is partnering with the Rwandan public sector, international aid agencies, and local NGOs to provide more nutritious, fortified foods in the country. Together, in 2017, they launched Africa Improved Foods (AIF), a private–public joint venture that has developed local farming and supply networks, manufacturing capacity, and a pan-African customer base.

The most mature stage of advantage involves *creating a new playing field, with reshaped boundaries of competition and stakeholder dynamics* enabling new value creation. One example is Yara's foray into digital farming, which unlocks new growth opportunities by shifting from selling crop nutrition products to solving broader agricultural and environmental problems.

Another is BIMA, a digital insurance provider that started operations in Ghana in 2010. Thanks to its innovative technology platform and partnership model with telecom providers, mobile money providers, and insurance underwriters, BIMA provides affordable, easy-to-manage life and health insurance to more than 35 million low-income customers across ten emerging economies. BIMA's customers have access to its services through their mobile phones. Many of them are lower-income families who earn less than $10 a day. About 75% of them are obtaining insurance for the first time in their lives.

Creating Environmental and Societal Benefits

The third dimension has to do with the magnitude and nature of environmental and societal benefits generated. In our work to holistically define impact, we identify six dimensions of environmental and societal value that companies can create through their products, services, operations, and value chains. These areas include economic vitality, environmental sustainability, lifetime well-being, ethical capacity, societal enablement, and access and inclusion.

In the initial stage, the environmental or societal benefit is still limited in scale and often oriented toward *mitigating the negative impacts of the business.* SBM-I addresses the symptoms of the environmental or societal issue rather than the underlying causes. For instance, collecting and recycling plastics is an excellent first step in reducing the impact of plastic waste. However, it does not achieve true sustainable packaging. That would require fully circular solutions in which all plastics are recycled, or even packaging-free solutions. Similarly, ensuring animal welfare at the food production stage is an essential early stage activity. Still, it does not address head-on the challenges of emissions-intensive production of cattle for food.

In the next stage, SBM-I delivers meaningful environmental and societal benefits by *targeting root causes of the environmental or societal challenge.* The company's activity generates net environmental or societal benefits, and there is potential for significant positive impact if it can scale. For instance, IBM's Food Trust blockchain-enabled technology platform establishes transparency around environmental sustainability for products in the grocery supply chain, ensuring product integrity and safety from production to consumption. This platform delivers meaningful environmental and societal surplus just by increasing the integrity or ethical capacity of the supply chain.

Finally, the most mature group of SBM-I efforts on this dimension *creates high, at-scale environmental and societal benefits,* addressing the root causes of the issue at hand. For instance, M-Pesa—a peer-to-peer mobile money service for people without a bank account—was born as a joint project between Vodafone and Safaricom. Launched in Kenya in 2007, M-Pesa has since increased the financial resilience of 40 million users in Africa, while creating income for 300,000 M-Pesa agents and a healthy business for the telecommunications venture.

By combining these three dimensions, a picture of the current competitive landscape of sustainable business model innovation emerges. Figure 6.2 shows the placement of all 102 SBM-I initiatives according to our three dimensions. It divides these initiatives into three groups, according to how far they have advanced.

Of the case studies, 45% were *"initiative leaders"* (shown at the lower left of Figure 6.2). These companies are often associated with a strong brand promise based on sustainability. They tend to invent or improve products to address consumer, regulator, or investor demands for more environmentally and socially mindful outcomes. While these SBM-I efforts can enhance and differentiate a company from its competitors, their advantage can fade as competitors replicate their approach or join industry coalitions. For example, most plastics recycling programs are no longer differentiating, because nearly all consumer packaged goods companies have made commitments to tackle that waste issue.

Moving to the center of the matrix, 25% of our cases qualify as *"ecosystem leaders."* Companies undertaking these SBM-I initiatives seek to provide environmental and societal benefits by reshaping the dynamics of suppliers, distributors, investors, policymakers, and customers. They are often visionary companies, seeking to turn environmental and societal challenges into new business opportunities. Some of them form novel cross-industry or cross-sector partnerships to build their new sustainable business models. For example, Microsoft's Airband initiative works with regulators and develops novel distribution partnerships with local telecommunications companies and Internet service providers (including small and medium-size enterprises) to extend broadband voice and data access across low-income and rural areas. Its goal is to reach more than 40 million additional people in the United States and abroad by 2022.

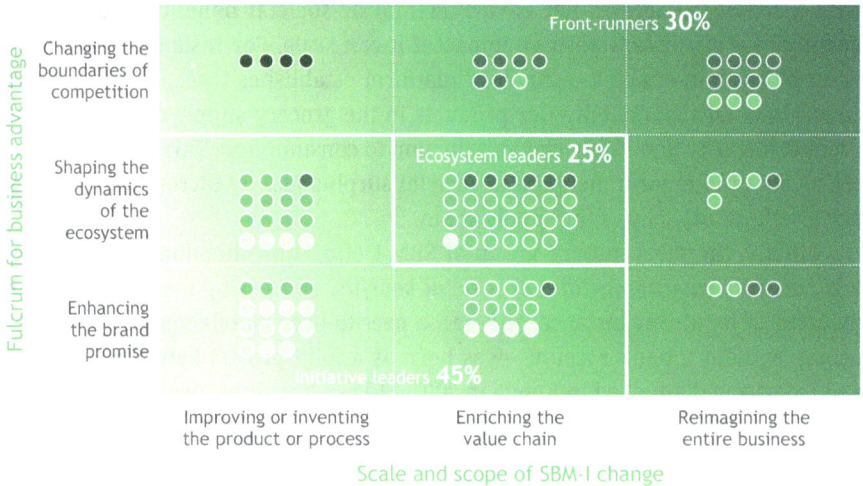

Magnitude of environmental and societal benefit
(each dot represents one of the case studies from our research)

Mitigating environmental and societal impacts; adding to the common good

Addressing the root causes of environmental and societal issues; significant potential for greater benefit through gains in scale

Addressing the root causes of environ-mental and societal issues, at scale

Source: BCG analysis
Note: Based on 102 case studies of SBM-I across geographies and industries; compiled from publicly available sources

Figure 6.2: Cases of Sustainable Business Model Innovation (SBM-I).

The Front-Runners of SBM-I

The final 30% of cases are *"front-runners."* They pave the way forward for their industries and markets, and they provide insight into what advanced SBM-I could look like. Front-runners have shifted their perspective from incremental "company-out" activities to more radical "societal needs-in" innovation. That is, they reorganize their capabilities, assets, products, services, and ecosystems to proactively solve for the UN Sustainable Development Goals, with close ties to their own business value drivers. Front-runners generate business outcomes (for example, total shareholder return) and environmental and societal outcomes in mutually reinforcing ways. They are closest to turning sustainability into a competitive business advantage.

In analyzing front-runner case studies, we found several factors that characterize them:

–   **They emphasize sustainability as part of their purpose.** All of the companies in our sample explicitly mention environmental or societal surplus in their formal purpose, vision, or mission statements.
–   **They build a robust, resilient business model and deploy it for all their goals.** The drivers of environmental and societal impact are directly linked to the drivers of business value and competitive advantage. These companies thrive as businesses because of their efforts to tackle the root causes of an environmental or societal issue.
–   **They optimize for holistic environmental and societal outcomes.** Rather than focusing on an isolated symptom of a particular issue, they seek a comprehensive solution that addresses its complex, systemic root causes. This differentiates them from competitors. It allows them to shape the stakeholder dynamics of the ecosystem and even reshape the boundaries of competition (the "rules of the game") to their advantage.
–   **They combine several sustainable business model innovations.** In "The Quest for Sustainable Business Model Innovation" we introduced common innovation archetypes for sustainable business models: Own the origins; Own the whole cycle; Expand societal content; Energize the brand; Relocalize/regionalize; Decarbonize for advantage; Exploit energy flexibility; Nudge sustainable consumption; Expand the value chains; and Build across sectors. By combining and layering these approaches, companies develop holistic strategies and models that increase business value and increase societal and environmental benefits simultaneously.
–   **They deploy advanced technology and digital capabilities**. This enables them to develop new solutions, break old economic constraints and tradeoffs, and amplify their reach and scale. Companies that demonstrate sophisticated

use of digital tools, analytics, and other advanced technology tend to score higher on the value drivers associated with business value and increase societal and environmental benefits.
- **They gain leverage from new cross-industry and cross-sector partnerships.** Front-runners partner with private, public, and social entities to pool resources, exchange capabilities, unlock new markets, and amplify their reach and scale.
- **They create value for a wide range of stakeholder groups.** They proactively consider the long-term interests of customers, suppliers, employees, shareholders and investors, government, and all of society, and in so doing they expand their basis of advantage.
- **They experiment with new ways of capturing value.** They look for innovative approaches to securing customer preferences and accessing new markets. They also experiment with novel ways to get returns on the stakeholder value they create—for example, leveraging blended financing to reduce risk and amplify their own investments.

Proficiency in any new field is a moving target, and sustainable business model innovation is no exception. The front-runners of today will be joined by many other companies. Many of them, like Schneider Electric, are finding ingenious solutions to pernicious societal and environmental problems. Along the way, they are demonstrating what a quality company will be like in the future.

The SBM-I landscape provides a quick way to understand just how far your company is leveraging sustainability as advantage. Start by looking closely at your current business model and sustainability initiatives, in light of the three dimensions of the SBM-I landscape. We've explored answers to some related questions in other articles in this series. What is the scale and scope on which you're innovating to drive environmental and societal impact? How much sustainable business advantage are you creating? What kind of environmental and societal surplus are you generating? Where do you start your SBM-I journey?

David Young and Marine Gerard

7 How to Tell if Your Business Model is Truly Sustainable

Throughout the pandemic, companies worked to rapidly adjust their business models to be more resilient and competitive in the face of uncertain economic recovery. As companies now build back, how can they assess which business model changes will enable the company to become genuinely more resilient and sustainable over time?

We believe that our insights from researching sustainable business model innovation (SBM-I) can help answer that question. Crossing all industries and geographies, our research analyzed more than 100 business models through which companies delivered both business value and environmental and societal benefits. We tested each business model against nine attributes to gauge its robustness and resilience, attributes identified through BCG's experience in helping companies create strategies and business models that yield sustainable business advantage.

The Nine Attributes of Sustainable Business Models

Below we discuss how various attributes fundamentally underpin business advantage and illustrate how they add to business resilience and sustainability, using examples of interesting companies that are pursuing sustainable business model innovations. In general, the better the business model scores on the nine attributes shown in the spider diagram of Figure 7.1, "Nine Attributes to Assess Sustainable Business Advantage," the more likely the company is well-positioned for resilience, sustainability, and competitive advantage over time.

The first five attributes in the list below can apply to many business models independent of their environmental or societal impacts, at least until their externalities result in new regulatory constraints or stakeholder backlash. However, it is the addition of attributes six through nine that forms the core of truly sustainable business models. And it is these attributes that are becoming increasingly important for all businesses to remain resilient and extend their advantage in the future.

https://doi.org/10.1515/9783111295268-008

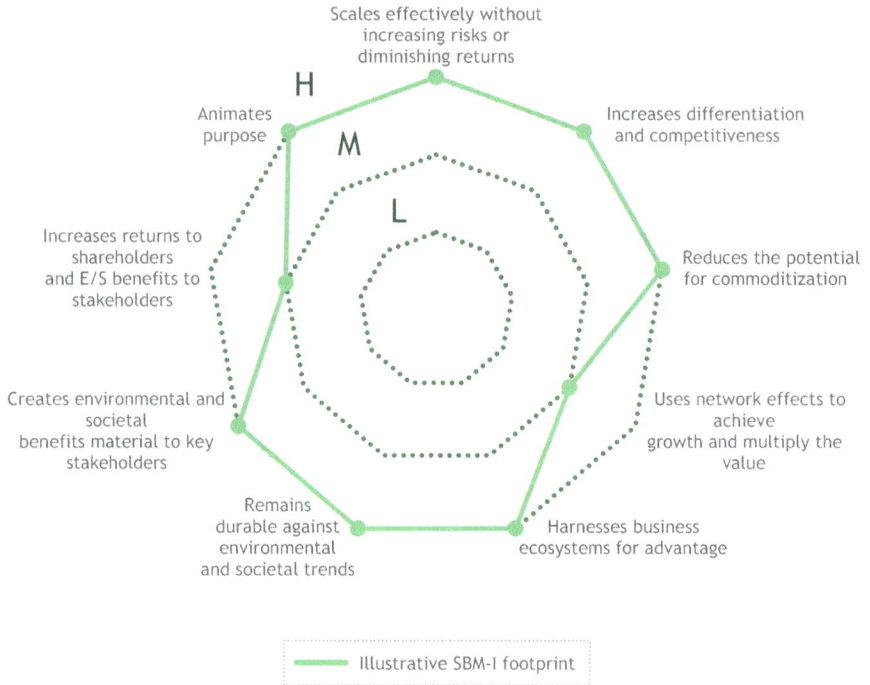

Figure with radial diagram showing nine attributes:
- Scales effectively without increasing risks or diminishing returns
- Increases differentiation and competitiveness
- Reduces the potential for commoditization
- Uses network effects to achieve growth and multiply the value
- Harnesses business ecosystems for advantage
- Remains durable against environmental and societal trends
- Creates environmental and societal benefits material to key stakeholders
- Increases returns to shareholders and E/S benefits to stakeholders
- Animates purpose

H, M, L

Illustrative SBM-I footprint

Source: BCG analysis of 102 case studies of SBM-I initiatives, based on publicly available data
Note: E/S = Environmental/societal; H = High; M = Medium; L = Low

Figure 7.1: Nine attributes to assess sustainable business advantage.

Scales effectively without increasing risks or diminishing returns. The business model allows the company to grow without reducing its capacity for value creation and profitability. In the case of SBM-I initiatives, as the business scales, so do the environmental and societal benefits it creates, without diminishing the economic returns.

For instance, since its launch in 1993, Jeanologia, which develops eco-friendly denim finishing technologies, has continuously broadened its operations. Many manufacturers and brands became customers as they grew more constrained in the amounts of energy, water, and chemicals they could use. In 2018, Jeanologia's technology was used in the production of 35% of the 5 billion jeans produced annually by the industry, saving more than 10.6 million cubic meters of water, an amount equivalent to the water supply for 584,000 people for a year.

Increases differentiation and competitiveness. The business model delivers product features and operational advantages that make its offerings notably stand out from competitors.

Lush has created an iconic cosmetics brand based on unique product formulations and formats (for example, vegan, packaging-free, and ethical cosmetics that stand out thanks to their vibrant colors), enabled by a robust Fair Trade-certified supply network. It operates factories in Toronto and Vancouver, where products are made by hand, and it trains sales representatives to deliver a distinctive, education-focused store experience.

Reduces the potential for commoditization. The business model enables the company to make its products and the efficiencies and effectiveness of its operating processes difficult for competitors to replicate over time, thereby providing an underpinning for sustainable advantage.

Schneider Electric's EcoStruxure platform leverages a unique combination of digital, IoT, analytics, and applications to deliver a powerful energy management and automation solution that becomes "smarter" as data and machine learning accumulate over time. Launched in 2007, EcoStruxure is (as of 2018) used across more than 500,000 installations. It is the foundation of a €27 billion business, helping customers save, on average, 20% of their CO_2 emissions. (Some save as much as 50%.) In one fiscal year, from 2018 to 2019, this added up to a total savings of 90 million metric tons of CO_2, equivalent to taking almost 20 million cars off the road for an entire year.

Uses network effects to achieve growth and multiply the value. The business model builds itself into the networks of the broader industry and customer ecosystem, enabling growth in the network to pull through growth for the business. For example, it may involve a distribution model—potentially in partnership with other companies—that quickly and cost-effectively accesses volumes of customers. The company may also become integral to the operation of a network, such as one providing health care, financial services, or telecommunications. As demand grows for the network, so does demand for the company's products and services.

Babyl, a subsidiary of Babylon Health UK in Rwanda, signed a ten-year partnership with the Government of Rwanda in February 2020. This partnership enables Babyl to roll out its telehealth platform and services through the government's community-based health insurance scheme, Mutuelle de Santé, and thus multiply its reach. To manage the challenge of a ratio of only 1 doctor to 10,000 inhabitants, Babyl's digital-first model connects and powers a digital health-care network, improving the country's quality and speed of care. It has already registered more than 2 million adults (from an overall adult population of approximately 12 million) across 30 districts, and it facilitates more than 3,000 consultations per day.

Harnesses business ecosystems for advantage. The business model leverages partnerships and collaborations within the business ecosystem. It does so in a way that strengthens its position and value proposition and shapes the dynamics of markets and stakeholders in ways that play to the company's strategic objectives.

The Jaza Duka initiative (the name means "fill up your store" in Swahili) was launched in 2017, jointly led by Unilever, Mastercard, and the Kenya Commercial Bank (KCB). Combining assets and capabilities across the business ecosystem, Jaza Duka helps micro-retailers digitize their transactions to build a proxy credit history and gain access to credit lines to expand their inventory and businesses. The program has helped 20,000 shopkeepers—of which the majority are women —grow their businesses and improve their livelihoods, which benefits all three companies by boosting revenues and lowering risks. The initiative expanded in 2019 with microinsurance and other rewards to encourage complete and timely orders and repayments from micro-retailers, furthering the social impact and business value of the full system.

Remains durable against environmental and societal trends. The business model reduces the constraints and risks that arise from changing environmental constraints and socioeconomic trends. These constraints might materialize in the form of new standards and regulations, supply chain pressures, or changes in consumer and stakeholder attitudes.

Interface evolved its business model over time—redesigning products to improve environmental footprint, developing sustainable sources of inputs (for example, by working with coastal communities to collect and recycle fishing nets into yarn), and setting up take-back and closed-loop recycling programs to turn used plastics into inputs for new carpet tiles. In this way, Interface can maintain its leading position on environmental issues and anticipate or even shape recycling standards and customer demands.

Creates environmental and societal benefits material to key stakeholders. The business model creates environmental and societal benefits that can be used for value creation over time. In another article, we explore the holistic sets of benefits that companies should seek to create.[1] As investors, customers, and other stakeholders increasingly scrutinize ESG risks and performance, companies that create environmental and societal benefits through their business model are better positioned to gain advantage by leveraging this trend.

Primark's Sustainable Cotton Programme creates environmental and societal benefits across a broad set of dimensions, connecting it to business value drivers. Since 2013, this program has trained cotton farmers in sustainable farming methods to reduce chemical pesticides, fertilizers, and water, helping farmers increase

---

1 https://www.bcg.com/publications/2021/maximizing-environmental-and-societal-benefits-from-your-business-model.

their yield and improve their livelihoods through increased income. In 2017, Primark started to use cotton from the program—which is traceable from farm to store—in its products at no extra cost to the consumer. The company started with one of its most popular lines, women's pajamas. In autumn 2020, Primark increased its number of sustainable cotton products to 60 million items, including denim, T-shirts, nightwear, duvets, and towels. By 2022, the program will equip more than 160,000 farmers with the knowledge and means to grow cotton using more sustainable methods, reflecting Primark's long-term ambition to ensure that all the cotton used in its supply chain is sustainably sourced.

Increases returns to shareholders and environmental and societal benefits to stakeholders. The business model is robust in a world of stakeholder capitalism by having a reinforcing cycle of competitive returns on capital and creating benefits to all key stakeholder groups. The business model does not sacrifice returns below what is competitive in the name of creating environmental/societal benefits—nor does it seek returns to the detriment of stakeholders. This positions the company for better long-run risk-adjusted returns.

Royal DSM has partnered with the public sector, international aid agencies, and local NGOs to set up a joint venture called Africa Improved Foods (AIF). This new enterprise tackles nutrition challenges in Rwanda while developing its local supply chain and manufacturing capacity and helping to expand the market for fortified foods. Besides employing 300 skilled factory workers, the venture's 45,000-ton-capacity facility is supplied by more than 35,000 farmers. AIF offers Royal DSM a strategic commercial position in Africa and returns profits above the agreed-upon commercial return to the government of Rwanda. The incremental value of the project over 15 years is estimated at $760 million. Finally, society benefits by having access to locally produced, affordable, and nutritious fortified grains and foods.

Animates purpose. The business model embodies and operationalizes the company's purpose. This boosts engagement and affinity with employees, customers, investors, and other stakeholders.

Jeanologia articulates a purpose that is more altruistic than being "the best company in the world." It wants to be "the best company for the world." Its business model and the resulting environmental impact—in 2018 alone, saving 10.6 million cubic meters of water, equivalent to the water supply for 584,000 people for an entire year—demonstrate and achieve the company's purpose.

A Call to Sustainable Innovation

In everyday practice, companies can use the robustness and resilience framework to determine if their business model provides them with business advantage that is likely to be sustainable over time. It can be used to identify potential vulnerabilities or gaps and to test how additional business model innovations could improve the attributes that underpin their business advantage and overall performance. Business leaders should particularly examine how the business model creates environmental and societal benefits, which are often not explicitly considered as attributes of resilience but are becoming increasingly important.

In the next section we explore how sustainable business model innovation can be done through a structured approach to improve and expand the robustness and resilience footprint of any business.

David Young and Marine Gerard

8 How to Tell if Your Business Model is Creating Environmental and Societal Benefits

The COVID-19 pandemic has been a singular challenge, testing the resilience and viability of many companies. Undoubtedly, there will be more dramatic challenges and opportunities to manage in the coming decade, including climate change and economic inequality. Fortunately, it is possible for business leaders to contribute to solving environmental and societal challenges through their core business, in ways that also generate new opportunities for business value and competitive advantage. This is the essence of *sustainable business model innovation* (SBM-I),[1] innovations that deliver returns to shareholders and benefits to stakeholders. As companies now build back in the recovery, how can they assess which business model changes and innovations will also create the most environmental and societal value for their stakeholders?

We believe our insights from researching SBM-I can help answer that question. Crossing all industries and geographies, our research analyzed 102 SBM-I initiatives through which companies delivered both business value and environmental and societal benefits. We evaluated each initiative on the basis of its competitiveness and resilience and then tested it against six dimensions of environmental and societal benefits (see Figure 8.1). We believe these six dimensions holistically encompass the range of societal values that a business can generate. In fact, in today's business context of increasing concerns about environmental and societal issues, a resilient and competitive business model must optimize for both business and social value. Generally, the traditional thinking on business model innovation has not sufficiently or rigorously incorporated how business models create value for stakeholders and the common good.

The Six Dimensions of Business Model Societal Impact

BCG identifies six dimensions of environmental and societal impact, all with implications for employees and for external stakeholders, including investors, cus-

---

1 https://www.bcg.com/publications/2020/quest-sustainable-business-model-innovation.

https://doi.org/10.1515/9783111295268-009

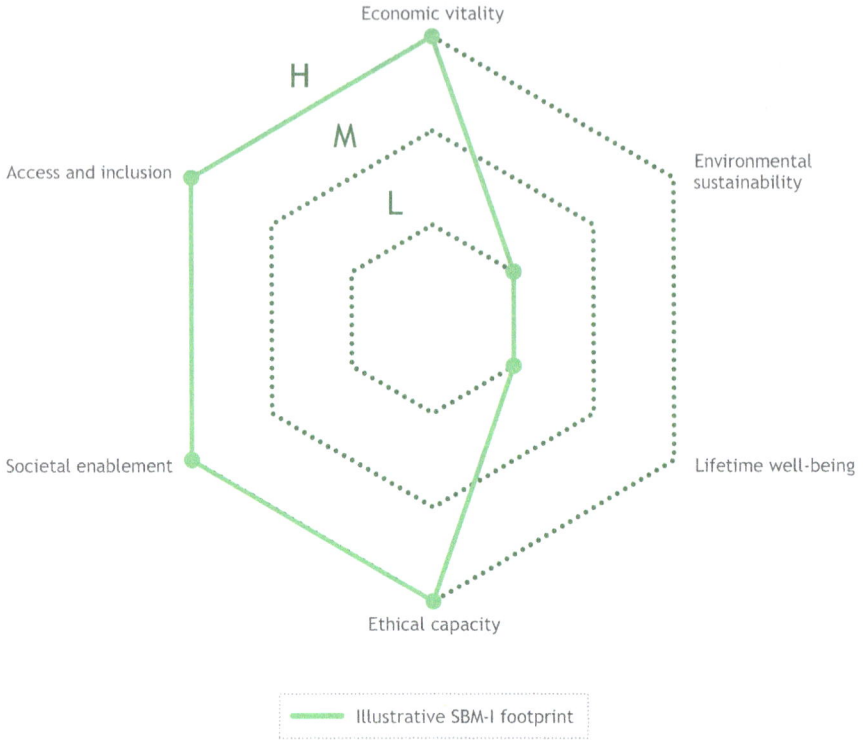

Figure 8.1: Six dimensions of environmental and societal impact: assessing the environmental and societal benefits created.

tomers, suppliers, and society. Below we discuss each dimension and illustrate how it creates environmental and societal benefits, using examples of companies pursuing sustainable business model innovations. In general, the better the business model scores on the six dimensions shown in the spider diagram of Figure 8.1, the more likely the company is well-positioned to deliver benefits to stakeholders and to remain durable under evolving environmental and societal trends, thus contributing to its resilience, sustainability, and competitive advantage over time.

Economic vitality. A company that scores high on this dimension promotes economic prosperity by creating livelihoods and economic opportunities for employees and workers in its supply chain and in its wider ecosystem. The company also contributes to the economic vitality of communities and society through the way it stimulates economic activity, pays taxes, makes investments, and generates other multiplier effects (such as providing a base for smaller businesses).

Companies supplying digital financial services—such as M-Pesa in Africa, Nubank in Brazil, and Ant Financial in China—help hundreds of millions of unbanked and underbanked customers build financial records, access micro-loans to buy goods and grow their small businesses, and build savings over time or use micro-insurance to protect essential assets or ensure their children's education. In the course of business, these companies make significant contributions to the economic vitality of society.

Environmental sustainability. A company that delivers environmental sustainability improves the environmental footprint of its operations, its products and services, and every aspect of its value chain (from sourcing, to use, to disposal). Internally, it develops systems that monitor and reduce its use of energy and materials, decrease its impact on biodiversity and water, lower its greenhouse gas emissions, and eliminate any remaining pollution and waste. Externally, it sets up product take-back and reuse and recycling programs to increase circularity and transform waste into new value streams. Companies at the leading edge of this dimension can solve environmental issues head-on through business models that create net environmental benefits, beyond just mitigating or reducing negative impacts. For example, they might restore natural habitats, regenerate resources, or provide transportation alternatives with a lower carbon footprint. Much of this is done through innovative use of digital and technological advances.

Interface, the world's largest manufacturer of modular flooring, now makes carpet tiles from recycled content and bio-based materials. These tiles store carbon, preventing its release into the atmosphere. Combining this technology with end-of-life take-back and recycling programs, Interface has developed the first "carbon negative" flooring products. It is moving closer to its vision of helping to restore the planet, reverse global warming, and leave a positive impact.

Lifetime well-being. Here a company generates improvements to the quality of life and well-being of employees, customers, and the wider communities where it operates. It provides employees with healthy, fair, and dignified working conditions, including benefits and opportunities for growth and self-actualization. Its products and services are safe, beneficial, and personally enabling; its community activities foster dignity, safety, health, and education. It thinks about well-being as a design principle in all its business activities, the experience of its customers, and the communication of its brand.

Nippon Insurance, based in Japan, is helping senior citizens live with dignity with a "Gran Age" program that pays out larger annuities to older policyholders. It also provides them with a constellation of complementary services to help prevent cognitive impairment, assist with daily life support, and engage them with social opportunities.

Ethical capacity. A company that consistently delivers on this dimension strengthens and enforces ethical practices in its own operations and in the wider ecosystem. It establishes robust governance structures, ensures board independence, and practices strong audit and compliance processes. It may put in place responsible sourcing and marketing practices, or systems to ensure data privacy and security. It mistake-proofs and corruption-proofs its products, services, and business processes. It also builds general trust in business by taking stands against corruption, actualizing human rights commitments (and living up to their ideals), and fostering strong ethical practices in communities and society in general. In this way, it enables transparency and accountability for its own actions and those of its industry.

Lush, a UK-based, privately owned cosmetics company that traversed the billion-dollar sales mark in 2017, has built an iconic brand based on environmental sustainability and ethical values, creating "a cosmetics revolution." All Lush items are composed of simple, ethically sourced, and vegetarian (80% vegan) ingredients. Lush distinguishes itself from competitors by denouncing animal testing of any sort and committing to engaging only with suppliers who adopt the same ethical stance. Lush applies its values across its own supply chain and operations, while also raising awareness around these issues with consumers, influencing their demand for ethical and sustainable products.

Societal enablement. A company that fosters societal enablement establishes core activities that promote and contribute to an open, well-functioning organization and society. Internally, this means promoting greater levels of workforce participation, strengthening processes to manage grievances and provide remedies, and increasing data transparency. Externally, this involves developing products and services that enable and support a well-functioning society—a society, for instance, that promotes social participation, ensures secure election and representation processes, supports the effective and efficient delivery of public goods and services, or raises awareness and education on specific issues.

Launched in 2018, Microsoft's Defending Democracy Program aggregates and expands the company's cybersecurity offerings to help governments protect election-related campaigns from hacking, defend against disinformation, and preserve the integrity of electoral processes in democratic societies.

Access and inclusion. A company that makes progress on this dimension ensures that its workers and employees have nondiscriminatory, inclusive, and equitable access to opportunities. These opportunities might include rewards, career options, recognition, and the ability to advance, regardless of social identifiers (for example, ability, age, ethnicity, gender, race, religion, sexual orientation, socioeconomic status, or class). Externally, the company designs and makes its products and services available to consumers and communities across the socio-demographic range. It consistently considers how to bring the best of what it does to more and more people.

With its Project Shakti initiative, launched in 2001, Hindustan Unilever Limited (HUL) has developed a capillary distribution network of more than 100,000 women micro-entrepreneurs. This effort has brought affordable Unilever products to tens of millions of Indian customers living in remote and underserved rural states and villages. The program not only increases access to goods for the customers but also promotes the economic inclusion and empowerment of women.

Companies should assess their business model against the footprint of their total environmental and societal benefits, holistically considering all six of the dimensions. Our own analysis shows that most companies under-develop their societal benefit (represented by five out of the six dimensions), potentially missing business opportunities that would come from contributing to the common good.

Close to two-thirds of the SBM-I initiatives we studied show a limited footprint across the six dimensions, while only a third create impact on three or more dimensions. Perhaps not surprisingly, the most common dimension of impact found among our sample cases is environmental sustainability (with more than half of cases optimizing for that dimension). Economic vitality ranks second and access and inclusion rank third.

By innovating to expand their scores across all six dimensions, companies can grow their environmental and societal benefit, the basis for new value creation and competitive advantage. They can also future-proof themselves against environmental and societal shocks and shifting trends. For example, a consumer packaged goods company could increase its portfolio of nutritious foods (lifetime well-being) while sourcing closer to its processing centers, thus providing more employment near its customers (economic vitality) and reducing transportation-related emissions (environmental sustainability). Similarly, a fintech that provides microfinance and already facilitates access and inclusion could also mitigate the carbon emissions from its servers or constrain debt-inducing consumption patterns and nudge microloans toward "green" goods and investments, thus boosting ethical capacity and environmental sustainability. Figure 8.2 shows the environmental and societal benefit footprint for two companies seeking to improve their track records.

Resilience Through Sustainability

In the aftermath of the pandemic, as many companies rethink their business models to solve for resilience over efficiency, sustainable business model innovation offers a powerful approach to ensure that business models are robust against future crises. Applying SBM-I requires a frank assessment of the environmental and societal value that your current business model creates for all stakeholders. This assessment should serve as a tool to spur innovation for a more resilient business model. Going forward, a company's ability to generate broad and demonstrable environmental and societal benefits from its core business model will be a key source of sustainable competitive advantage.

A food manufacturer develops an extensive fortified foods portfolio to address nutrient deficiencies in emerging markets

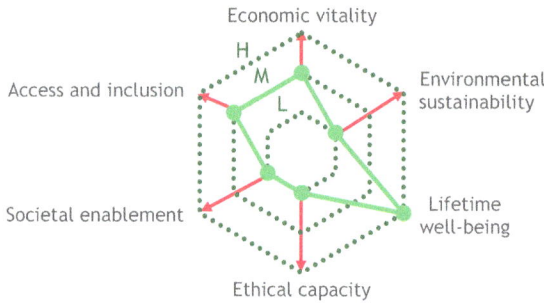

A fintech company provides access to high-quality, low-cost, digital financial services to unbanked and underbanked populations

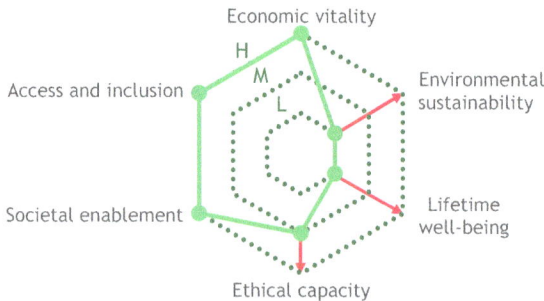

Source: BCG analysis of 102 case studies of SBM-I initiatives, based on publicly available data
Note: H = High; M = Medium; L = Low

Figure 8.2: Examples of environmental / societal benefit footprints.

Part 3: **How to Apply Sustainable Business Model Innovation**

David Young and Marine Gerard

9 Four Steps to Sustainable Business Model Innovation

You may have noticed that every day there's another announcement about companies making new climate commitments, asset managers outlining their plans for ESG integration, or regulators proposing new disclosures or extending producers' responsibilities. Corporate coalitions like the World Economic Forum (WEF) International Business Council (IBC) and the U.S. Business Roundtable endorse a more stakeholder-inclusive corporate capitalism while industry coalitions work to solve their members' shared sustainability challenges. And employees and consumers call on employers and brands to take environmental and social challenges seriously. All of this makes clear that we have entered a new era for business, one in which sustaining competitive advantage requires companies to transform their business models for sustainability.

Company leaders need a broader, more systemic understanding of these dynamic sustainability challenges and the ways that their companies can play a part in addressing them. Fortunately, as some farsighted businesses are discovering, the most powerful opportunities for profitable innovation are embedded in these same challenges. Let's consider three examples.

The first is Telenor, the leading Norwegian mobile operator. In 2008, having entered Pakistan three years earlier, it joined forces with the microfinance bank Tameer. With support from the Bill & Melinda Gates Foundation, the International Finance Corporation (IFC), and the Consultative Group to Assist the Poor (CGAP), they launched a new service called Easypaisa, providing mobile-based financial services to the unbanked and underbanked. By the end of 2019, Telenor Microfinance Bank (the result of Telenor's acquisition of Tameer) boasted the largest branchless banking service in Pakistan, growing its Easypaisa mobile wallet user base to 6.4 million, its depositor base to 17 million, and the transactions volume through its agent network to about PKR 1 trillion (approximately $6 billion). This service has significantly advanced financial inclusion in Pakistan and established Telenor as a major telecom enterprise there.

Or consider Ajinomoto, a global food and biotech company based in Japan. It produces seasonings, sweeteners, and pharmaceuticals. As part of its 2030 vision and growth strategy to "help one billion people worldwide lead a healthier life," Ajinomoto is exploring a new "personalized nutrition for health" business. Combining its core nutrition expertise and new technology, the company aims to provide customers with digitally enabled diagnostics, analytics, and product recommenda-

https://doi.org/10.1515/9783111295268-010

tions. These would guide people toward the kind of well-balanced amino acid intake that boosts cognitive and physiological functions and helps prevent aging-related diseases like dementia—a prominent societal issue in Japan.

Another example is Indigo Ag, a United States-based agricultural technology startup that was valued at $1.4 billion in 2017. In 2019, the company launched a service called Indigo Carbon to help incentivize farmers to remove carbon from the atmosphere and sequester it in their soil. The service provides technologies and recommendations for regenerative agriculture practices. The ultimate goal is to pay farmers for each ton of carbon captured and then sell certifications to companies looking to offset their carbon footprints. By supporting a transparent carbon credit marketplace, Indigo Carbon creates benefits for all participants: the farmers, the companies buying the offsets, the planet, and its own business.

What do these three companies have in common? Regardless of industry, geography, or size, they (and dozens of others like them) are innovating business models—building on and expanding beyond their core assets and capabilities—to address significant environmental and societal challenges in their local contexts. In this way, they create new sources of value and competitive advantage for their business.

The Four-Step Innovation Cycle

In our research, we have studied more than 100 cases of companies that are practicing what we call sustainable business model innovation (SBM-I). We have found that the most advanced of these companies, the "front-runners," combine environmental, societal, and financial priorities to re-imagine their core business models and even shift the boundaries of competition.

One might expect the front-runners to consist mainly of smaller enterprises, branded through their visible social or environmental missions. But most of them are actually global corporations that have gradually developed new business models that create both sustainability and long-term competitive advantage.

The core practice for SBM-I is an iterative innovation cycle, shown in Figure 9.1. With each round, the company gains scale, experience, and market presence for its initiative; these reinforce both the business advantage and the environmental and societal benefits generated.

1

Expand the Business canvas

Expand the business canvas through stakeholder discovery and scenario analysis, and identify vulnerabilities and opportunities that are tied to a changing environmental and societal context

2

Innovate

Explore the 10 archetypes of innovation and lessons of SBM-I leaders to ideate more robust and resilient business models that generate notable environmental and societal benefitses

4

Scale

Scale to expand impact and realize advantage. Strive to reshape the stakeholder ecosystem and alter the boundaries of competition

SBM-I

3

Link to drivers of Value & advantage

Test and refine business model innovations to expand environmental and societal benefits, and connect them to drivers of advantage and business value

Source: BCG analysis
Note: SBM-I = Sustainable business model innovation

Figure 9.1: A structured innovation cycle unlocks the full potential of SBM-I.

Expand the Business Canvas

So how can you bring this cycle to life in your company? The first step is to develop a rich understanding of the broader stakeholder ecosystem in which the company operates and of the environmental and societal issues and trends that might affect this ecosystem. As part of this diagnosis, you explore the potential impacts of ecosystem dynamics and issues on your business model. This will allow you to identify a range of business vulnerabilities and opportunities tied to environmental and societal issues. Some of these are good starting points for focused SBM-I.

More specifically, we recommend the following:

– **Expand the business canvas by mapping the wider ecosystem of stakeholders and societal issues in which the business operates.** Ask yourself: who are the key stakeholders in the system? What are the material environmental and societal issues and trends? How do stakeholders and environmental and societal issues directly or indirectly impact all the different parts of the business model?

– **Stress-test the business model (current or potential) within this broader map.** How do stakeholder dynamics and environmental and societal issues constrain or hold back your business model? Where do limitations in the system create vulnerabilities for the business model?

– **Extrapolate trends and build materiality scenarios.** Look at today's environmental and societal trends and think about how they might evolve over time. In addition, build scenarios to envision completely different, more extreme versions of the future (as opposed to linearly projecting trends) to stretch your thinking. And then, under these scenarios, ask yourself: how might environmental and societal issues change over time? How might stakeholders' perceptions of and attitudes toward those issues shift? What would be the effects on the system map and the business model?

– **Explore scaling up the business.** Imagine the business model at different scales of activity. Suppose your business grew three- or five-fold over the next few years. Where might breaking points or opportunities arise? What happens to the externalities the business creates? How do risks and opportunities change?

– **Identify innovation opportunity spaces or "strategic intervention points" (SIPs).** These are points at which targeted action or innovation could alter stakeholder dynamics, positively impact the environmental or societal issues, reduce the vulnerabilities of the business model, or even create new business value opportunities.

Look for difficulties, gaps, and risks to arise from the analysis. For example, your company's own lines of business might contribute to the environmental or societal issue and impact the growth of the business today. Also, don't just rely on your own thinking. Cultivate outsiders who can provide complementary and thought-provoking perspectives.

In a recent interview[1] Christine Rodwell, former vice president for Business Development Cities, Veolia, explained that "to walk the talk on sustainability, companies need to listen to their external stakeholders. They should create a committee of critical friends (across public, social, and academic sectors) who will challenge them and advise them to develop business solutions that create meaningful environmental and societal benefits."

To understand what expanding a business canvas looks like in practice, consider the hypothetical example of a consumer packaged goods (CPG) manufacturing company engaged in a real-world dilemma: the toxic effect of plastic packaging on natural habitats, particularly in the world's oceans. About 18 billion pounds of plastic waste enter the world's oceans each year. This is equivalent to five grocery bags of trash on every foot of coastline. Plastic pollution causes extensive damage to life on land and at sea, including toxic contamination, strangulation, blockage of digestive passages, and endocrine-related reproductive problems for people as well as animals. Concerns about this problem reached a tipping point in the mid-2010s, as studies confirmed the damage.

As industrial leaders in this field know all too well, the complexities of gathering, cleaning, sorting, recycling, and reusing plastics have made it costly and difficult to address this issue. Companies that step forward with effective and financially viable solutions will not only gain enormous goodwill but are also likely to build high-growth businesses.

But where do you start? And where do you focus innovation efforts and investments to tackle such a complex, multifaceted environmental issue? Reflecting the SBM-I cycle approach, Figure 9.2 shows what a stakeholder-centric systems map for the plastics issue could look like from the point of view of a CPG company. This map uses basic systems dynamics principles to capture the most significant interrelationships among the CPG company, the environmental issue at stake, and key stakeholders (consumers, policymakers, civil society, waste collectors and recyclers, and plastics manufacturers). The arrows show patterns of cause and effect. For example, when urbanization increases, so does the cost of landfilling.

The power of this diagram (versus more traditional, linear depictions) comes in part from its ability to reveal where delays, rebound effects, or tipping points might be active in the system. For instance, the node labeled "environmental and recycling awareness" will influence changes in several consumer habits—but only after a delay. Such awareness cannot be seen as a quick-fix solution, but over time it will help change the dynamics of the entire system.

---

1 https://bcghendersoninstitute.com/lessons-from-veolia-and-renault-with-christine-rodwell/.

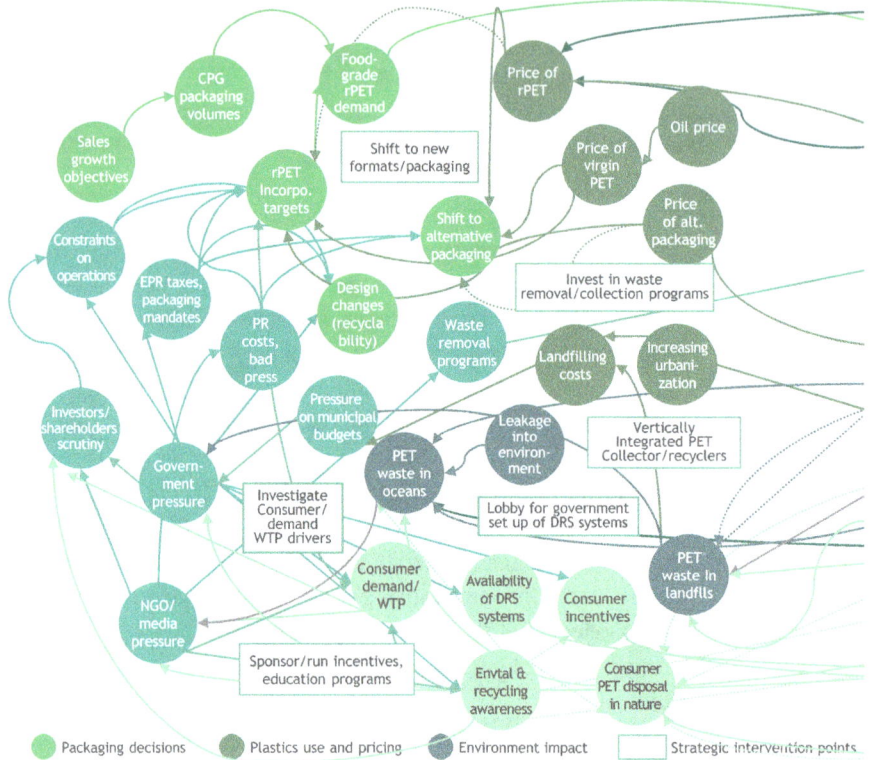

Figure 9.2: An expanded business canvas related to the plastics challenge.

The boxes in Figure 9.2 represent the opportunity spaces or strategic intervention points (SIPs) that become evident during this step. In this example, a few of the SIPs for our CPG company are as follows: shifting to new packaging formats; setting up plastic collection initiatives; lobbying for government programs like deposit return systems; joining precompetitive coalitions that invest in recycling infrastructure and new recycling technology; and educating and nudging consumers to consume and dispose of packaging in more sustainable ways.

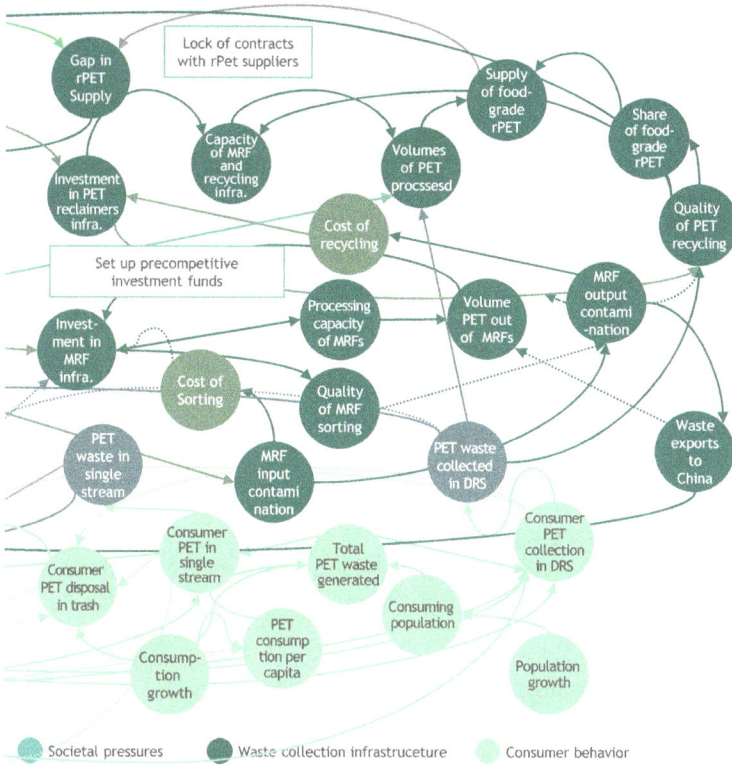

Figure 9.2 (continued)

Innovate for a Resilient Business Model

The first step in the cycle will have led you to identify the opportunity spaces that hold potential for both financial returns and societal value. You must then transform your business model, or imagine an entirely new one, so that you can seize these opportunities. In this second step, you innovate and develop new aspects of that new business model. You are seeking to bypass current constraints, break tradeoffs, deploy technological advances, and perhaps integrate activities that were previously kept separate. You should ideate a new business model to integrate and reinforce both business advantage and environmental and societal benefits.

In related research[2], we introduced and defined several archetypal business models. We have updated this research, and defined ten archetypes—building blocks as sustainable business model innovation—that optimize for both societal and business value. Here we illustrate how they might apply to the plastics waste challenge.

– **Own the origins.** Change production inputs to generate societal and environmental benefits. For instance, HP is working with waste collectors in a partnership with the First Mile Coalition in Haiti. HP has invested $2 million in a local facility to produce clean, high-quality recycled plastics that can then be used as input in an array of HP personal computer products and ink cartridges, reducing the environmental footprint of those products. Four years after its launch in 2016, the program had already diverted approximately 1.7 million pounds (771 metric tons) of plastic materials (equivalent to more than 60 million plastic bottles) from waterways and oceans and created income opportunities for 1,100 Haitians (with 1,000 more expected in coming years). Thanks to this and other efforts, HP boasted the world's most sustainable PC portfolio in May 2020. This included, for example, the HP Elite Dragonfly, the first PC manufactured with ocean-bound plastic.

– **Own the whole cycle**. Create environmental and societal impact by influencing the product usage cycle from cradle to grave. Since the 1990s, Grupo AlEn, a leader in home cleaning products based in Monterrey, has invested and scaled up its in-house plastic recycling operations to become one of the largest plastic recyclers in Mexico. AlEn now operates 30 routes and 6,200 collection points in the Monterrey area, recycling more than 50,000 tons of polyethylene terephthalate (PET) and high-density polyethylene (HDPE) per year. This business expansion has given AlEn an exclusive supply of recycled plastics, enabling it to create distinctive, greener packaging at a relatively stable cost.

– **Expand societal value**. Expand the environmental and societal value of products and services, and capture value in pricing, market share, and loyalty. In 2018, PepsiCo acquired Sodastream, the world's leading at-home sparkling water maker. Building on this technology, PepsiCo has begun to bring packaging-free, customizable beverages to workplaces, college campuses, and airports. This new business positions PepsiCo to win in the increasingly personalized beverage market and to save an estimated 67 billion single-use plastic bottles by 2025.

---

2 https://www.bcg.com/publications/2020/quest-sustainable-business-model-innovation or chapter in book "The Quest for Sustainable Business Model Innovation."

– **Decarbonize for advantage**. Differentially decarbonize operations and products faster and deeper than competitors and capture value in pricing, market share, and loyalty. As part of its Climate Take Back mission, Interface, the world's largest manufacturer of modular flooring, offers the world's first 'carbon negative' flooring products. Made from recycled contents and bio-based materials, these tiles store carbon, preventing its release into the atmosphere. This offering is supported with other initiatives across the value chain (that is, working with coastal communities to collect and recycle fishing nets into yarn; setting up takeback and recycling 'ReEntry' program) and allows Interface to (i) move closer towards its vision, (ii) maintain its position as an environmental leader in the market, and (iii) anticipate or even shape recycling standards and customer demands.

– **Exploit energy flexibility**. Engineer operating and ecosystem energy/power supplies to take advantage of volatility in energy source pricing and capacity for advantage in cost and mix. UPM is a global forestry, pulp and paper company which produces a range of sustainable forestry products – such as sustainable packaging papers that are an alternative to plastics packaging. UPM began exploring energy flexibility in its Finnish paper mills by identifying the physical flexibility of thousands of pieces of equipment to support varied energy usage and analyzing their operating markets' varied energy sources. It then exploited existing opportunities, invested in new assets to continue dynamically optimizing fuel usage and electricity costs, began directly participating in a range of electricity markets (such as day-ahead markets, balancing markets, and frequency markets) and incentivized production teams to optimize for profit rather than volume to capture the full energy flexibility potential.

– **Expand the value chains**. Innovate by layering onto the business ecosystems of customers or of partners in other industries. In Chile, Algramo's innovative bulk distribution system replaces single-use plastic with radio frequency identification (RFID)-equipped reusable containers. Since 2013, the startup has scaled up its business by partnering with more than 2,000 family-owned stores across Santiago. They dispense affordable food and staple products *"al gramo"* (Spanish for "by the gram") and reward customers for reusing containers. Algramo's model not only helps the environment but also benefits the urban poor, who previously had to pay high prices for small quantities of products, in wasteful, individually wrapped packets.

– **Re-localize and regionalize.** Shorten and reconfigure global value chains to bring societal benefits closer to home. In Brazil, BASF has developed a solution to a local issue: waste certificate fraud. Some collectors and recyclers claim credits for recycled materials that they didn't actually process or that aren't actually recycled. Partnering with Kryha, a digital blockchain studio, and Recicleiros, an NGO that supports waste collectors and their cooperatives, BASF developed an online platform called ReciChain. This platform enables accurate and secured data tracking throughout the recycling value chain, to improve the quality of operations and guarantee the validity of manufacturers' certificates and claims.

– **Energize the brand**. Encode, promote, and monetize the full environmental and societal value of products and services, and use that leverage to engage customers in novel ways. The innovative manufacturing company 3M released the latest version of its Thinsulate insulation product in 2019. This is "100% recycled featherless insulation" made from recycled plastic bottles. Building on this accomplishment, 3M worked with the high-end apparel brand Askov Finlayson to create "the world's first climate-positive parka," producing 3,000 parkas in 2019 as an inspiring demonstration project.

– **Nudge sustainable consumption.** Apply technology for behavioral insights and economics to nudge and enable consumers to make more sustainable choices in ways that propel the portfolio. Fairphone is a Dutch social enterprise, which is reimagining the consumer electronics business model to produce and sell a more ethical and durable smartphone. The Fairphone is composed of sustainable materials, including responsibly sourced and conflict-free tin and tungsten and recycled copper and plastics; it has a modular design that can be upgraded and repaired by swapping out components. When customers go to purchase, the default excludes items most customers already own like chargers and cords, and includes a "nudge" to recycle their phone. The company also has a cradle-to-grave phone leasing model to recover and reuse old devices.

– **Build across sectors.** Create new business models in collaboration with government and nonprofit organizations, particularly in rapidly developing economies, to improve the business ecosystem and societal proposition. Together, SC Johnson and the social enterprise Plastic Bank have opened nine recycling centers in Indonesia to collect and recycle plastic before it reaches the ocean. This partnership also plays an important societal role, helping families in impoverished areas who collect plastic waste by buying it at a premium from them. In 2019, the partnership announced a ground-breaking, three-year deal to create 509 plastic collection points, including locations in Thailand, the Philippines, Vietnam, and Brazil. In aggregate, these points are expected to collect 30,000 metric tons of plastic over three years—the equivalent of stopping 1.5 billion plastic bottles from entering waterways and the ocean. On the business side, among other benefits, this collaboration will secure a steady supply of high-quality recycled plastics and help SC Johnson meet its 2025 packaging goals.

These ten archetypes can be starting points for developing your own business model innovation. Adapt them, and combine several together to develop a more comprehensive solution to environmental and societal issues relevant to your enterprise. Interestingly, among the 102 in-depth SBM-I cases that we explored in our research, 75% of the SBM-I leaders (the "front-runners") combine three or more archetypes. This contrasts with less than 30% in the two other groups—the "ecosystem leaders" and the "initiative leaders"—whose efforts tend to be more narrowly focused.

In addition to exploring the possibilities inherent in these LEGOs, take inspiration in the lessons learned from SBM-I front-runners. Front-runners see sustainability as a source of competitive advantage. In line with their long-term strategies, they continuously iterate and fine-tune their business models, always seeking to deepen their beneficial impact. They explicitly seek to understand and fix the root causes of environmental and societal challenges—as some of our plastics recyclers did, addressing not just the environmental concerns but also the social aspects of the issue. These companies also use digital technologies wherever possible, to break economic constraints and unlock new solutions. They practice an intensive form of stakeholder engagement: partnering with nonprofits and governments, operating across organizational boundaries, and pooling resources with other enterprises, even competitors. Last but not least, they experiment with new forms of value capture, such as blended financing sources, to de-risk and amplify their own investments. After all, notwithstanding their environmental and social track records, the front-runners are still in business to show a profit and return investment to shareholders.

Link to Drivers of Value and Competitive Advantage

In the third stage of the cycle, test, iterate, and refine your business model ideas or concepts (from the second step) to ensure that they will yield the environmental and societal benefits intended, and that the benefits will translate into value and advantage for the company. A business with weak profit margins cannot invest in innovation to amplify and scale environmental and societal benefits.

The objective of this step is to keep assessing and reengineering the business model, so that it continually improves the resilience of the business and the benefits to society. The following questions, based on our research into the character-

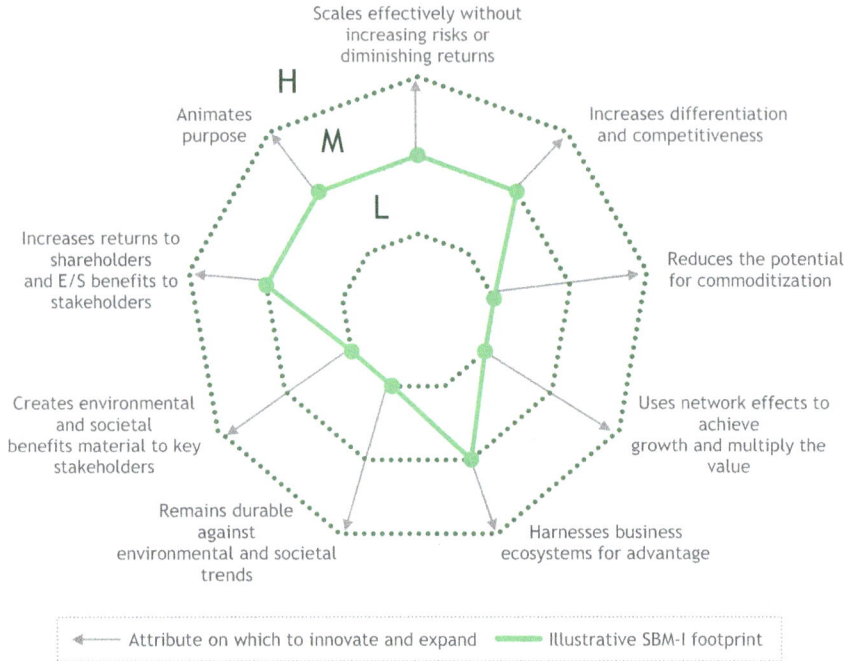

Figure 9.3: Nine attributes drive advantage in sustainable business models.

istics of robust, resilient business models,[3] can help you navigate this part of the process:

- Can the business model scale effectively? Can it be replicated across all your business units or the markets you serve, without diminishing returns?
- Will the business model differentiate your brand or product and make it more competitive in the marketplace?
- Will it reduce the risk of commoditization, by being hard for others to imitate? Will its distinctiveness help you retain some control over pricing?
- Can it leverage network effects? For example, can it attract the kinds of customers and suppliers that make other customers feel compelled to join?
- Does the business model harness business ecosystems—including the larger industry, the value chain, and everyone who interacts with your products, services, and practices—for advantage and sustainability?

---

3 https://www.bcg.com/publications/2021/nine-attributes-to-a-sustainable-business-model.

- Does the business model naturally create meaningful environmental and societal benefits?
- Will the environmental and societal benefits remain durable against changing trends over time, even as the business model scales up?
- Does the business model increase returns to shareholders as well? Are the financial benefits linked to the environmental and societal benefits in some significant way?
- Finally, does the model animate your company's purpose? Does it boost engagement and loyalty between the company and its employees, customers, investors, and other stakeholders?

Figure 9.3 shows how a company might assess its business model against these nine questions. The resulting footprint reveals how robust and resilient the business model is and identifies where it could be improved to unlock further advantage and value for the company.

The fuller the footprint, the better. Among the front-runners in our sample, 90% score "high" on at least five of the nine attributes, as opposed to only 30% in the other groups. The front-runners also show superior average scores on every single dimension.

Scale the Initiative

The full potential value of sustainable business model innovation is achieved only when the new business model is brought to scale: engaging people in the company, across the supply chain, in the company's networks, and in its ecosystems to expand impact and advantage.

To accomplish this, companies can leverage three enablers. First, partnerships with other organizations, within or across industries or sectors, can help a company pool resources, fill capability gaps, and unlock new markets. Almost 90% of the front-runners have broadened their efforts this way. Second, digital technology (leveraged by 80% of the front-runners) can help create new distribution channels that reach previously unserved or underserved populations at a fraction of the cost of their predecessors. Third, companies that adopt SBM-I tend to develop cultures and leadership values that attract and engage people inside and outside their boundaries. Indeed, all of the front-runners explicitly mention the environmental and societal impact they seek to deliver in their vision, purpose, or mission statements.

Consider the example of BIMA, a mission-driven provider of mobile-delivered health and insurance services that started operations in Ghana in 2010. Its innovative digital technology platform and its partnership model (which comprises telecom providers, mobile money providers, and insurance underwriters) have enabled it to rapidly scale its innovative business model. BIMA now provides affordable, easy-to-manage life and health insurance to more than 35 million low-income customers across ten emerging economies. BIMA's customers have access to its services through their mobile phones. Many of them are lower income families who earn less than $10 a day. About 75% of them are obtaining insurance for the first time in their lives. These societal benefits are at the core of BIMA's strategy and mission; the company's website says explicitly that its "purpose is to protect the future of every family."

The four-step innovation cycle we propose in this article offers companies a way to systematically integrate and solve for social and business value in one business model. Most of the companies that begin this journey are already skilled at optimizing for business advantage. They may already recognize the importance of taking into account their environmental and societal impacts. With this approach, they are now ready to take on innovation for a business that optimizes for both business and social value.

Part 3.1: **Expand the Business Canvas**

David Young
10 An Applied Example of Expanding the Business Canvas in Plastics

The first post in this series introduced an approach to *expand the business context* using a stakeholder perspective of the environmental and societal challenges in the ecosystem and the competitive dynamics—a first step in the Quest for Sustainable Business Model Innovation.[1] A novel expanded understanding of the business context can identify potential disruptions and opportunities; and find *strategic intervention points* for positive environmental and societal impact while generating a more resilient and valuable business.

This note illustrates how consumer packaged goods (CPG) companies could use that approach to expand their business context to find opportunities that help address the plastics challenge they face. The goal is to gain new insights to better inform business and packaging strategies and corporate actions that can help mitigate global plastic waste, stakeholder pressures, and the related business risks. Our approach here develops illustrative maps of the business and stakeholder ecosystem to analyze select dynamics.

Step 1 | Identify the trends and E/S issues of material concern to stakeholders and facing the business ecosystem
Identify the pressures from consumers, investors, governments, NGOs, and the media regarding PET waste piling up in landfills and leaking into soils, water, and oceans (represented in pink in our diagrams). To keep the exercise practical, we narrow the scope to PET (mainly plastic bottles) and focus on the U.S. market, given the attention to the issue, the market size, and the CPG company's ability to act there.

Step 2 | Systematically map out all key stakeholders and their interests relevant to the E/S issues
In our example, there are four stakeholder sectors critical to the dynamics of PET waste and illustrated through the systems map: *Consumers* (in orange in our diagram), *State and local governments, NGOs, the media, and investors and shareholders* (in yellow), *CPG companies and their packaging suppliers* (in bright green), and *Waste managers and PET recyclers* (in dark green). For simplicity, we focus on *Materials Recovery Facilities (MRFs)* and *Specialized PET recyclers,* two main stakeholders in the plastics waste value chain. MRFs sort the

---
1 https://www.bcg.com/publications/2020/quest-sustainable-business-model-innovation.

https://doi.org/10.1515/9783111295268-011

"recyclable" waste collected by waste haulers into different streams, including paper, glass, aluminum, and plastics, sell the value streams on to specialized recyclers, and discard the remaining mixed/contaminated waste in landfills or export it to developing countries (mainly China until 2018). Specialized PET recyclers buy the sorted PET waste from MRFs, clean and recycle it into recycled PET (or rPET) sold to plastics packaging manufacturers.

We then identify where and how the stakeholders act in the ecosystem and the dynamics that they create. The goal here is to stay relatively high level but represent the essential forces to aid analysis.

Some of these stakeholder dynamics are represented in Figure 10.1 and include:

Government, NGO, and the media pressures grow with mounting PET waste in landfills, strained municipal budgets, degraded coastal properties, threatened biodiversity, and increased health risks. Governments respond with taxes and penalties (for example, extended producer responsibility (EPR) taxes) on CPG companies, and attention from NGOs and media expose them to negative press and reputational damage.

Institutional investors and shareholders, perceiving risks, increase scrutiny of their investments in CPG companies, and push for changes in packaging to reduce investment risk, for example, increasing rPET incorporation targets into plastic packaging.

Consumers, influenced by government and NGO awareness campaigns and incentives to collect and sort PET bottles in the appropriate recycling bins or deposit return schemes (DRS), change their recycling demands and behaviors. This change creates higher and cleaner volumes of recyclable PET waste over time, thereby improving the volume and quality of the rPET supply.

Some *consumers* also start "voting with their wallets" to demand more sustainable packaging formats from CPG companies and become allies for more stringent actions from governments and NGOs.

In turn, *CPG companies* explore changing their packaging design and purchasing decisions to incorporate more rPET into their packaging, escalating the demand, and, depending on supply balances, the price of rPET.

Responding to that dynamic, *MRFs and PET recyclers* evaluate investments to upgrade the capacity and quality of their sorting and recycling infrastructures. More capacity increases the quality and volume of supply of rPET to the market and, over time, reduces the flow of "recyclable" waste sent to landfills and leaked into the environment.

Illustrating this as a systems dynamics picture facilitates thinking, analysis, and discussion. But going deeper is necessary to uncover more actionable ways for the company to create change and advantage.

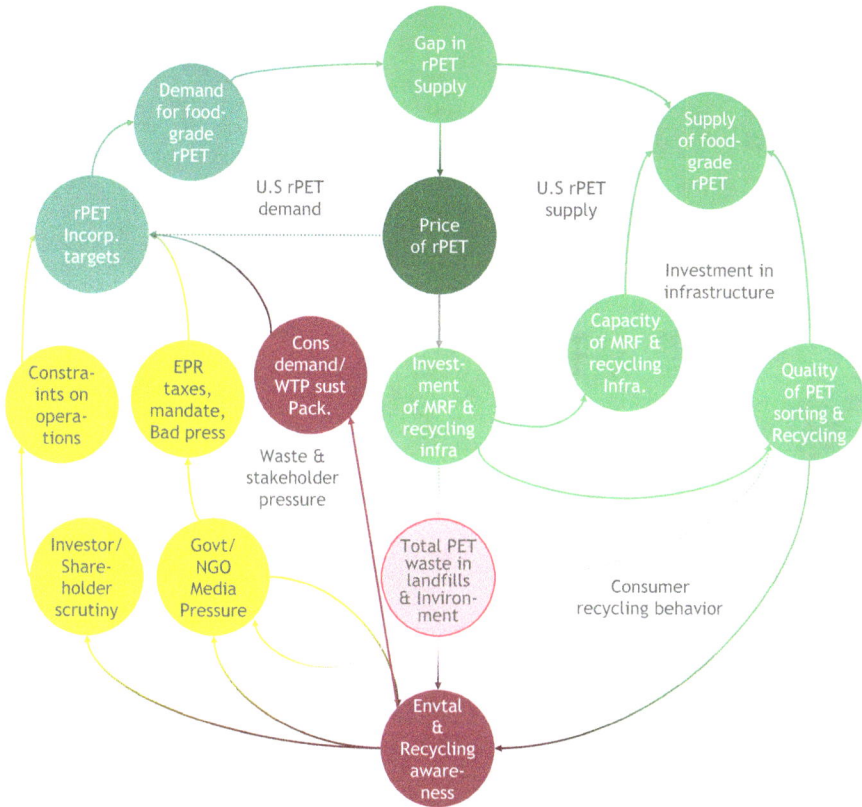

Figure 10.1: Main factors and dynamics linking key stakeholders to the E/S issue.

Step 3 | Detail and explore the stakeholder dynamics to broaden and deepen the context map

Identify the different actors, dynamics, feedback, and behaviors in the system, all the actions and reactions of stakeholders, and the consequences of possible actions by the company. Explore each "sector" of the context map to understand their interconnections and dynamics.

(I) Consumers

Consumer plastics demand and waste increases with consumption fueled by population growth, disposable income, and a culture of convenience that sustains single-use disposable products (as shown in Figure 10.2).

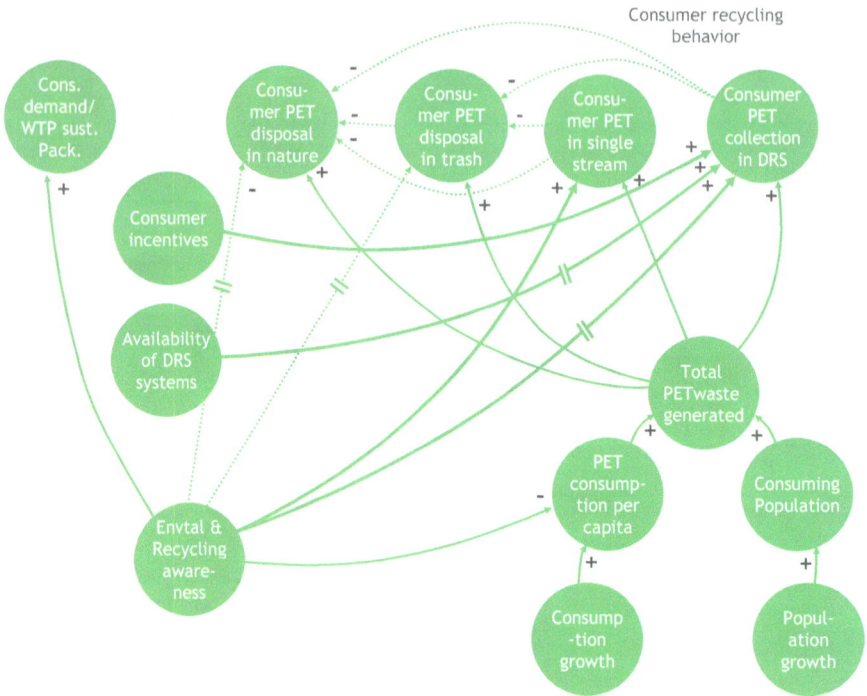

Figure 10.2: Consumer dynamics.

Consumer behavior also contributes to low plastics collection and recycling rates. Overall, there is little awareness of waste disposal guidelines,[2] confusion around the types of recyclable waste and their appropriate channels, and limited knowledge on proper sorting and cleaning guidelines. The lack of consumer incentives to sort and recycle is also notable in the United States. For instance, even though they have proven very effective across Europe, Deposit Return Schemes (DRS) systems, which could allow broader and cleaner PET collection and recycling, are only available in ten states across the United States today and offer typically only $0.05 return per PET bottle. As a result, most U.S. consumers today discard their PET waste in the main trash, the single-stream recycling bins (which have a high degree of mixed and contaminated waste), or in nature (see Figure 10.3).

---

2 https://www.theguardian.com/environment/2018/jul/30/dizzying-array-of-recycling-symbols-is-confusing-consumers.

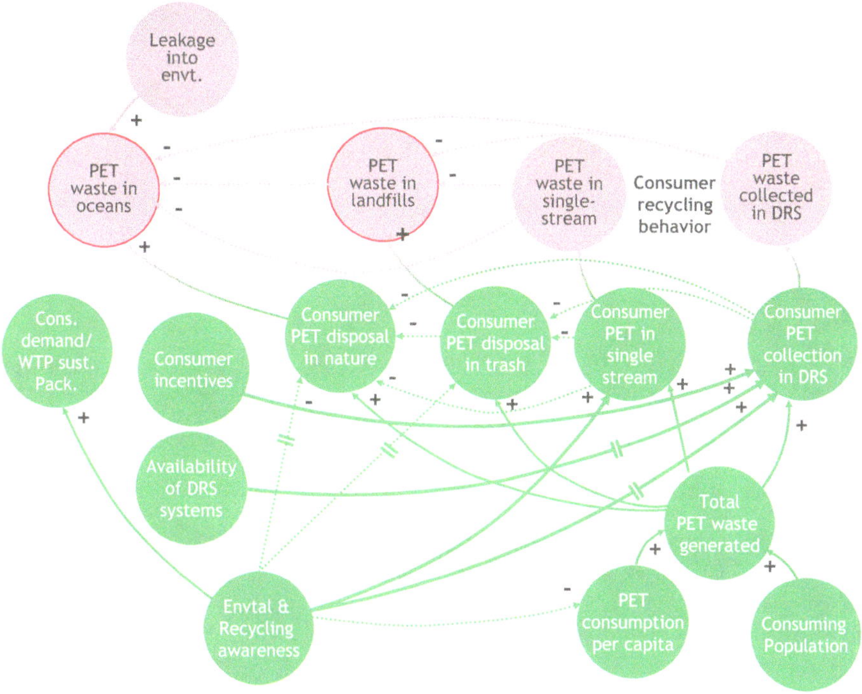

Figure 10.3: Waste accumulating in landfills and the environment.

To give a sense of magnitude, Americans throw away between 20 billion[3] and 35 billion plastic bottles every year. Of these, a little less than 30% are collected for recycling[4] (going down to less than 10% when considering plastics containers and packaging overall[5]). Apart from a small share of bottles that ends up incinerated in waste-to-energy plants, the vast majority of PET bottles (60%+) end up in one of the 2,000 municipal solid waste landfills across the United States[6] or leaked in the environment. Globally, approximately 8 million tons of plastics flow into the ocean each year,[7] causing negative impacts on hundreds of marine species and humans, as micro-plastics to permeate our food system (see Figure 10.3).

---

3 https://www.recycleacrossamerica.org/recycling-facts.
4 https://www.americanchemistry.com/chemistry-in-america/chemistry-in-everyday-products/plastics.
5 https://www.epa.gov/sites/default/files/2019-11/documents/2017_facts_and_figures_fact_sheet_final.pdf.
6 https://www.epa.gov/landfills/municipal-solid-waste-landfills#whatis.
7 https://ourworldindata.org/plastic-pollution.

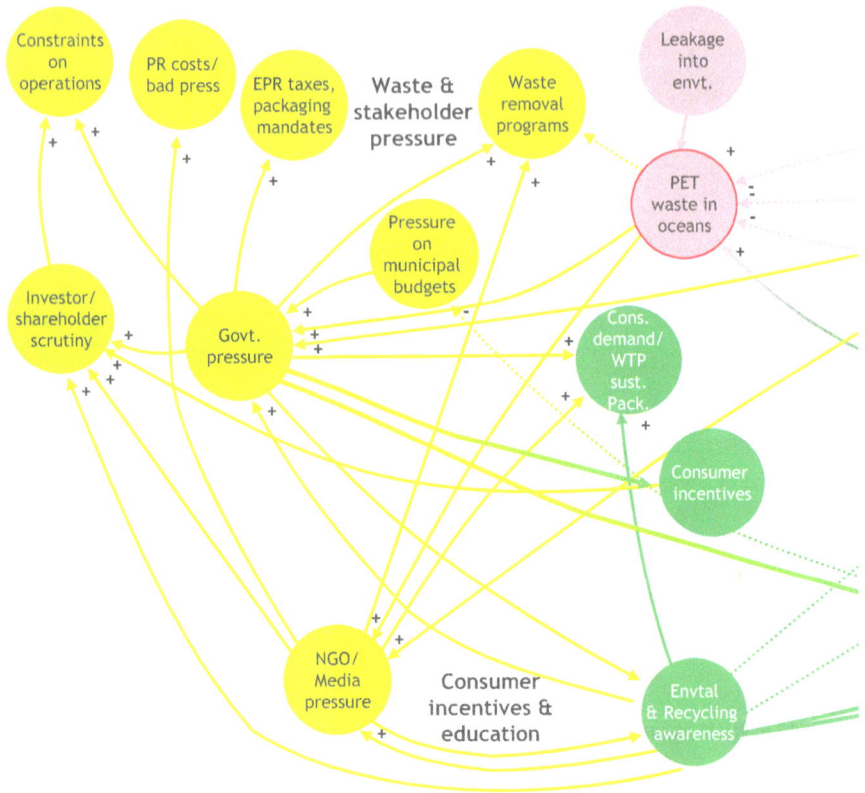

Figure 10.4: Accumulation of waste increases key stakeholder pressure.

 With no systematic, at-scale removal processes, plastic waste in landfills and the oceans increase. Following this trajectory, the plastics issue reached a tipping point during the last decade. Oceans plastics became very visible; studies and statistics on environmental, animal, and human health became alarming; and disposal and cleaning costs started becoming untenable for governments. (For example, landfill costs that averaged $43.3/ton in 2010 across the United States are now projected to reach $53.53 in 2021,[8,9]—straining municipal budgets).

---

8 https://sweepstandard.org/cost-to-landfill-waste-continues-to-rise-through-2016/.
9 https://sweepstandard.org/no-end-in-sight-to-us-landfill-cost-increases-pacific-region-to-experi
ence-highest-growth/.

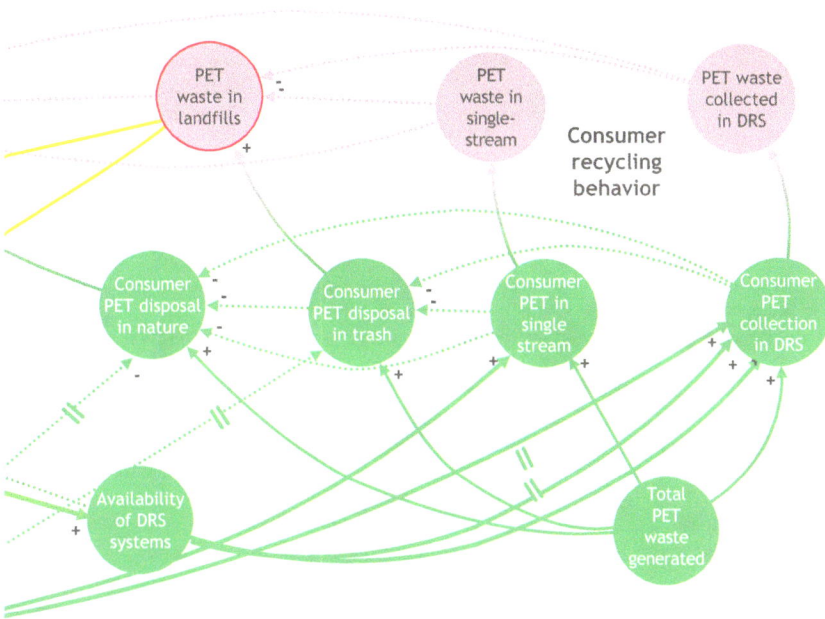

Figure 10.4 (continued)

(II) Key stakeholders: governments, NGOs, the media, and institutional investors/shareholders

As the perceived risks from plastics waste increase, so do the actions of governments, media, NGOs, and, consequently, institutional investors and shareholders. Governments at all levels pass regulations (for example, the EU is leading with bans on plastic bags and single-use items; California, Washington, and Northeastern states are following suit). Activists and the media call out many of the world's largest food and beverage and CPG companies as the main culprits, raising the risk of reputational damage. NGOs pressure large players across the plastics value chain to commit to ambitious goals of plastic waste reduction (for example, the Ellen MacArthur Foundation launched the New Plastics Economy Global Commitment in 2018). And institutional investors and shareholders demand more from their investees (for example, in 2018, twenty-five institutional investors with a combined $1 trillion assets under

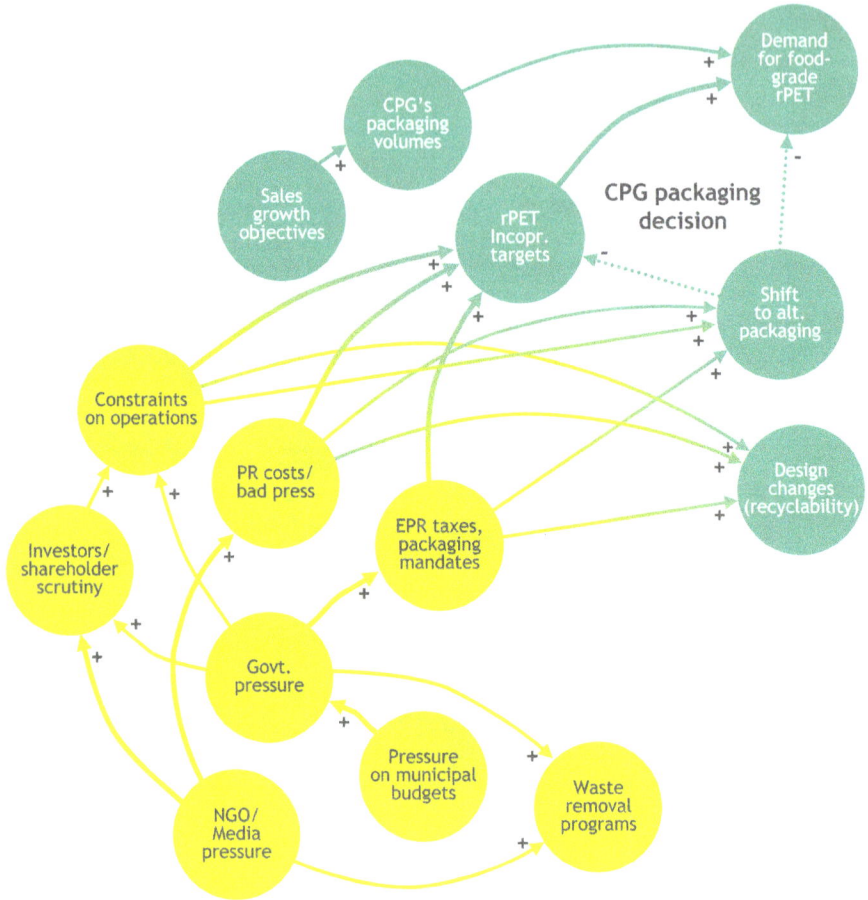

Figure 10.5: Stakeholder pressure triggers CPG actions.

management signed a declaration citing plastic pollution as a clear corporate brand risk; they also pledged to interact with leading companies to find solutions through new corporate commitments, programs, and policies[10]).

Stakeholder actions change the dynamics in the ecosystem, and with CPG companies and their packaging suppliers. For example, Environmental Permitting (England and Wales) Regulations (EPR) make CPG companies financially responsible for the plastics waste they generate. Recycled content mandates change demand and

---

10 https://static1.squarespace.com/static/59a706d4f5e2319b70240ef9/t/5b99f3ec758d4663942c3686/1536816112564/Investor+Declaration+on+Plastic+Pollution+20180613.pdf.

supply chains. Negative press risks reputations and rights to operate. Constraints on operations or capital alter the infrastructure across the system. In 2019, California was exploring the possibility of prohibiting any packaging that would not be 100% recyclable, reusable, or biodegradable from being sold by 2030[11]—these bills are still under debate today. Figure 10.4 shows how the accumulation of waste triggers critical stakeholder pressure and impacts CPG companies.

(III) CPG companies and their packaging suppliers

In response to these mounting pressures, CPG companies (in green in Figure 10.5) act by reviewing and improving their packaging choices, investing in R&D of new materials, and forming industry and cross-sector coalitions. Most of them have plans to incorporate more rPET into their packaging and to redesign packaging for recyclability, ensuring it can be effectively sorted and recycled through the existing infrastructure. Companies are acting in coalitions to explore alternative packaging materials (for example, glass, aluminum, biodegradable materials) and packaging formats (for example, packaging-free hydration fountains and systems).

However, as all CPG companies make similar decisions and announcements, they create a very sharp and sudden increase in rPET demand, unlikely to be met. Insufficient consumer collection rates and recycling system capacity constrain the total supply of food-grade rPET produced (see Figure 10.5).

(IV) Waste managers and PET recyclers

Investigating the system root causes of insufficient rPET supply today (see Figure 10.6), we note three main dynamics at play. First, for decades virgin plastic was extremely cheap, demand for rPET was low, and packaging and waste were not top of the key stakeholder agendas. Consequently, the price of rPET was low, so PET recyclers had no economic incentives to invest in building and upgrading their infrastructure.

Second, consumer recycling rates were low and single and dual-stream collection systems sent mixed "recyclable" waste to MRFs for sorting, leading to increasingly contaminated unrecyclable waste streams. Waste Management estimates that today 25% of waste sent for recycling is nonrecyclable and goes to landfills.[12] Higher contamination rates translate into higher sorting costs at MRFs, more inferior values of output streams, increased rejection rates by PET reclaimers, and thus lower rPET

---

11 https://www.cnbc.com/2019/02/23/california-proposes-phaseout-of-single-use-plastics-by-2030.html.
12 https://sustainability.wm.com/.

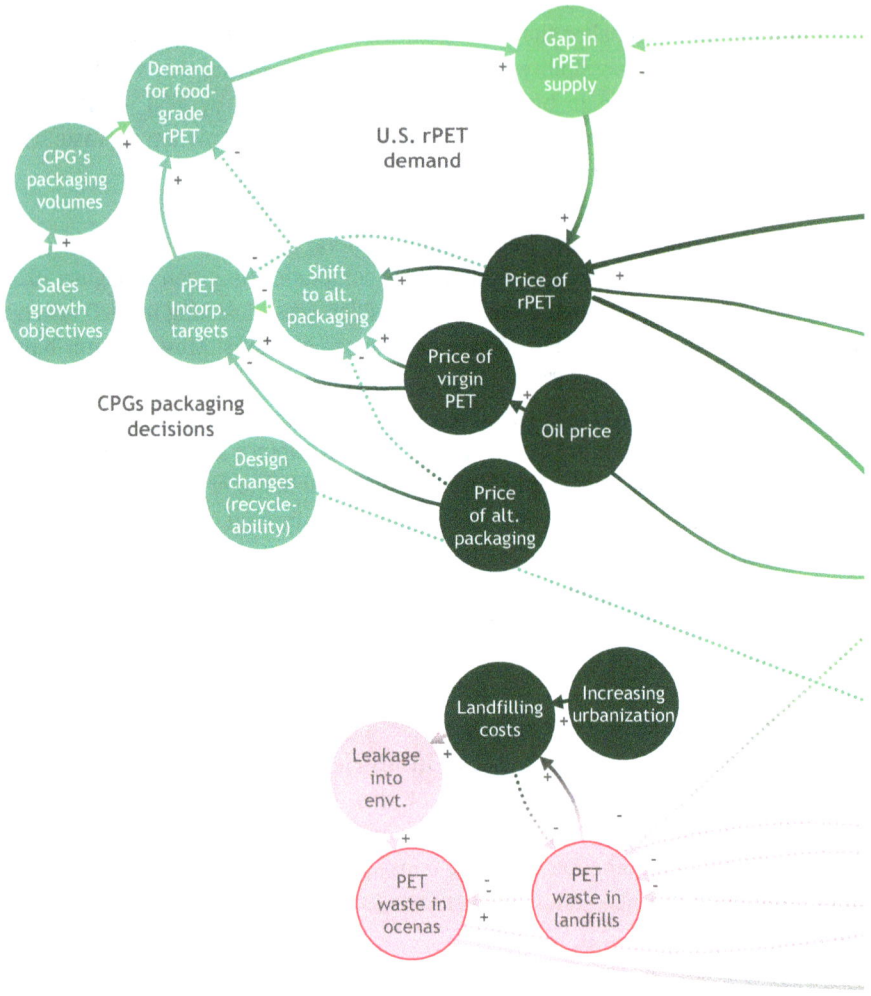

Figure 10.6: rPET supply value chain and economic dynamics.

output volumes. This degradation of MRF economics also meant that MRFs had fewer financial incentives to invest in building and upgrading their infrastructure.

Third, as capacity and profitability of MRFs and PET recyclers decreased, waste exports offshore to China and other developing markets became the preferred option over domestic processing in the 1990s and 2000s. (During that period, China imported waste plastics to recycle to meet its national demand for plastics.) While economically rational, sub-par industry practices and weaker regulatory standards resulted in higher leakages into the environment.

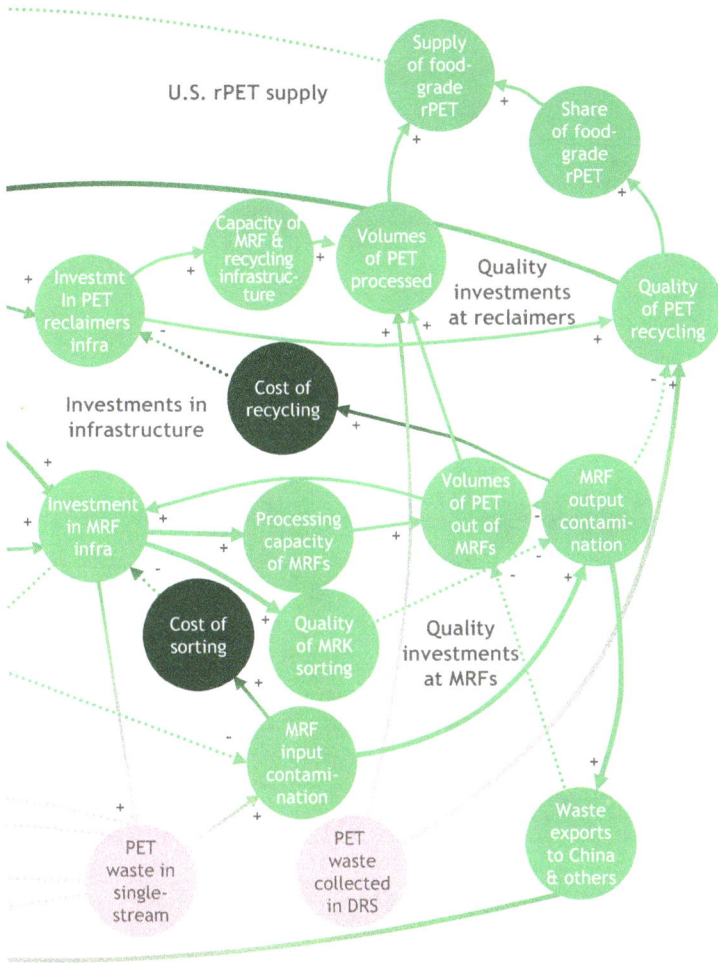

Figure 10.6 (continued)

These three dynamics hurt recycling economics in the United States and delayed critical infrastructure investments by MRFs and PET reclaimers. As a result, only 30% of total PET bottles get collected and recycled, and only ~20% of those get recycled into food-grade rPET. The other 80% is recycled into lower-grade applications (for example, fibers, sheets, films),[13] further reducing the rPET sup-

13 https://bottledwater.org/rpet-facts/.

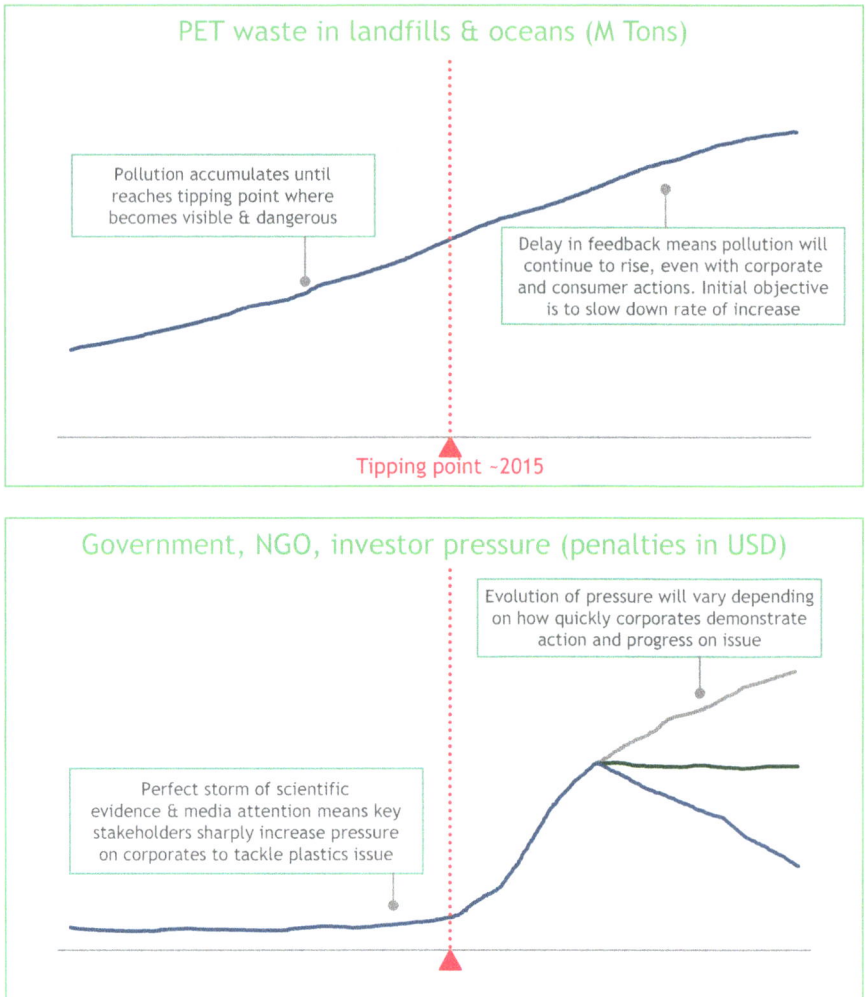

PET waste in landfills & oceans (M Tons)

Pollution accumulates until reaches tipping point where becomes visible & dangerous

Delay in feedback means pollution will continue to rise, even with corporate and consumer actions. Initial objective is to slow down rate of increase

Tipping point ~2015

Government, NGO, investor pressure (penalties in USD)

Evolution of pressure will vary depending on how quickly corporates demonstrate action and progress on issue

Perfect storm of scientific evidence & media attention means key stakeholders sharply increase pressure on corporates to tackle plastics issue

Figure 10.7: Accumulation of PET waste triggers tipping point response.

ply available for CPG companies that demand food-grade rPET. A sudden increase in rPET demand and prices might create the incentive to invest, but it will take time for the capacity to catch up on years of delayed technological investments.

We can model the dynamics within and across each "sector" to build a holistic view of the system and investigate how the dynamics play out (linear or nonlinear, delays or acceleration, reinforcing or stabilizing forces). Figures 10.7–10.10 represent the likely behaviors of key variables under the current system structure (these can be molded analytically using systems dynamics tools).

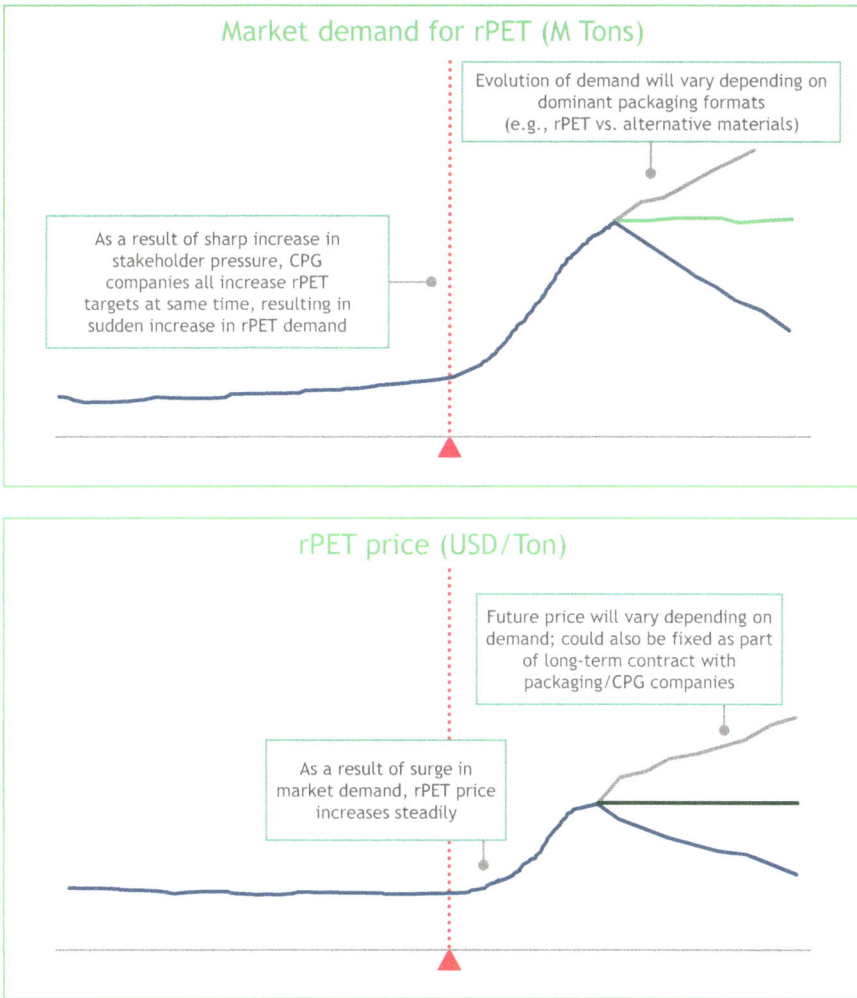

Market demand for rPET (M Tons)

Evolution of demand will vary depending on dominant packaging formats (e.g., rPET vs. alternative materials)

As a result of sharp increase in stakeholder pressure, CPG companies all increase rPET targets at same time, resulting in sudden increase in rPET demand

rPET price (USD/Ton)

Future price will vary depending on demand; could also be fixed as part of long-term contract with packaging/CPG companies

As a result of surge in market demand, rPET price increases steadily

Figure 10.8: Increasing demand for rPET causes surge in price.

As PET waste in landfills and oceans accumulates, it reaches a tipping point where the issue becomes highly visible and threatens environmental, animal, and human health. With increased media and scientific attention, the system witnesses a sharp, rapid increase in key stakeholder pressure.

In response to mounting pressures from key stakeholders, CPG companies aim to incorporate more rPET into their plastics packaging (while exploring other formats or material options). The surge in demand creates a sharp increase in the price of rPET.

Sorting and recycling capacity in U.S. (M Tons)

Over the years, limited investments in MRF/PET reclaimers infrastructure made (due to low demand, increasing contamination rates and costs)

While higher demand and rPET prices will incentivize capacity build-up/upgrading, likely to be lower and slower than demand (recyclers will want to avoid over-building)

Consumer collection rates for recycling (in %)

Long feedback time means consumer education will take time to translate into significantly higher collection rates and sorting cleanliness

Could explore how could be boosted with incentives and other media campaigns

Figure 10.9: Recyling capacity increases but lags demand for rPET.

Following the surge in rPET demand and price, MRFs and PET reclaimers start expanding and upgrading infrastructure to produce more rPET. Similarly, with mounting stakeholder pressures, consumers' recycling behavior improves. However, both these dynamics show time delays and resistance effects. Thus, capacity is unlikely to build as high or as fast as rPET demand, and consumer collection rates are expected to take significant time to rise.

While food-grade rPET supply will increase in the United States, because of these delays and resistance in the system it is likely to lag demand so that incor-

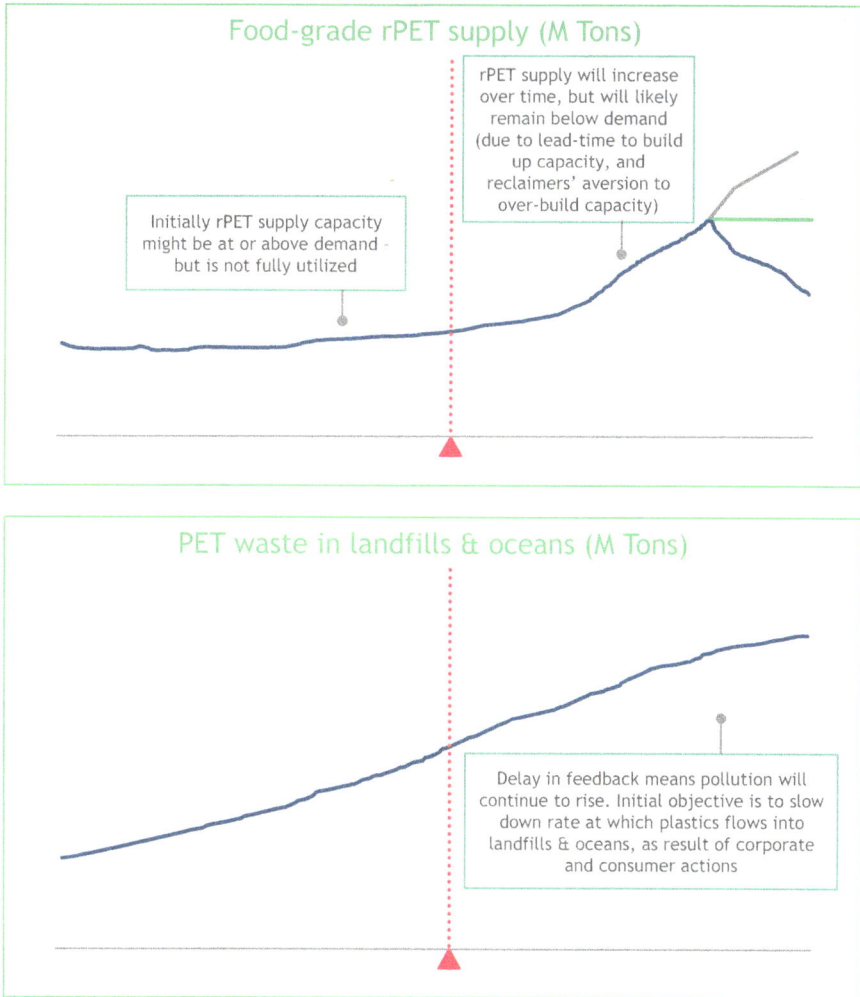

Food-grade rPET supply (M Tons)

rPET supply will increase over time, but will likely remain below demand (due to lead-time to build up capacity, and reclaimers' aversion to over-build capacity)

Initially rPET supply capacity might be at or above demand - but is not fully utilized

PET waste in landfills & oceans (M Tons)

Delay in feedback means pollution will continue to rise. Initial objective is to slow down rate at which plastics flows into landfills & oceans, as result of corporate and consumer actions

Figure 10.10: Increase in rPET will slow, but not halt, flow of PET to landfills.

porating rPET into packaging alone is unlikely to quickly reduce PET waste going into landfills and the oceans—at best, it will slow down the inflows of plastics waste. It will take additional actions to tackle the plastics issue.

Step 4 | Identify what trends and shocks might disrupt the context, create break points, or new opportunities in the ecosystem or for the company
Next, consider the system in its entirety (Figure 10.11) to see places where a few potential "shocks" could occur and cascade through the ecosystem to disrupt the

"normal" system behavior and create new risks and vulnerabilities for stakeholders and the business. For instance (circled in blue):

- China and other developing markets stop their waste imports suddenly—this creates high pressure on the U.S. waste management system. Higher volumes of mixed/contaminated waste go to landfills, increasing strain on municipal budgets and governments and adding to pollution. Precisely this happened throughout the 2010s and more strikingly in 2018 with the Chinese National Sword policy.
- Governments and NGOs then intensify the pressure on the plastics industry and CPG companies through high fines, packaging requirements, and high public relations (PR) costs for CPG companies, which has been happening around the world since 2015.[14]
- Prices of virgin plastics could increase or drop due to an oil shock or embargo on producer nations, and this would impact companies' CPG packaging costs and decisions if it persisted over time.

Beyond "shocks," delays in the system accumulate over time that create resistance to change. Here are a few examples:

- As already noted, MRF and PET recyclers have delayed building capacity, so today's infrastructure doesn't have the scale or quality to produce high volumes of food-grade rPET. While increased demand will drive capacity investment, it takes about 12 to 24 months to install new sorting and recycling lines. Even then, MRFs and recyclers are likely to limit the capacity to hedge themselves and ensure rPET pricing allows returns on capital, given the uncertainty in the past.
- There is a lag, of course, between CPG companies' packaging decisions and their implementation. While companies might all aim for more recyclable packaging that incorporates more recycled content, a key to better recycling will be to harmonize packaging standards and characteristics across companies. Reaching agreement will take time, as will the individual companies retooling production lines, which would slow progress.
- Consumer behavior causes the third source of delay: packaging preferences, recycling habits, and their willingness to pay for more sustainable packaging.

---

14 https://www.theguardian.com/environment/2014/dec/10/full-scale-plastic-worlds-oceans-revealed-first-time-pollution.

Step 5 | Identify "strategic intervention points" in the system to change the context, alter stakeholder dynamics, impact the E/S issues, or open new business opportunities.
Using a full understanding of the system, identify points where targeted interventions could create an outsized impact on the ecosystem to change the amount of PET waste going to landfills and into the ocean while improving the resilience and sustainability of the business. Another way to achieve a strategic intervention is to look for ways to fundamentally re-wire the ecosystem to advantage the company, possibly bypassing current system constraints and actors.

Based on our example, here are several strategic intervention points (SIPs) that would benefit both the ecosystem and the company:

At the company packaging level
–   Design for recyclability to ensure PET packaging is easily recyclable within the current infrastructure to increase the overall share of PET waste that is sorted and recycled (up from ~30% today). Examples include standardizing packaging formats and removing dyes and chemical adhesives. This is a relatively easy and cost-effective lever.
–   Increase targets on rPET incorporation and communicate those across the supplier base to signal new demand and incentives for waste managers and recyclers to build capacity. While this is important, it might not be enough by itself to trigger enough capacity building.
–   Shift to alternative packaging materials and formats to bypass plastics waste entirely by switching to materials recyclable within the current infrastructure (for example, glass, aluminum) or to new, packaging-free forms. While this lever might involve time for further R&D, it also holds the potential for much more transformative environmental impact and could open the door to entirely new business models and growth areas for CPG companies—and could thus be a good point to explore SBM-I opportunities.

At the waste collection and recycling infrastructure level
–   Lock in long-term supply contracts with PET reclaimers to fix the quantities and price for food-grade rPET for a given period, thereby giving reclaimers more guarantees and security to make the needed investments. Another option here could go as far as pursuing backward or forward integration, acquisition, or strategic collaboration with a PET collector and recycler. While this could be effective and implementable in the short term, there will likely be significant competition among CPG companies to secure such options.
–   Set up a pre-competitive industry fund or co-investment facility to directly invest in MRF and recycling infrastructure. Companies could rally funding

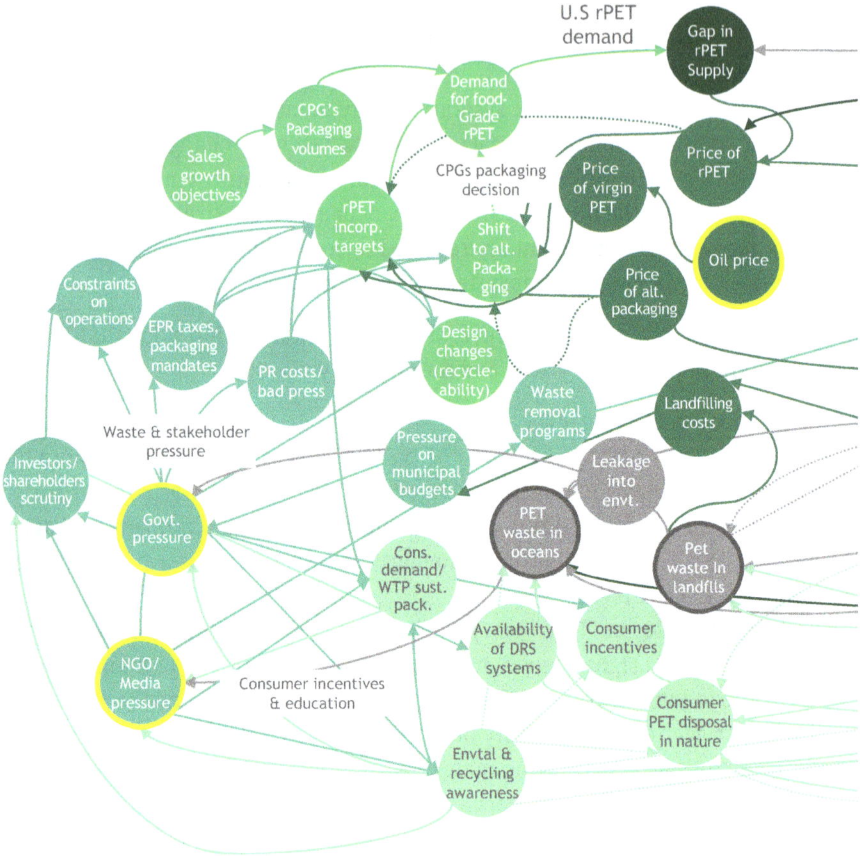

Figure 10.11: Complete view of the systems map (with potential shocks circled in yellow).

and unlock public capital to accelerate capacity building and share the risk, particularly in key states with high waste volumes and government pressures. While this effort would require collaboration, it could have a high impact by accelerating infrastructure capacity building.

- Lobby governments to fund DRS systems and move away from costly EPR regulations and drive limited environmental impact. Instead, promote DRS systems, which have proven effective around the world, and could be a powerful lever to increase the supply and cleanliness of PET waste collected for recycling.
- Invest in new models of waste removal and collection. Consider new supply chains—potentially as part of coalitions—to remove plastics from the oceans and landfills or collect it directly from consumers, to supply recycling processes for more rPET. While this would likely require coordination to reach meaning-

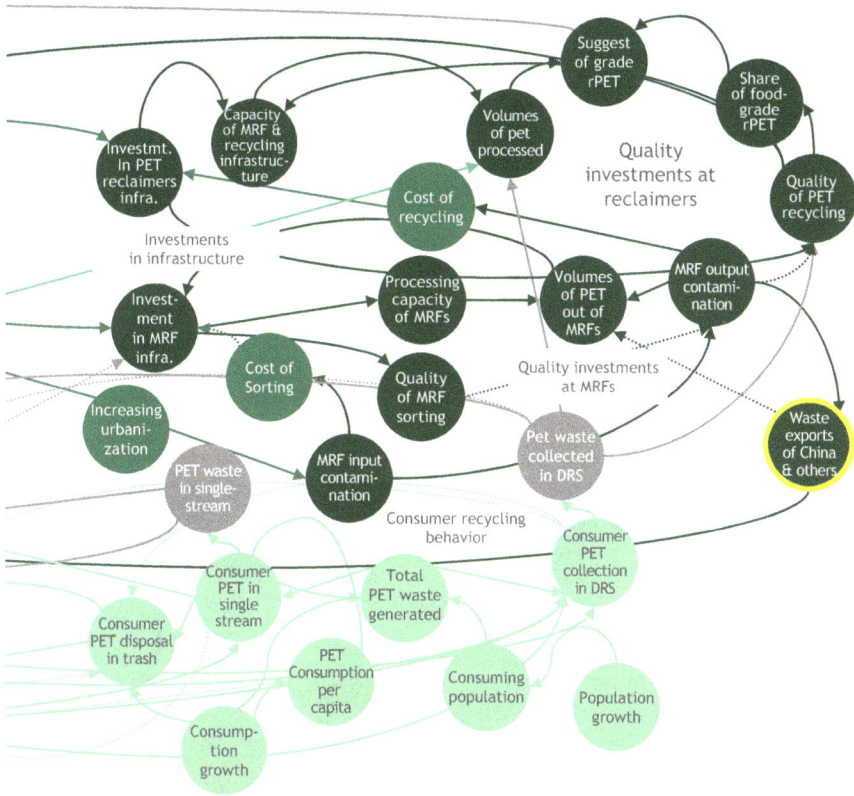

Figure 10.11 (continued)

ful scale, emerging initiatives like the NextWave Coalition demonstrate high potential with companies like Dell, IKEA, HP, and General Motors joining in and tens of millions of plastic bottles already removed from the ocean.

At the consumer behavior level

– Investigate motivators for consumer demand and willingness-to-pay for packaging options, and the intrinsic behavioral tactics to nudge consumption toward more sustainable choices.

– Sponsor and run consumer education and incentive programs in partnership with other stakeholders to generate higher and cleaner volumes of PET waste collected for recycling. While behavior change is a potent and essential lever,

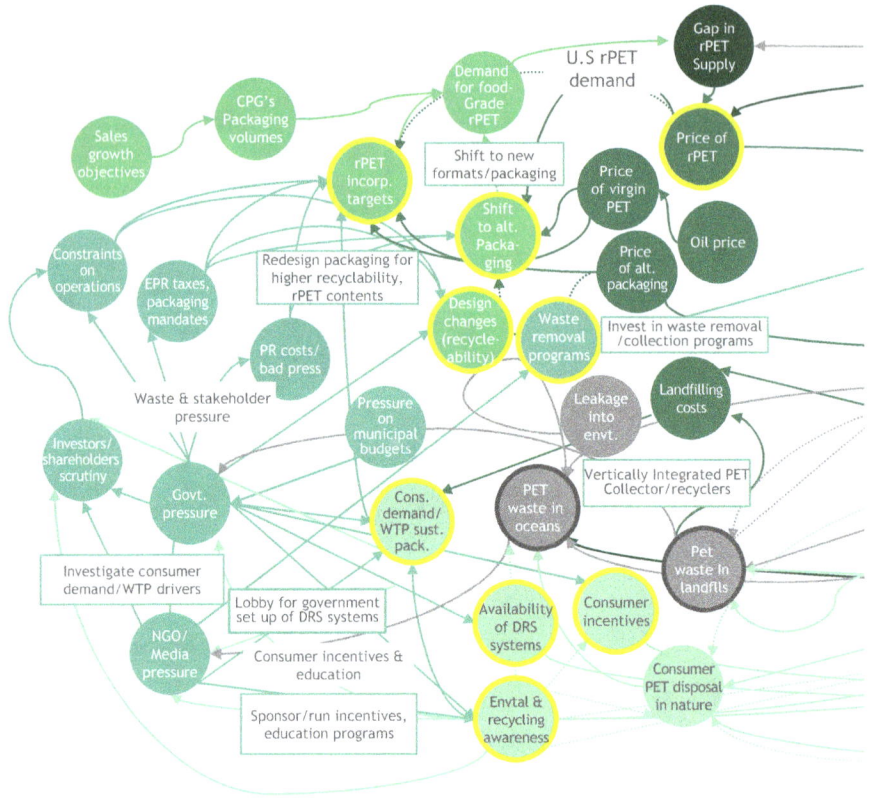

Figure 10.12: Strategic intervention points in system (circled in yellow) with possible actions for CPG's.

the significant and systematic impact will likely materialize over a more extended period.

By interrogating the expanded business context, this example showed how CPG
companies could gain novel and expanded insights on the dynamics of their ecosystem, and the challenges and opportunities facing their business model (see
Figure 10.12).

Conducting this exercise to span different levels of analysis and consider all
loci of decision (for example, global/regional versus state/local) will be important
ultimately, to identify and refine the understanding of dynamics, risks and opportunities. Indeed, what makes the plastics packaging challenge particularly complex is the discrepancy between corporate decisions (for example, packaging
designs, materials) being made at the regional or even global level, and the reality
of highly localized waste management systems and consumer behaviors at the

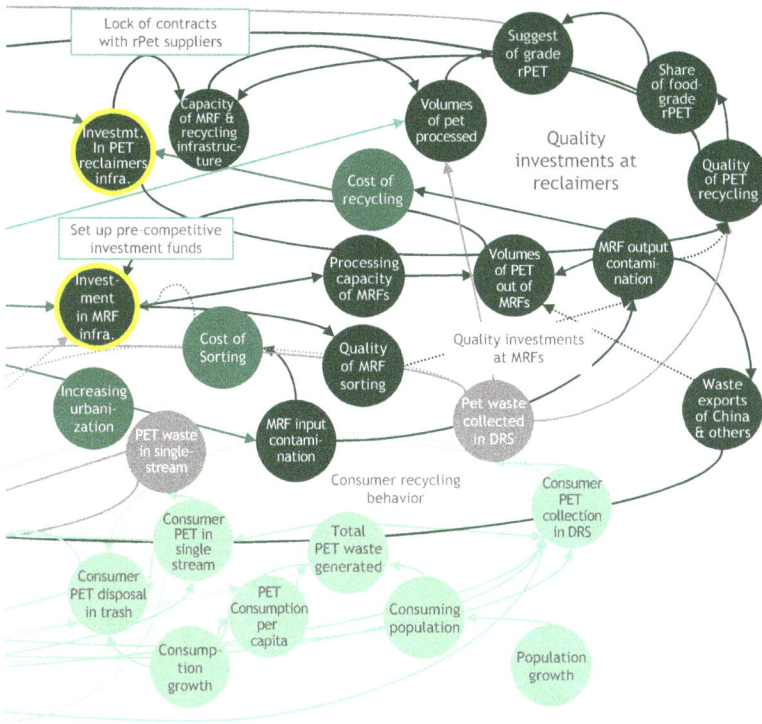

Figure 10.12 (continued)

state or even municipal level. Additional BCG work—to be published soon—will discuss that issue in detail and how to design coalitions that span grain sizes of action in a system to take a new approach to the plastic challenge.

Insights gained from expanding the business context will help inform near-term agendas for strategy, government affairs, public relations, and investor relations. For example, should Procurement negotiate new long-term contracts with rPET suppliers? Should the company set up or acquire PET collectors and recyclers? Should Government Affairs lobby for DRS systems in key states? Should Corporate Foundations sponsor at-scale consumer education and incentive programs and contribute to existing ocean waste removal coalitions? Companies should also leverage them to identify Sustainable Business Model Innovation opportunities to achieve both sustainable competitive advantage and a more sustainable world. This will be explored in-depth in our following posts.

David Young, Rich Hutchinson, and Martin Reeves

11 The Green Economy Has a Resource-Scarcity Problem

The sustainability race is on. Corporations, investors, and governments worldwide have made ambitious commitments to reduce their operations' negative environmental and social impacts.

But there's a problem: new solutions will inevitably trigger bottlenecks for the very resources, infrastructures, and capabilities upon which they depend. While the supply of these sustainability-related resources will expand due to investment and innovation, in many categories, rapid growth in demand will likely outstrip supply, heightening competition and pushing up prices.

The result is that the world is entering a period of sustainability-driven scarcities, bringing new risks and opportunities—and the potential to change the dynamics of competition in many industries for the decade ahead.

Consider carbon credits, for example. Many companies rely on them as a near-term bridge or as a long-term primary strategy for offsetting greenhouse gas emissions. But, at BCG, we anticipate that a significant shortage in carbon credit availability will emerge over the next decade. Under even a conservative scenario, the net supply of credits annually coming onto the market will fall short of supply by 300 million metric tons of carbon dioxide equivalent ($MtCO2e$) in 2030, according to our analysis. This market shortage will likely be exacerbated by a compounding effect in which deficits from prior years stack on top of one another as companies fight to offset both current and historical emissions.

Other impending sustainability scarcities are already visible in several categories.

- **Recycled plastics:** According to BCG analysis, about 45% of the demand for recycled polyethylene terephthalate (rPET) will be unmet by 2025. This will be a problem for consumer-packaged goods companies that have set ambitious rPET packaging goals.[1]

---

1 https://www.bcg.com/publications/2020/global-agreement-to-address-plastic-pollution.

Note: "The Green Economy Has a Resource-Scarcity Problem" was earlier published at hbr.org, July 8, 2021. Reprinted with permission. Copyright 2021 by Harvard Business Publishing; all rights reserved.

https://doi.org/10.1515/9783111295268-012

- **Battery inputs:** The current supply of raw materials, such as lithium, nickel, cobalt, manganese, and graphite, is less than one-third of what will be required to meet battery demand in 2030, according to Cairn Energy Research Advisors. This poses a significant risk to companies that manufacture electric vehicles and energy storage systems.
- **Green hydrogen:** This has been touted as a promising method of decarbonizing heavy industries, such as steel and cement manufacturing, chemical and petrochemical refining, and large-scale shipping. Industry projections of supply and demand of green hydrogen[2] suggests production capacity will need to grow by a factor of 100 to 200 over the next 30 years to meet demand. However, that level of growth in supply could be challenging, given potential bottlenecks in the production of equipment and factory inputs, such as platinum needed for the cathodes in electrolyzers, as well as in the renewable energy input required to produce green hydrogen.
- **Sustainable cotton:** The vast majority of major fashion brands have committed to using 100% sustainable cotton by the end of 2025. In 2018, however, just 21% of cotton worldwide was grown sustainably.[3] And industry experts don't expect the supply of sustainable cotton to expand rapidly enough to meet demand,[4] owing to such factors as the financial challenges that small farmers face in adopting sustainable growing practices.

Forward-looking companies are already trying to secure the resources they will need before sustainability scarcity becomes the norm. For example, Apple, Tesla, and Volkswagen have acted to ensure access to future supplies of critical metals through long-term contracts with producers. Meanwhile, other companies are taking steps to address the looming shortage of recycled plastics. Nestlé and Unilever have invested $30 million and $15 million respectively[5] in a private equity fund that invests in and supports the development of companies in the plastics recycling value chain. PepsiCo and Coca-Cola have invested heavily in the R&D of plastics alternatives, consumer education, and recycling infrastructure to get in front of the expected rPET shortage.

By identifying and anticipating critical bottlenecks, forward-looking companies can take the moves necessary to alleviate constraints and turn them to competitive advantage.

---

2 https://www.bcg.com/publications/2019/real-promise-of-hydrogen.
3 https://sustainablecottonranking.org/market-update.
4 https://www.iisd.org/system/files/publications/ssi-global-market-report-cotton.pdf.
5 https://resource-recycling.com/recycling/2021/03/30/unilever-invests-in-fund-that-acquires-recycling-companies/.

Steps Companies can Take Now

Faced with sustainability scarcity, companies will need to develop a portfolio of strategic and tactical responses to mitigate risk and capitalize on opportunities. Depending on the specific resources in question, these responses should include:

– *Securing supply* through long-term contracts with existing or new suppliers. This should not only focus on mitigating shortage, but also on making the relevant supply chain more resilient.

– *Owning the origins* by acquiring suppliers or developing new sources to ensure that companies will be able to satisfy their future demands for critical inputs while potentially also building new businesses to supply others.

– *Forcing innovation* to turn constraints into opportunities by redesigning goods and services to reduce or eliminate the need for the resources in question.

– *Extracting value* through price premiums on products that rely on sustainable materials or by building entirely new businesses that provide sustainable resources to others.

– *Arbitraging the options* to create advantage from playing off the different supply and pricing dynamics for sustainability scarcities across different geographies.

– *Seeding the market* and hedging new scarcity risks through a portfolio of venture investments in technologies and companies aiming to resolving resource bottlenecks.

– *Broadening the market* by advocating for public policy and investments that enable technological innovation, expand supply, or incentivize alternatives of prospectively scarce inputs.

– *Acting collectively* by catalyzing or participating in industry and cross-sector coalitions to address supply constraints, including with governments and NGOs.

While such moves can make business models more durable, they will only create competitive advantage and value by being fully baked into business strategy and business model innovation. Our research to date finds that less than one-fifth[6] of companies pursuing sustainability outcomes have done so in ways that reinforce advantage and value creation. Fewer still, less than 10%, are using sustainability to reshape the boundaries of competition or reimagine their businesses. It may

---

6 https://www.bcg.com/en-ca/publications/2021/keys-to-being-a-leader-in-sustainable-business-model-innovation.

sound crass to seek profit and advantage in sustainability, but reconciling these apparently opposing forces will leverage the power and innovative potential of the corporate economy to accelerate and scale the sustainability agenda.

Capture Advantage Through Sustainable Business Model Innovation

We suggest that companies adopt the technique of continuous sustainable business model innovation[7] to address and leverage sustainability scarcities.

– Start by *expanding the business model canvas* and mapping the flows, resources, and impacts (positive and negative) for the current business model. The canvas should be broad enough to encompass extended business ecosystems and all relevant stakeholders. It should also cover long-enough time scales to visualize supply dynamics, innovation, and regulation.
– Next, *stress test the current business model* by simulating its expansion, identifying where significant sustainability scarcities could arise and understanding their impacts on advantage and value creation.
– *Model and test business model innovations* that break through scarcity constraints. Explore transformations of the business model by applying moves like vertical reintegration or circularity. Work through the mix of possible responses described above to resolve constraints or open new opportunities. Understand also how to link proposed sustainability improvements to drivers of advantage and value creation for the business.
– *Determine which moves need to be addressed collectively* at the level of an industry or an economy, and which ones are best addressed individually at the company level.
– *Shape the context to ensure success* by scaling strategies across supply chains and business ecosystems, building coalitions to create awareness or collective action, stimulating demand, and advocating for policy change.
– *Scale and repeat.* Continuously refine your worldview on how the race for sustainability will play out for your business model, in your business ecosystem, and in your industry. Dynamically innovate and adjust your business model and portfolio of responses.

---

7 https://www.bcg.com/publications/2020/quest-sustainable-business-model-innovation

The world is at a tipping point on sustainability. Investors are increasing their focus on ESG, consumers are demanding transparency and accountability, governments are setting legally binding targets, and companies are stepping up with bold commitments.

To win through sustainability, a company must move swiftly, mapping out a plan for delivering on its promises, securing the required inputs, and capturing the value that new sustainable business models offer. Besides benefiting the company, these actions will accelerate the world's investment in and development of scarce resources—propelling us toward a sustainable future.

David Young and Simon Beck

12 Identifying Resource Scarcities in the Race to Sustainability

In the past year, sustainability commitments have gone mainstream. Hundreds of corporations have publicly taken a stand on Net-Zero emissions, some of the world's largest asset managers[1] are calling on companies to align with the Net-Zero economy, and the upcoming COP26 summit will undoubtedly spark even greater sustainability commitments from the public sector that will have ramifications for businesses.

While this surge of commitments is clearly a boon for the global community, there is a problem.[2] As companies race to fulfill their sustainability commitments,[3] they may quickly find that much-needed resources, infrastructures, and capabilities are not readily available. In the coming years, we anticipate periods during which demand for the inputs to sustainable solutions will surpass supply —creating troubling scarcities of resources.

To ensure access to critical resources, leaders must move quickly. Companies that can identify novel ways to address their scarcity issues will mitigate risk, build resilience, and capture economic premiums. Scarcity advantage will help determine the winners in the race to sustainability.

For example, the current extraction of raw materials is less than one-third of what will be required to meet battery demand in 2030; BCG analysis suggests that the net supply of carbon credits coming onto the market will fall short of demand by 300 million metric tons of carbon dioxide equivalent in 2030; and industry experts estimate that the production of tree seedlings in the United States will need to increase 2.4-fold to keep up with demand for reforestation and carbon offsets.

In this article, we highlight the dynamic factors that businesses must examine to determine where, when, and how significant scarcities will emerge. With these insights, companies can not only mitigate business risks but also capture new opportunities to innovate and drive forward the green economy.

---

1 https://www.bcg.com/publications/2021/interview-with-blackrock-ceo-larry-fink.
2 https://hbr.org/2021/07/the-green-economy-has-a-resource-scarcity-problem.
3 https://www.bcg.com/about/commitments.

https://doi.org/10.1515/9783111295268-013

Identify Risks, Bottlenecks, and Scarcities

To identify potential business risks, bottlenecks, and scarcities, companies must first expand the business canvas[4] by mapping the wider socioeconomic ecosystem of stakeholders and societal issues in which the business operates. This involves mapping out the full set of players in the system—and their value chains. The goal is to identify key inputs, including the goods (such as raw materials, manufacturing tools, and storage facilities) and services (such as expertise and critical capabilities) that are likely to face a surge in demand.

Next, companies must stress-test the business model to understand where rapid changes in demand, driven by environmental and societal trends, will create critical shortages in the system—and therefore vulnerabilities to the business. A company should simulate an increase in demand for sustainable resources or products, based on actual projections, to anticipate effects on the ecosystem and the business model. If demand for a particular input increased by a factor of ten, could the company still easily acquire it? Would this create pressure on the value chain? Are critical inputs in the ecosystem also important to other industries and ecosystems? For example, graphite is essential for scaling up green hydrogen, but it is also a critical input for scaling up electric vehicles, so it's critical to stay on top of emerging trends across industries that may be competing for the same sustainable resources.

Using this approach, companies can identify strategic intervention points at which targeted action or innovation can alter stakeholder dynamics, positively impact environmental or societal issues, reduce vulnerabilities within the business model, and create new business opportunities.

Understand Which Scarcities Will Affect Your Sustainable Business Strategy

After identifying potential scarcities, companies can then assess the risk and materiality of each potential scarcity by analyzing ten dynamic factors (see Figure 12.1).

Our approach analyzes how the actors within the wider socioeconomic system—and the dynamics among them—create or alleviate sustainability scarcity. The system actors are organizations or groups whose actions and strategies will

---

4 https://www.bcg.com/publications/2021/four-strategies-for-sustainable-business-model-innovation.

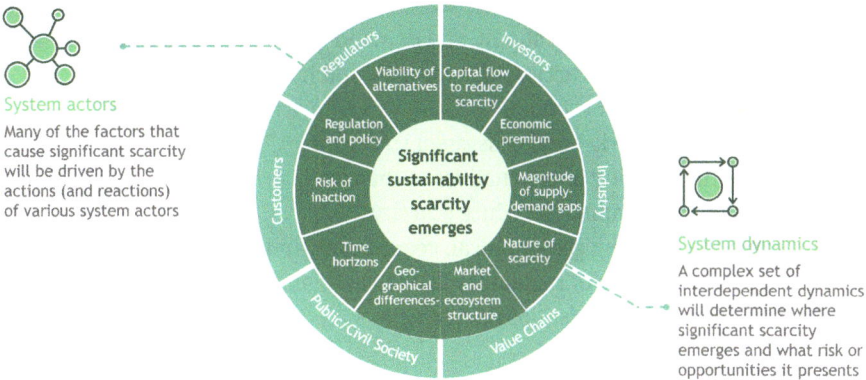

Source: BCG analysis

Figure 12.1: Resource scarcity is driven by system actors and system dynamics.

affect the availability of sustainable resources. This includes investors, industry players, suppliers, value chain participants, the public, customers, and regulators. System dynamics come into play when individual actors make unilateral or multilateral decisions that affect the entire system. For example, if regulators respond to an emerging scarcity by adjusting regulations and policies, this may increase the flow of capital toward a particular resource scarcity or boost the viability of alternative resources or production processes, thereby relieving scarcities by changing the underlying economics. Regulators are more likely to intervene if they believe that the risk of shortages is high enough that it should not be left purely to market forces. For example, governments have identified certain commodities, such as lithium, as essential to national security and the green transition.

By evaluating each segment of the wheel (as depicted in Figure 12.1), leaders can grasp which scarcities will be the most problematic, which will be most relevant for their business or their customers, and that will create the biggest competitive advantage—and act accordingly.

Understand the Wider System Dynamics that Create Resource Scarcities

We have identified ten dynamic factors that companies can analyze to evaluate the business impact of potential scarcities in sustainable resources, infrastructures, and capabilities—and to support their quest for sustainable business model innovation.

1. Determine the exact nature of the scarcity.
2. Quantify the gap between supply and demand under various scenarios.
3. Determine when the scarcity will emerge—and how long it will last.
4. Evaluate the effect of economic premiums and pricing fluctuation.
5. Understand the market and ecosystem structure.
6. Calculate the viability of alternatives to the scarce resources.
7. Track the flow of capital to reduce scarcity.
8. Examine the evolving geographical, geopolitical, and cultural contexts.
9. Anticipate the effects of regulatory frameworks and policy incentives.
10. Evaluate the business risks of inaction.

Determine the exact nature of the scarcity. Scarcities come in many shapes and sizes. There may be a shortage of raw material (like lithium or cobalt), a limitation in current production methods (as in sustainably produced cotton), a problem with scaling up quickly, a shortage of expertise or talent, or an underdeveloped infrastructure. It's essential to pinpoint the exact source of the scarcity problem so that you can respond appropriately.

For example, large-scale reforestation is required to help countries combat climate change. A recent study found that the United States is already short more than two billion seedlings per year—and that's just to meet 50% of the country's reforestation goals by 2040. One of the challenges is accessing skilled labor. Very few people know how to collect seeds, and those who do are in high demand. The United States also faces a shortage of workers who know how to process seeds, nurse seedlings, replant trees, and maintain forests. So the nature of the scarcity, in this case, is not just a production problem. It's also about the underlying talent and skills needed to scale production. The Biden Administration's Civilian Climate Corps offers one example of the way the United States is attempting to bridge this talent gap by training a new generation in climate-related public-works projects, including reforestation.

Quantify the gap between supply and demand under various scenarios. As the sustainability movement accelerates, supply and demand patterns will change. Companies need to understand where demand will increase—and where it will decrease—within their own ecosystem and in adjacent ecosystems. This requires a dynamic systems perspective because the demand for any single resource may rise and fall at the same time, depending on context.

For example, the global platinum supply has been at a deficit for the past three years, but future supply and demand issues are complicated. Demand for platinum is expected to rise as the transition to clean energy and green hydrogen ramps up, given that the element is a key input for hydrogen electrolyzers and hydrogen fuel cells. At the same time, as clean mobility gains traction and fuels the transition from internal combustion engines to electric vehicles, the demand for platinum in catalytic converters will decline. When quantifying the supply–demand gap, companies must account for such opposing market forces.

Determine when the scarcity will emerge—and how long it will last. By understanding when a scarcity will emerge and how long it will last, companies can manage economic premiums and operational constraints, identify the alternatives that could arise to fill the gap, and arbitrage options across different geographies. They can also identify opportunities for acquisition and investment. The key is to move quickly while multiple options still exist. Companies should run scenarios on the duration of each scarcity and develop a clear strategy. From the standpoint of operational resilience, a short and severe bottleneck may be tolerable with limited action, but a prolonged shortage presents serious operational and financial risks if it's not addressed in a timely manner.

BCG analysis suggests that demand for carbon credits will begin outpacing supply by 2024. Even in a conservative scenario, the net supply of credits coming onto the market will fall short of supply by 300 million metric tons of carbon dioxide equivalent in 2030, according to our analysis. This deficit over the next decade could have a significant impact on companies' ability to achieve their Net-Zero commitments, particularly those aimed at a 2030 horizon.

Evaluate the effect of economic premiums and pricing fluctuation. When a scarcity arises, companies will likely need to pay a premium for the resources in short supply. By understanding which resources will be in short supply and recognizing whether competitors are in a good position to pay a premium for that resource, companies can assess their risk and adjust the business model accordingly. What's more, if a resource scarcity leads to high economic premiums, it can trigger a flow of capital toward alternative technologies that are more economically viable. Companies must anticipate these types of shifts.

Take battery-grade lithium for example. It has experienced significant price volatility over the past few years, but as demand from electric vehicles (EVs) and stationary energy storage rapidly increases, industry experts are warning of "perpetual deficits." Although price forecasts vary significantly, Fitch Solutions notes that "green lithium," which is sourced through more sustainable practices (using lower carbon intensity and lower water usage), will sell at a premium compared with conventional mining approaches. Bolstering this forecast, the EU's regulations will require EVs and industrial batteries to have a declared carbon footprint beginning in July 2024.

Understand the market and ecosystem structure. The structure of the value chain, markets, and the broader ecosystem has a significant bearing on how quickly companies can respond to scarcity issues. A highly fragmented ecosystem with multiple players and varying regulatory frameworks will be much more difficult to navigate than a concentrated value chain. Companies should conduct a comprehensive survey of their value chain, not only to identify potential bottlenecks and mitigate shortages but also to make the supply chain more resilient.

Consider the challenges in scaling production of sustainable palm oil. In 2020, the Consumer Goods Forum (CGF) launched the Forest Positive Coalition of Action, a CEO-led initiative representing 20 CGF member companies who are committed to removing deforestation, forest degradation, and conversion from key commodity supply chains, including that of palm oil. Previous attempts to achieve Net-Zero[5] deforestation targets with sustainable palm oil have been challenging, in part because small farmers account for 40% of palm oil production. This means large palm oil suppliers need to convince millions of small farmers to change their agricultural practices. With this market structure, it can be very difficult to systematically achieve sustainability targets.

Calculate the viability of alternatives to the scarce resources. Once companies grasp the fundamental nature of a scarcity and its significance, the next step is to evaluate the technical and economic viability of alternatives. The need for innovative alternatives is especially pronounced when it comes to limitations on raw materials because this type of scarcity cannot be solved by investing in and scaling up production or shifting to new production methods. If the scarcity is expected to last a long time or create a significant supply–demand gap, an entirely new solution that eliminates the need for the scarce resource may be needed. For each scenario, companies must understand where to invest to ensure access to critical resources.

For example, current battery manufacturing processes rely heavily on pure, high-quality graphite, but extracting high-quality graphite is challenging, and recycling at scale is not yet a well-established practice. Additionally, a great deal of waste occurs during EV battery manufacturing; approximately 30 times more graphite is required to make a battery than is present in the final product. Companies like Tesla and Unifrax are experimenting with alternatives such as silicon anodes to significantly reduce the need for graphite in EV batteries. As technology advances, silicon anodes may entirely replace the need for graphite.

Track the flow of capital to reduce scarcity. The amount of capital directed toward scarce resources signals how long a shortage may last and how severe it might be. The more capital that is deployed to address the scarcity, the higher the likelihood is that production will ramp up quickly or new alternatives will be developed. Lower levels of investment indicate that companies may face more diffi-

---

5 https://www.bcg.com/about/net-zero.

cult obstacles in resolving the scarcity. By tracking the flow of capital, companies can see where and how shortages are being addressed and find the best path forward to secure the sustainable resources they need.

For example, according to the World Energy Outlook 2020 report,[6] more than $3 trillion in investment will be needed between now and 2050 to scale up carbon capture, utilization, and storage (CCUS) infrastructure. Oil giants, multinational corporations, governments, and multilateral organizations are all investing in the CCUS economy, but the investments are falling far short of what is needed. In 2020, Europe, the Middle East, and Africa invested just $2 billion in CCUS. Unless large, transformative investments are made soon, CCUS capacity will not meet the demand.

Examine the evolving geographical, geopolitical, and cultural contexts. Some scarcities occur within a specific context owing to changing government regulations, export restrictions, natural disasters, or geopolitical turmoil in a resource-rich region. They may also be driven by cultural context, consumer mindsets, and global demand trends. Companies must recognize the short-term and long-term effects of these potential disruptions and changes and make the moves necessary to alleviate or capitalize on any constraints— or create advantage by actively managing the different supply and pricing dynamics for sustainability scarcities across various geographies.

Again, sustainable palm oil offers a useful example. In some emerging markets, the demand for products containing palm oil is growing quickly; however, efforts to shift consumer preferences and promote the use of certified sustainable palm oil in these markets are still nascent.

Anticipate the effects of regulatory frameworks and policy incentives. Government policy interventions can have a significant effect on sustainability scarcities. Government incentives, subsidies, and direct investment can increase the flow of capital for alternatives to sustainability resources, increasing investment, availability, and their economic viability. Over the past two decades, for example, government tax incentives have increased investment in wind turbine technology and production capacity in the United States, accelerating adoption of this renewable energy. Companies should develop scenarios on possible regulatory changes—and strategize ways to manage disruptions or capitalize on potential changes.

Looking ahead, the worldwide lithium-battery market, for example, is expected to grow by a factor of five to ten in the next decade. In response to this vast increase in market demand, the US Department of Energy released a "National Blueprint for Lithium Batteries" in June 2021. The blueprint guides invest-

---

6 https://www.iea.org/reports/world-energy-outlook-2020.

ment in a domestic lithium-battery manufacturing value chain to ensure that US companies benefit from domestic and global market growth and avoid the risk of "long-term dependence on foreign sources of batteries and critical materials." Companies that can capitalize on government investments can gain a strong competitive advantage in this fast-growing global market.

Evaluate the business risks of inaction. Sustainability can be a source of competitive advantage, and, when devising a company strategy, it's important to understand how competitors are pursuing sustainability. As more and more companies pledge Net-Zero commitments, for example, a certain subset will inevitably fall short of their targets. When these companies scramble to meet their goals, the scarcity of sustainable resources will worsen, ramping up risk for companies unprepared for these changing dynamics. Inaction can present obvious operational risks (you can't access the talent you need to fulfill a sustainability commitment) and financial risks (you will be fined for using unsustainable resources). But the risks aren't always so clear cut (you miss sustainability targets and draw negative press coverage, but this doesn't harm sales or investor sentiment).

Historically, companies that fall short of sustainability targets have not faced serious repercussions, but the risk is growing now that broader accountability mechanisms exist for investors, consumers, and regulators. Running cost–benefit scenarios reveals the true cost of not taking action to address sustainability scarcities.

For companies to meet—or even exceed—their sustainability goals, they must continuously monitor the sustainability landscape. The ten-factor analysis described here offers a clear view into the ways that various actors across all industries and geographies will affect availability of the resources necessary to achieve sustainability commitments.

Time is of the essence. Sustainability commitments are surging, but sustainability-related resources are in limited supply. Companies that continuously scan their ecosystems for sustainability scarcities will be prepared to circumvent shortages—or capitalize on them—and unlock new opportunities for long-term growth and competitive advantage.

David Young and Simon Beck

13 Solving the Puzzle of Sustainable Resource Scarcity

As more and more companies commit to adopting climate conscious practices, the available supply of suitable resources and infrastructure is shrinking.

Corporate climate commitments have taken off worldwide in recent years, catapulting from 52 commitments to science-based targets in 2015 to more than 1,000 in 2021. The commitments are becoming more ambitious, too. In 2020, for the first time, the number of companies committing to limiting the global temperature rise to 1.5 °C surpassed the number committed to a limit of 2 °C. In addition, we are seeing commitments across other issues of sustainability, ranging from deforestation, biodiversity, and land conversion to green steel usage and elimination of internal combustion engine vehicles.

As commitments multiply and the targets become more aggressive, however, the green economy is developing a resource scarcity problem.[1] With thousands of companies simultaneously shifting to more sustainable practices and innovating new products and services to enable sustainability, the need for sustainable resources is becoming urgent. But inputs such as organic cotton, sustainable aviation fuel, recycled plastics, and seedlings, as well as the infrastructure necessary to ensure their widespread availability, are in limited supply.

There is also a shortage of people with green skills. Companies and governments are struggling to hire qualified talent, such as retrofitters to create energy-efficient buildings and power grids, ecologists to design and plan sustainable development, and seed collectors to scale up reforestation efforts.

In an earlier article,[2] we explained how companies can identify where, when, and how significant scarcities will emerge in their ecosystem. In this article, we focus on strategies that companies can adopt to overcome resource scarcities (see Figure 13.1).

---

1 https://hbr.org/2021/07/the-green-economy-has-a-resource-scarcity-problem.
2 https://www.bcg.com/publications/2021/identifying-resource-scarcities.

https://doi.org/10.1515/9783111295268-014

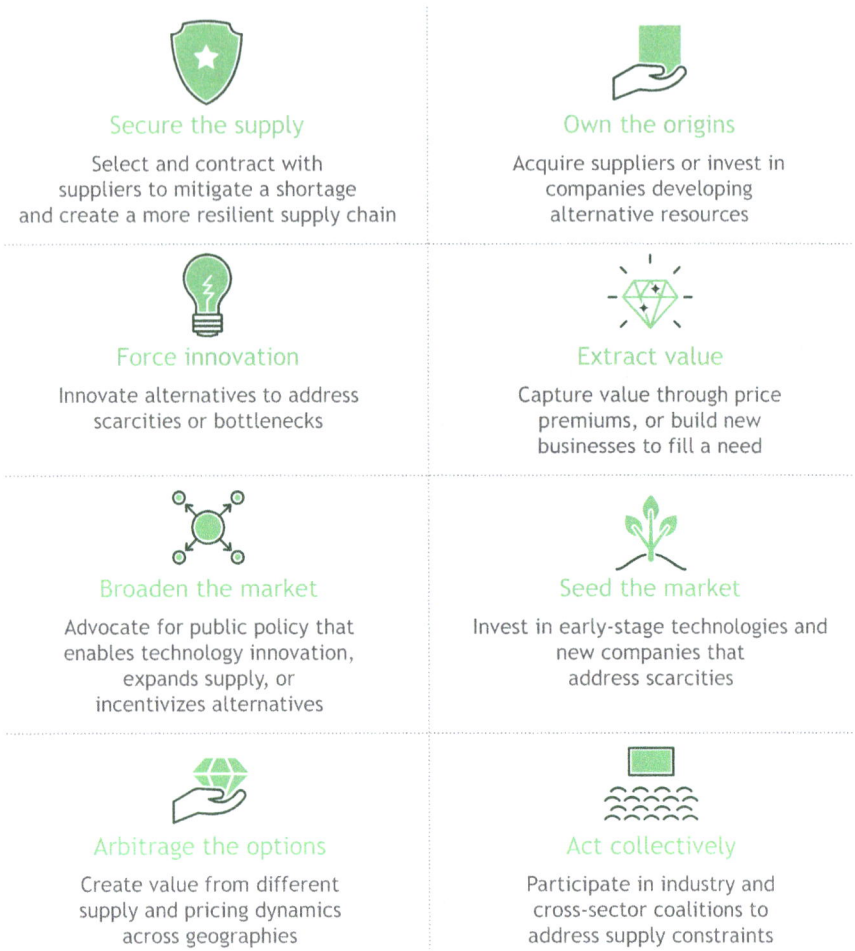

Secure the supply

Select and contract with
suppliers to mitigate a shortage
and create a more resilient supply chain

Own the origins

Acquire suppliers or invest in
companies developing
alternative resources

Force innovation

Innovate alternatives to address
scarcities or bottlenecks

Extract value

Capture value through price
premiums, or build new
businesses to fill a need

Broaden the market

Advocate for public policy that
enables technology innovation,
expands supply, or
incentivizes alternatives

Seed the market

Invest in early-stage technologies and
new companies that
address scarcities

Arbitrage the options

Create value from different
supply and pricing dynamics
across geographies

Act collectively

Participate in industry and
cross-sector coalitions to
address supply constraints

Source: BCG analysis

Figure 13.1: A portfolio response to overcome resource scarcities.

Eight Core Strategies

Leading companies are adopting a portfolio-based response to resource scarcities —an approach that allows them to pick and choose the strategies that best fit their unique business model and ecosystem. From our work with clients, we have found that eight strategies yield the best results.

Secure the supply. Develop long-term contracts with existing or new suppliers, not just to mitigate shortages, but also to make the supply chain more resilient. For shortages of critical talent and capabilities, explore the possibility of augmenting traditional staffing with new fluid sources of talent, including hidden internal talent pools, global sourcing, returnships (internships for adults reentering the workforce), and employee sharing. As sales of electric vehicles (EVs) have taken off, demand for cobalt, a necessary ingredient in EV batteries, has increased dramatically. As a result, the mineral's price has surged and supplies are scarce, in part because the pandemic created logistical supply chain issues. Knowing that their need for cobalt was likely to triple from 2020 to 2025, BMW negotiated a five-year contract with Managem, a Moroccan mining group. This new contract secures 20% of BMW's cobalt demand through 2025.

Own the origins. Acquire suppliers or invest in new sources to ensure access to critical resources. Where feasible, build new businesses to supply others with scarce resources.

The demand for lithium is expected to outstrip supply within four years, according to Benchmark Mineral Intelligence. General Motors responded by taking an ownership stake in Controlled Thermal Resources' Hell's Kitchen lithium extraction project. By 2024, this project could produce 60,000 tons of lithium per year, enough to supply 6 million electric vehicles and make Hell's Kitchen the United States' largest producer of lithium.

Force innovation. Turn constraints into opportunities by redesigning goods and services to reduce or eliminate the need for scarce resources.

To deal with cobalt shortages, Panasonic has reduced the cobalt content of its vehicle batteries to less than 5%, and the company expects to develop cobalt-free batteries within the next two to three years. Meanwhile, researchers at King Abdullah University of Science and Technology (KAUST) have developed a process for extracting lithium from seawater, where the element is relatively plentiful.

Extract value. Build entirely new businesses or products that provide sustainable resources to others, or capture price premiums for products that rely on sustainable materials.

Growth in the EV market has created a surge in demand for nickel. Mining companies that have a clean and traceable supply chain for high-quality, green, Class 1 nickel are in high demand and should command a price premium. Tesla signed a contract with BHP, a multinational mining firm, to secure a long-term supply contract for sustainable nickel. Beyond securing the supply, the two companies have also agreed to work together to increase battery supply chain sustainability, reduce carbon emissions from their respective operations, and focus on end-to-end raw material traceability via blockchain.

Broaden the market. Advocate for policies and investments that enable technological innovation, expand supply, or incentivize the development of alternatives to scarce resources.

To address the anticipated shortage of recycled plastics, nearly 100 companies have signed the US Plastics Pact, a consortium led by The Recycling Partnership and World Wildlife Fund. The group brings together plastic packaging producers, brands, retailers, recyclers, waste management companies, and policymakers to reduce plastic waste through industry-led innovation, infrastructure upgrades that scale recycling capacity, and a unified framework for a circular economy for plastics across the United States.

Seed the market. Mitigate emerging scarcity risks by investing in technologies and companies that aim to resolve resource bottlenecks.

Companies with plans to increase recycled plastic content in their packaging face a shortage of recycled materials. BCG analysis suggests that by 2025 approximately 45% of demand for recycled plastics will be unmet. Unilever established ambitious targets to ensure that 100% of its plastic packaging is fully reusable, recyclable, or compostable, by 2025. To boost the supply of postconsumer recycled plastics, Unilever has invested in multiple funds, including the Closed Loop Partners' Leadership Fund, a private equity fund that acquires companies along the value chain to increase recycling, reduce waste, and build a circular economy.[3]

Arbitrage the options. Create competitive advantage by arbitraging supply scarcities and price dynamics across different geographies.

California's Low Carbon Fuel Standard, which seeks to slash the carbon intensity of transportation fuels by 20% by 2030, has created strong demand for renewable natural gas. In response, dairy farmers in several midwestern states invested millions of dollars in biogas projects. Amp Americas, a renewable energy company, is capitalizing on this new market by developing and managing dairy biogas projects throughout the Midwest and then selling renewable natural gas to California's fuel transportation market.

Act collectively. Catalyze or participate in industry-wide and cross-sector coalitions, including governments and NGOs, to address supply constraints.

---

3 https://www.bcg.com/capabilities/climate-change-sustainability/circular-economy-circelligence.

Sustainable aviation fuel (SAF) could reduce the carbon intensity of flying by 80%, but currently it accounts for only 0.1% of global supply. To build the market for high-quality SAF, corporate members of the Sustainability Aviation Buyers Alliance are working in collaboration with the Environmental Defense Fund and Rocky Mountain Institute to develop a SAF certificate system, expand SAF investment opportunities, and accelerate the use of SAF to reduce aviation emissions. In October 2021, ten global airlines and Boston Consulting Group established the Aviation Climate Taskforce to accelerate breakthroughs in emerging technologies such as hydrogen technologies and synthetic fuels, to help the industry achieve Net-Zero emissions.

Adapting the Business Model for Sustainability

The first step in identifying, overcoming, and creating competitive advantage in cases of resource scarcity is to use sustainable business model innovation (SBM-I).[4] SBM-I enables companies to combine environmental, societal, and financial priorities; reimagine their core business model; and turn sustainability into a competitive advantage.

In our examination of more than 115 SBM-I case studies, more than 20% addressed areas of known scarcity, and more than 50% employed at least three of the strategies described above in their portfolio.

But many leading companies aren't just using SBM-I to overcome scarcities within their own supply chains. They are pursuing new business opportunities by alleviating scarcities that their customers face. Twice as many of the companies we studied focused on addressing scarcity for their customers as on alleviating the risk of scarcity in their own production lines. In other words, SBM-I is not merely a defensive move. It's an opportunity to create business advantage.

The demand for sustainable resources, capabilities, and infrastructure is poised to grow exponentially in the coming years. Companies that act now to leverage a portfolio-based response will be able not only to overcome resource scarcities but also to turn them into a competitive advantage.

---

4 https://www.bcg.com/publications/2021/four-strategies-for-sustainable-business-model-innovation.

—

Part 3.2: **Apply Modular Transformations**

Bryann DaSilva, Julia Dhar, Sana Rafiq, and David Young

14 Nudging Consumers Toward Sustainability

We each make choices every day—about what to buy, what to eat, when to recycle, and whether to walk, drive, or take public transportation. While these can feel like highly individual choices, behavioral economics has shown that consumers are highly susceptible to environmental and social cues. Given that consumers' decisions have consequences—for personal well-being and the health of the planet—companies could play a role in steering consumers to make sustainable choices. It's as simple as giving them a nudge.

Popularized by Richard Thaler and Cass Sunstein in their book *Nudge: Improving Decisions about Health, Wealth, and Happiness,* nudges are simple, low-cost interventions that can alter people's decision making without attaching a substantial economic reward or penalty to the process.

One purpose of nudges is to help people be the best version of themselves—to make the choices that they would make if their executive function, willpower, and long-term thinking were firing on all cylinders. As consumers increasingly demand more environmentally and socially conscious choices, nudges can nurture and facilitate their desire to live sustainably, accelerating demand for sustainable products and services. That demand, in turn, can help build attractive markets for investment and propel the sustainability transformation forward.

Whether they intend to or not, companies already shape behaviors, so they could encourage environmentally and socially conscious ones instead. A travel portal may rank comparable flights on the basis of price and flight time, for example, but it could rank them on the basis of carbon emissions. Food delivery platforms may promote popular restaurants or their sponsors, but they could elevate climate-friendly food options instead. By examining the current options offered to customers and seeking ways to nudge them toward sustainable choices and behaviors, a company can empower its customers to meet their personal sustainability goals, enhance the company's brand, help build sustainability markets, and protect the planet.

From a Behavioral Surplus to a Societal Surplus

With access to an abundance of consumer data, organizations that digitally engage with their customers now have what Professor Shoshana Zuboff calls a behavioral surplus. Zuboff coined the term to describe the concentration of excess

https://doi.org/10.1515/9783111295268-015

information companies have captured about consumers that is above and beyond what they need to improve their products or services—information that could be used to predict and steer future purchasing behavior and launch new products.

Companies that build this behavioral surplus (and, along with it, the power to predict and shape consumer behavior) could and should use it for the greater good —to create what we call a societal surplus: the sum of the benefits that accrue to society by advancing economic vitality; environmental sustainability; lifetime well-being; access, equity, and inclusion; ethical capacity; and social progress. Companies could use their behavioral data to nudge customers toward more sustainable choices, thereby building market demand for sustainable offerings and helping society achieve sustainability targets. A societal surplus is generative; it benefits consumers, shareholders, and society as a whole.

In our assessment, there's an ethical imperative here: if companies are cultivating a behavioral surplus, then they also have a responsibility to cultivate a societal surplus. Recent advances in data and analytics,[1] data segmentation, machine learning, and artificial intelligence (AI)—combined with raised awareness of the environmental and social impacts of lifestyle choices—mean that companies have the technology and data[2] that they need to help consumers make the responsible choices that the best versions of themselves would make.

By cultivating a societal surplus, companies can gain a sustained competitive advantage that is not easily replicated. By understanding and aggregating the environmental and societal benefits created by their customers' use of more sustainable products or services, companies can quantify their own societal impact. Are nudges in an online marketplace increasing the number of transactions for more sustainable products? Does a credit card that shows the emissions associated with each purchase reduce the amount of carbon per dollar spent? Is a manufacturer experiencing significantly higher growth because of its nudges to buy energy-efficient appliances? Is a sustainability campaign that is allied with social media influencers seeing an uptick in sustainable purchasing patterns? In the same way that an organization[3] calculates its CO_2 footprint, water savings, or diversity, equity, and inclusion impact, companies should quantify the effect of their nudges by measuring the impact that their customers' choices have on the sustainability market and the community at large.

---

1 https://www.bcg.com/capabilities/digital-technology-data/data-analytics.
2 https://www.bcg.com/capabilities/digital-technology-data/overview.
3 https://www.bcg.com/capabilities/organization-strategy/overview.

Enhancing a Sustainability Strategy

The right portfolio of sustainability nudges should help a company accelerate its sustainability strategy. This can be done, for example, by nudging its customers toward more sustainable product lines, capturing inputs that help it meet the goals of a circular economy, or providing greater transparency into product sustainability and choices that further differentiate the company.

Before building a portfolio of sustainability nudges, companies must first understand which issues are most material to their stakeholders and to the performance of the business. If a product's total life-cycle emissions is central to a company's sustainability strategy, for example, the goal could be to create a suite of initiatives that will nudge its customers to make choices that reduce those life-cycle emissions. This can be done by nudging customers toward the company's lower-emission products or its Internet of Things[4] energy-optimization service, for example. At the same time, it's important to think about how the nudges could also contribute to other important social goals, including improving customers' lifetime well-being, advancing equity and inclusion, and operating ethically.

Addressing sustainability also requires collective action to shape the wider ecosystem. Companies are increasingly joining alliances to jointly make fundamental changes, such as expanding the recycling infrastructure, building market demand, and strengthening their influence on standards and policy. The use of sustainability nudges also applies to corporate-led sustainability alliances.[5] A sustainability alliance can share the load on some sustainability nudges by educating consumers, for example, and disclosing environmental costs.

For example, an alliance could create a shared advertising campaign that encourages consumers to adopt a sustainable behavior, such as recycling plastic beverage bottles. Then, each member company could complement that campaign with its own set of recycling nudges. Or the alliance could promote a logo usable by all members that conform to certain sustainability practices, such as abiding by fair-trade arrangements or sourcing from conflict-free areas. Every sustainability alliance should explicitly think through how it will use nudges to amplify members' sustainability efforts and accelerate end-market transformations.

---

4 https://www.bcg.com/capabilities/digital-technology-data/internet-of-things.
5 https://www.bcg.com/publications/2022/how-to-build-sustainability-alliance.

Putting Nudges into Action

So, how can companies use nudges to engage customers and advance sustainability? There are four main ways.

Highlight sustainable options throughout a customer's purchasing journey. Behavioral economics research shows that given a choice, people opt for the status quo—they have a preference for the default option. But, with the right type of prompting, they can be encouraged to adopt new behaviors. Companies could find creative techniques to highlight sustainable products and services, particularly approaches that showcase their unique value.

- **Draw attention.** Make it easy for consumers to find and purchase sustainable options. Travel search engines could list the flights with the lowest carbon emissions first, stores could make the most sustainable products easy to spot on racks and shelves, and parking garages could put parking spots for electric vehicles closest to the entrance.
- **Leverage branding.** Develop a brand that allows consumers to quickly gauge a product's level of sustainability. Companies could create brands around sustainable themes, such as planet friendly, sustainable sourcing, or water-smart options.
- **Create contrast.** Present a sustainable choice next to alternatives to positively influence the consumer's perception of the value of the sustainable option. By offering a consumer a nonorganic, an organic, and a local organic version of a product—two sustainable choices along with a nonsustainable one—companies could nudge consumers to select a sustainable option.

Simplify sustainable choices. Successful companies take into account consumers' tendencies to act and think automatically, nudge them when they're open to making a change, and enable them to take small steps that aren't difficult.

- **Remove barriers.** Eliminate digital and physical barriers or additional steps so as to streamline the sustainable decision. Meal kit services could offer curated vegetarian or carbon-neutral options that could be ordered with a single click.
- **Change defaults.** Decrease the friction of choosing the most sustainable option. Food delivery platforms could set the utensils default to "no plastic cutlery and napkins."
- **Provide automatic prompts or encouragement.** Guide sustainable decision making through real-time prompts. E-commerce platforms could suggest that a customer consider a product that offers the same features but has a smaller carbon footprint. Additionally, the platform could offer customers the choice to "round up" to contribute toward offsetting carbon emissions.

Educate customers and disclose environmental costs. Companies could use nudges to share data and insights that highlight the value of sustainable options —and the costs associated with nonsustainable options.

- **Remind.** Keep sustainability top of mind for customers. Show customers their purchases and emissions in an app or at the bottom of their receipt. Send them periodic reminders about the impact of their sustainable choices and the company's commitments to sustainability. Or, post reminders in stores or at checkout counters highlighting the value of sustainable choices.
- **Educate.** Help customers learn more about the production of the products that they buy and the importance of sustainable choices. Produce a video that highlights the local farm or the factory where an item is produced, that talks about the sustainable and ethical practices of the brand, or that analyzes the steps of the production life cycle and reveals opportunities for customers to drive sustainability. Then make the video accessible via a quick response, or QR, code.
- **Disclose.** Be transparent about the resources that were required to produce an item. Using the nutrition labels on foods and beverages as a model, clearly and consistently present a product's sustainability metrics on the packaging in a way that allows for easy comparison.

Engage customers and communities in actions that reinforce their commitments. Companies could use nudges that reflect socially acceptable group behaviors, inducing customers to think or act differently.

- **Encourage precommitment.** Encourage customers to actively commit to sustainable choices early on. Use commitment strategies (such as asking customers to sign a pledge when they contract for a service or to press a button as they walk into a store) to encourage sustainable choices.
- **Tap into positive social pressure.** Use individuals' desire to uphold social norms and maintain a positive image to drive sustainable choices. Consider ranking and grading customers' purchases for sustainability relative to their peers, convey the percentage of customers who have switched from a less sustainable product to a more sustainable product recently, or congratulate the most sustainable customers.
- **Gamify.** Frame sustainable decision making as a game, and reward good choices. Invite customers to ring a bell when their cart contains sustainable choices, incentivize sustainable purchases that unlock a new level within a loyalty program, or offer rewards for meeting certain targets (such as making three consecutive carbon-neutral purchases).

Whether companies run traditional advertising campaigns or use the latest in machine learning and behavioral science, they tap into the behavioral surplus they have accumulated as a matter of course.

The urgent question is whether companies should nudge consumers toward more sustainable choices, thereby helping to create a societal surplus for the well-being of individuals and the world. Getting consumers on the path to sustainable living can't wait. There is an ethical imperative for companies to help them.

By recognizing the opportunity and building a portfolio of sustainability nudges, companies can drive consumer demand, accelerate their sustainability strategy, and build sustainability markets—not only to benefit the company's bottom line but also for the good of individuals, society, and the planet.

Massimo Russo, David Young, Tian Feng, and Marine Gerard

15 Sharing Data to Address Our Biggest Societal Challenges

Achieving most, if not all, of the UN's 17 sustainable development goals (SDGs) will require the use of data from multiple public and private sources. In this sense, the SDGs are the embodiment of what we call "data mega-use-cases": complex problems and opportunities affecting many different individuals, companies, organizations, and governments. Financial inclusion, crisis response, resource conservation, public health, and climate change are all examples of data mega-use-cases encompassed by the SDGs. But data can only contribute to the solution of these problems if it is readily available and shared.

The good news is that there is increasing focus on using big data to support the SDGs. The UN has put forth specific big data mega-use-cases and has launched the Global Pulse initiative to bring the power of big data and artificial intelligence to bear on the SDGs. Many of the UN's use cases leverage telecom, mobile, search, and sentiment data from social media. Over the last four years, UN experts and business leaders have met annually at the UN World Data Forum to discuss these and other opportunities.

For their part, businesses have so far focused primarily on economic value creation from data. But with data's expanding role in achieving environmental, social, and governance goals, companies need to broaden their horizons. Sharing data—from the Internet of Things and other sources—with companies and organizations participating in ecosystems and public–private partnerships can be both a key part of a company's total societal impact[1] strategy and a foundation for sustainable business model innovation.[2]

The Value of Data Sharing

BCG explored more than 550 data-sharing projects and innovative or sustainable business initiatives. Of these, we identified 220 examples of data sharing for mega-use-cases (see Figure 15.1).

---

1 https://www.bcg.com/publications/2017/total-societal-impact-new-lens-strategy.
2 https://www.bcg.com/publications/2020/quest-sustainable-business-model-innovation.

https://doi.org/10.1515/9783111295268-016

73 Health

38 Education/Social

66 Economic development

33 Agriculture/Food

65 Mobility/Information Infrastructure

32 Humanitarian

53 Environment

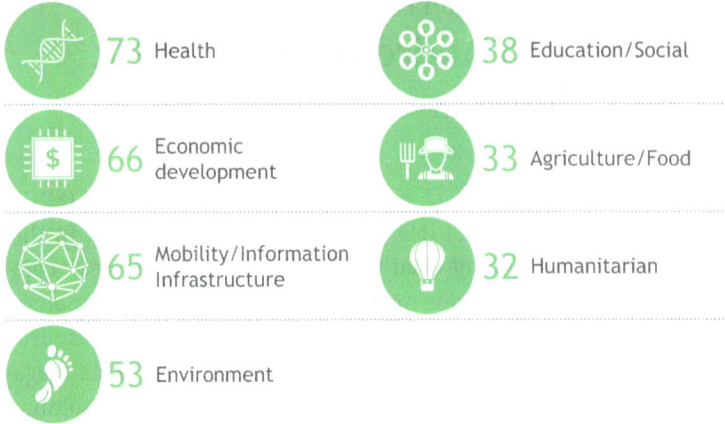

Example of data sharing in each sector, out of 220 reviewed

One-third

Tackle problems from two or more sectors

Sources: New York university GovLab, Data Collaborative Explorer, desk research; BCG analysis
Note: Several examples are included in more than one category owing to their broad applications; some may be included in all seven categories for the same reason

Figure 15.1: Data sharing in Mega-Use-Cases.

The scope of these initiatives is broad, covering more than seven sectors. Since the same shared data can be used for many purposes, it is not surprising that a third of the projects we identified benefit two or more sectors. For example, a shared geolocation data set helps with efforts to track the potential spread of a virus (health), informs measures to reduce air pollution (environment), and helps with data-driven infrastructure decision making (mobility). Figure 15.2 illustrates the ways in which value can be generated from data sharing for mega-use-cases.

Below we examine five mega-use-cases that illuminate a few of the ways in which data sharing is helping to address some of the world's most challenging problems.

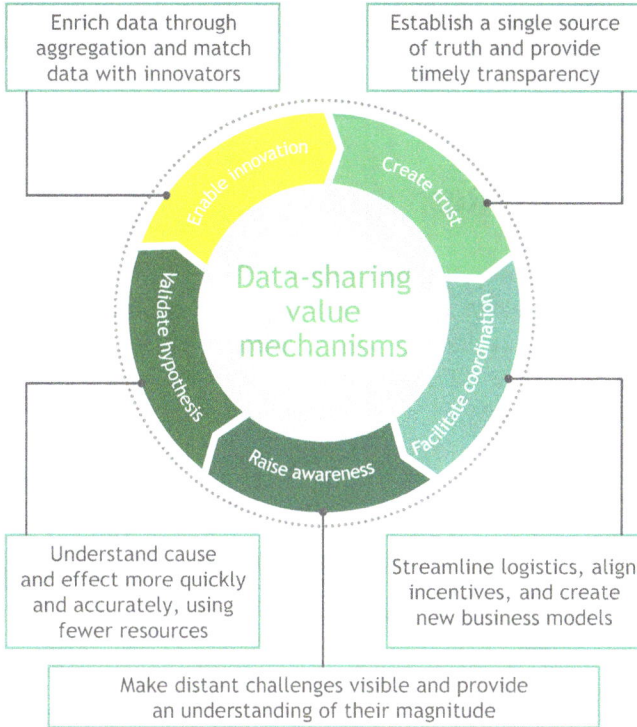

Source: BCG analysis

Figure 15.2: Five ways to generate value from data sharing.

Financial Inclusion

In 2018, the World Bank estimated that there are some 1.7 billion unbanked adults worldwide. While many factors contribute to this problem, three of the biggest are the cost of banking, the need for documentation, and people's lack of trust. Underlying these is the need for financial institutions to accurately assess the risk profile of potential customers. For many individuals with limited or no credit history, providing the required information has long been an insurmountable hurdle.

Financial institutions have recently succeeded in expanding access through microfinance and other channels thanks to data shared by and about consumers. China's Ant Financial and Chile's Destácame use novel data sources (platform payments and utility bills, respectively) to build alternative credit scores for the financially underserved. By finding creative ways to use data intended for other purposes[3]—such as e-commerce or payment—to assess an individual's ability to pay back a loan, these companies are able to extend credit access to the unbanked and underbanked.

Disaster and Incident Response

In the event of an epidemic, earthquake, hurricane, or other disaster, the UN's Humanitarian Data Exchange allows governments and relief organizations to share data and coordinate response efforts so that support gets to the people and places that need it most. During the COVID-19 pandemic, more than 100 data sets have been released on this exchange, from government response information to case counts to mobility data.

At a local level, the Waze Connected Citizens Program is a two-way data exchange involving millions of users in more than 1,000 cities, along with public-sector partners in multiple countries, to facilitate coordinated responses to traffic accidents. Data on accidents and road conditions sourced from users is subsequently anonymized and shared with governments for use in infrastructure planning. Government agencies, in turn, provide data on maintenance efforts back to users through the exchange, allowing for better route planning.

Data sharing can also help validate hypotheses about postcrisis realities. Following Hurricane Katrina, for example, volunteer groups in New Orleans were able to save time and money on their rebuilding efforts by comparing pre- and post-storm mailing data from marketing company Valassis. The data enabled volunteers to shift hours away from labor-intensive population surveys and toward actual rebuilding efforts. Similarly, Valassis data was used to demonstrate the return on investment in revitalizing Detroit neighborhoods in a faster and more resource-effective way than ground surveys would have allowed.

Resource Conservation

In the last 20 years, the world has lost 10% of its forest cover. Deforestation and other types of resource loss can be insidious because they occur over geographically dispersed areas, often over long periods of time, and because harvesting typically takes place far from the point of consumption. Demand for rhino horns in

---

3 https://www.bcg.com/publications/2020/exploring-the-alternative-data-use-landscape.

Asia, for instance, fuels poaching in Africa, with devastating effect on the species. Demand for palm oil in the United States leads to unsustainable harvesting in the forests of Borneo. It is challenging for people around the world, as well as in the affected countries, to grasp the full extent of the problem or to act in a timely fashion.

The World Resource Institute's Global Forest Watch raises awareness by closing the gap between deforestation sites and supply chain decision makers. Through satellite imaging and data shared by partner organizations and governments, the system alerts NGOs, governments, and individuals of deforestation taking place around the world. Its PALM (Prioritizing Areas, Landscapes, and Mills) risk tool lets companies spot deforestation in their palm oil supply chain before it happens, enabling them to intervene in time.

By aggregating data from multiple locations, Global Forest Watch also raises awareness of the problem's magnitude. Visualization of historic data allows users to grasp the extent of deforestation across time and space. Users can review historic trends worldwide or delve into specific countries to understand the impact of such factors as logging and conservation policy. This kind of data aggregation can help connect pockets of anecdotal data to reveal a compelling narrative.

Cisco has partnered with the World Wildlife Fund, Dimension Data (part of NTT), and FLIR Systems, a producer of night-vision cameras, to track wildlife populations and notify rangers of potential poaching activity in a number of game reserves. Cisco contributes networking and IoT technology and develops solutions tailored to specific endangered species and their locations. Data from satellite imagery and tracking devices that indicates poaching activity is shared with authorities to raise awareness. Rhinoceros poaching in protected areas has plummeted 96% since the solution was implemented.

Data sharing can also facilitate coordination and foster trust among multiple parties in a supply chain, enabling new business models in a circular economy. For example, BASF's reciChain platform combines blockchain technology with functions that enable accurate tracking and secured sharing of data to improve the sorting, tracing, and monitoring of plastics throughout the supply chain. Manufacturers of polymers create a "digital badge" for their products, which are then tracked by consumer goods manufacturers, waste collectors, and recyclers. Blockchain enables and validates the sharing of data from the digital badges. Overall, reciChain enables a more circular supply chain for recycled plastics by helping to quantify recycled content, improve sorting quality, assess recycling economics, and monitor polymer life cycles.

Public Health

In the early months of the COVID-19 crisis, governments and public-health organizations scrambled to understand the characteristics of the novel coronavirus. Very quickly, global databases were established to monitor not only case counts but also the actions that governments were taking in response. With this data, researchers could study the effects of one country's policy decisions, such as lockdowns and contact tracing, to inform policy decisions in others. Data sharing helped validate hypotheses at speed and scale.

Many organizations have contributed data drawn from their businesses to help researchers and others paint a more complete picture of the crisis. Cuebiq, a location data research company, transformed global positioning system (GPS) data into a personal-mobility index. In the early months of the pandemic, Carnegie Mellon University used self-reported symptoms data from Facebook and Google surveys to compile interactive maps of COVID-19 indicators in the United States. Kinsa, a health technology company, leveraged data from smart thermometers to forecast hotspots. Scripps used biometric data from wearable devices to better understand the leading health indicators of COVID outcomes. Since the crisis is far from over in many countries, this kind of real-world data gathering, aggregation, and sharing is still contributing to the evolving public-health response.

Data sharing also enables coordination between public-health officials and private citizens. Some 500 contact-tracing applications[4] have been developed worldwide. While these differ in level of success—and some raise privacy concerns—best-practice examples allow public-health officials to inform citizens of local COVID risks and allow citizens to help public-health officials paint a more complete picture of local COVID rates.

Climate Change

Combating climate change requires a combination of existing solutions with new insights and technologies. Data sharing can further innovation by allowing the aggregation of data from a variety of sources and by easing access for innovators and scientists. Aggregation can involve combining multiple instances of the same data (such as time series and large samples) or different types of data (such as machine performance and energy consumption).

---

4 https://www.bcg.com/publications/2020/contact-tracing-accelerates-iot-opportunities-and-risks-2.

Precision agriculture showcases the power of aggregating and analyzing data from many sources in the development of new technologies. The data on which it is based can come from equipment and field sensors, survey instruments, and field robots, as well as from satellite imagery and drones. It can be used not only to increase farmers' yields and profits, but to tackle climate change.

In 2019, Indigo Ag launched Indigo Carbon with the goal of incentivizing farmers to remove carbon from the atmosphere and sequester it in their soil. In the first phase, Indigo partners with other organizations to use data shared by farmers to quantify soil carbon, along with methane and nitrous oxide emissions, and accelerate carbon sequestration. In the future, Indigo plans to pay farmers who embrace regenerative agriculture for each ton of carbon captured and to sell certifications to companies that want to compensate for their carbon footprints. By working with established market regulators, Indigo is supporting a transparent marketplace and acting as an intermediary, thereby injecting trust into the carbon credit market.

Broader data sharing can harness talent for innovation. Schneider Electric is aggregating data from partners and customers on its EcoStruxure Platform, facilitating data sharing with application developers on its Schneider Electric Exchange, and sponsoring competitions on DrivenData for new energy management solutions.

In previous articles in this series, we argued that effective data-sharing ecosystems achieve a balance among the value, risks, and costs involved in accessing and using participants' data. There are still many barriers, but given the potential value shown by the mega-use-cases described above and many others, public- and private-sector leaders should think hard about where they can contribute and how they can overcome the hurdles. Leaders of companies looking to broaden their total societal impact strategies can assess which data assets they can contribute by asking themselves these questions:

– Where can our enterprise data be used for greater transparency? Can we help generate trust among parties to develop novel solutions to society's most critical problems?
– Can our data be used to raise awareness? To measure outcomes?
– Can we share our data on a platform or in an ecosystem to promote greater innovation? Can we participate in developing new solutions by leveraging sources of data outside our company?

Addressing these questions can help businesses find opportunities to share their data directly for the good of society. It can also help identify opportunities to develop new business models that will promote both business advantages and social benefits. Participating in data ecosystems as a data or solution provider can be a critical part of a comprehensive strategy for total societal impact and sustainable business model innovation.

Martin Reeves, Jack Fuller, and Gerardo Gutiérrez-López

16 The Playful Corporation

We don't usually think of play as being an essential part of business. Play, in a business context, looks like an optional extra: something you do after you've finished your work, rather than being an integral part of work itself. There are certainly many gestures toward playfulness in the modern office: bean bags, *LEGO*® corners, foosball tables, and so on. But these are more often attempts to create a comfortable working environment rather than to make the work itself more effective.

The fact that innovation productivity[1] appears to be declining, and workplace disengagement[2] rising, might suggest a need to become more productively playful. But it is when we look closely into the dynamics of play, and what play can do for business, that we see its true importance.

Especially when facing uncertain environments, we should understand the value of play and the steps that we can take in order to foster more genuine play in our organizations.

Why We Need Play

Play is an activity that can be realized in many forms. We can define it as deploying *improvisation* and *imagination*, to *inspire* ourselves and others toward more effective exploration of possibilities. Each of these three components—improvisation, imagination, and inspiration—is increasingly important in today's business contexts.[3]

Improvisation is needed the more an environment becomes unpredictable. The less we can rely on plans, the more we need the mindset and skill of improvisation, to respond rapidly to novel situations. *Imagination* is needed the more an environment becomes malleable: the more opportunities we have to shape patterns of demand and competition. In such open-ended situations we compete on our ability to envision new products or areas of unmet need. *Inspiration* is required the more we involve others, as in building and orchestrating a complex

1 https://www.brookings.edu/research/technology-and-the-innovation-economy/.
2 http://www.gallup.com/file/services/176708/State%20of%20the%20American%20Workplace%20Report%202013.pdf.
3 Reeves, M., et al. *Your Strategy Needs a Strategy*, 2015, Harvard Business Review Press.

https://doi.org/10.1515/9783111295268-017

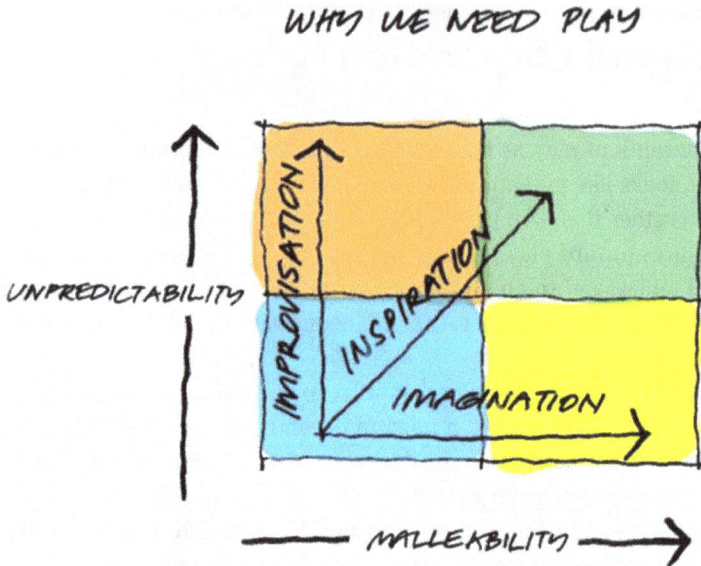

Sources: Henderson (1970), Lockridge (1981), Nadler & Tushman (1994, 1995), Abell (1999), Wiltbank et al. (2006) and Reeves et al. (2011, 2012, 2015).

Figure 16.1: Why we need play.

and dynamic business ecosystem. In each case, the more our environment departs from orderly stability, the more we need to cultivate play (see Figure 16.1).

What Play Can Do for Us

Diving in more detail into these interconnected elements of play, let's examine the value that play can bring.

Improvisation

Play involves improvisation, meaning doing something quickly and with minimal preparation in response to an external stimulus or internal "hunch." Many of us will understand this personally from toying with Play-Doh as children—making shapes without much premeditation, following whatever thoughts come to mind.

Psychologist Mihalyi Csikszentmihalyi argues[4] that play occurs when we do things immediately that are within our ability. The piano player improvises when she plays new chords and melodies—things she *can* do but might not have done before in precisely that form. In the landscape of possibility, we are exploring "nearby" moves rather than long-distance "moonshots."

Interestingly, the invention of Play-Doh[5] itself is an example of this in business. Play-Doh (then called Kutol Cleaner) began as a product to clean wallpaper, until the inventor Joe McVicker heard a teacher saying that kids found modeling clay too tough to manipulate. On a whim, McVicker shipped some wallpaper cleaner to the school, and the kids loved it. We can suppose he thought something like "might as well try it." This moment illustrates a key aspect of the mindset of play. McVicker was improvising with potential applications for his product, in this case with successful results.

Google Maps[6] also began with play. In 2003 then-CEO of Google Eric Schmidt was reportedly in a meeting discussing whether Google should acquire Picasa. But Schmidt was not paying attention; he was fiddling around on his computer with a satellite mapping tool called Keyhole. Following his own hunch and sense of excitement, Schmidt interrupted the meeting and demonstrated Keyhole. The executives forgot the official agenda and spent the time playing with the new tool. A lot of systematic activity was later required to develop a business, but the original idea came from play. To take another, historical example, the basic design of the telescope is thought to have come about from two children playing with different lenses in the shop of the inventor Hans Lippershey.[7]

We can't measure how many possibilities we miss when we *don't* play (when we stick strictly to the agenda, or never play with the lenses), but we do know that play can lead to innovation. We also know that businesses that innovate less are less likely to succeed[8] in the long term. Play should thus be seen as a personal, whimsical, and yet legitimate path to uncovering new ideas, ones we might not have found through more systematic, goal-oriented approaches alone.

---

4 Csikszentmihalyi, Mihaly, and Stith Bennett. "An Exploratory Model of Play." American Anthropologist, vol. 73, no. 1, 1971, pp. 45–58. JSTOR, http://www.jstor.org/stable/671811. Accessed 24 July 2023.

5 https://www.toyhalloffame.org/toys/play-doh/.

6 Ten Years of Google Maps, From Slashdot to Ground Truth – Vox https://www.vox.com/2015/2/8/11558788/ten-years-of-google-maps-from-slashdot-to-ground-truth.

7 https://en.wikipedia.org/wiki/Hans_Lipperhey.

8 Fink, T. M. A., et al. "Serendipity and strategy in rapid innovation." Nature Communications 8.1 (2017): 2002. https://arxiv.org/pdf/1608.01900.pdf.

Imagination

Another key element of play is the imagination. Australian software company Atlassian is famous for cultivating a playful, collaborative mindset among its employees. One game they play is called Premortem,[9] in which the team is encouraged to think of terrible outcomes. "All depths of doom and despair are encouraged." The instruction manual explicitly prompts the imagination: "Close your eyes and picture your CEO holding a press conference. A pack of hungry journalists and irate customers are in front of your building. What does she say?" They explore a landscape of dangerous scenarios.

The rationale for this kind of activity has been described by biologists, in analyzing how and why mammals play. Animals[10] invent handicaps, or mock dangerous situations, and then try to escape them, to be prepared for real-life dangers. Thus, while the play itself is fun, it has an essential function in the long run. The underlying mental skill here is the ability to hold in mind what is *not* true. Often in business we are much more comfortable with questions of the form, "What can my bank do next year?" versus, "What could a bank be (that no bank currently is)?" Play happens in the subjunctive mood—relating to what is imagined or wished. We need playful conversations to envision possible futures, negative or positive.

The imaginative aspect of play is also valuable in customer research. As the CEO of GE, Jeff Immelt[11] emphasized the need for "imagination breakthroughs" and "dreaming sessions" with customers. If we can create free, improvised state of play with customers, it helps us move beyond questions about existing products (what kind of chocolate someone prefers, or how they sold their last house), to what can be imagined. With the rise of virtual reality in customer research,[12] opportunities will only increase to design imagination-spurring playful experiences, to reveal unmet and hitherto unimagined needs.

---

9 https://www.atlassian.com/team-playbook/plays/pre-mortem.
10 Spinka, Marek, et al. "Mammalian Play: Training for the Unexpected." The Quarterly Review of Biology, vol. 76, no. 2, 2001, pp. 141–68. JSTOR, http://www.jstor.org/stable/2664002. Accessed 24 July 2023.
11 https://www.fastcompany.com/53574/fast-company-interview-jeff-immelt.
12 https://online.rutgers.edu/master-business-admin/virtual-reality-business-marketing/?program=mba.

Inspiration

Inspiration is the other strand that runs throughout genuine play. The mental skill here was defined by the philosopher Aristotle, who pointed out two bad extremes in discussions: being too serious and dull, and being too frivolous—which is dull in its own way. Between these two lies a mental quality Aristotle[13] called *eutrapelia,* or "good-turning": being able to change direction playfully from serious to fun and back, engaging others in a rich but also lighthearted discussion. Somewhere between the tedium and buffoonery lies inspiration, where sparks of interesting thought arise in ourselves and spread to others.

Creating the space where inspiration happens is crucial whenever we work with others. Sharing imaginative thoughts with colleagues creates much more inspiration than one person instructing others. One well-known proxy marker of the need for more play is workplace disengagement: according to Gallup, 70% of US employees are not engaged,[14] meaning "sleepwalking through their workday, putting [in] time—but not energy or passion." The most important area for inspiration, however, lies in reaching out to others. If we can practice striking the right balance of playfulness in day-to-day office interactions, we can take this skill outside the corporation, in getting to know clients or building ecosystems of collaborators. When we work with external partners it is critical to be able to spark people's personal engagement, to co-create and share ideas, since we have less control and are more reliant on the voluntary engagement of others.

Play, then, does a lot for us, whether in impromptu conversations, brainstorming sessions, unplanned tinkering with products, customer focus groups, or client presentations. Play helps us in discovering new products and markets, imagining scenarios, exploring a vision, and creating shared inspiration and ownership of ideas. The underlying mental skills are ones we need the more we face unpredictable and open-ended environments—when we need new ideas and to bring others along with us.

How to Get More Play

There is no set of instructions to guarantee effective play—to be too instrumental and mechanical about it would be self-defeating. But we can draw lessons from

---

13 Ardley, Gavin. "The Role of Play in the Philosophy of Plato." Philosophy, vol. 42, no. 161, 1967, pp. 226–44. JSTOR, http://www.jstor.org/stable/3749078. Accessed 24 July 2023.
14 http://www.gallup.com/file/services/176708/State%20of%20the%20American%20Workplace%20Report%202013.pdf.

cultural and biological research, to identify the actions you can take as a leader, to create the conditions for more play.

Derisk Play

As we learn from mammalian play,[15] a basic condition for play is that the negative consequences of action are reduced. We can improvise and imagine more broadly when we give play a break from the ordinary responses and judgments of the world. In the workplace, we should seek to create what management professor Amy Edmondson calls psychological safety:[16] "a sense of confidence that the team will not embarrass, reject, or punish someone for speaking up." Play can be odd, foolish looking, even mischievous; it is no coincidence that Hermes was the ancient god of wordplay but also the god of trickery. We should seek to encode in our organization's communications (our statement of values, all-staff emails, induction programs, introductions to meetings) a tolerance for what happens in playful discussions and situations, recognizing it as a somewhat wilder mode than ordinary interactions.

Suspend Goals

Most corporate work is rightly linked to a goal, which aligns intentions and prioritizes what we emphasize and communicate. In play we invert this. It's interesting when intentions *don't* align and minds wander off in different directions. A prerequisite for play is to suspend the idea of an objective, to allow conversation to be driven more by people's personal impulses and imagination. Yet temporarily abandoning goals is mentally difficult. Psychological studies show that a strong predictor of adult playfulness is *low* levels of prudence, and yet prudence—practical judgment—is an admired virtue[17] in business. A playful corporation, therefore, has to cultivate (and hire) minds that can cross between the prudent and the

15 Spinka, Marek, et al. "Mammalian Play: Training for the Unexpected." The Quarterly Review of Biology, vol. 76, no. 2, 2001, pp. 141–68. JSTOR, http://www.jstor.org/stable/2664002. Accessed 24 July 2023.

16 Edmondson, Amy C. Managing the risk of learning: Psychological safety in work teams. Cambridge, MA: Division of Research, Harvard Business School, 2002. https://www.hbs.edu/ris/Publica tion%20Files/02-062_0b5726a8-443d-4629-9e75-736679b870fc.pdf.

17 Proyer, R.T., Ruch, W. The virtuousness of adult playfulness: the relation of playfulness with strengths of character. Psych Well-Being 1, 4 (2011). https://doi.org/10.1186/2211-1522-1-4.

playful: from careful, goal-directed communication, to whimsical, aimless—but ultimately valuable—reverie.

Create Thresholds

A famous study of play, the book *Homo Ludens* by Johan Huizinga, notes that all cultures set aside special zones for play: "The arena, the card-table, the magic circle, the temple, the stage, the screen, the tennis court, etc., are all in form and function play-grounds, isolated, hedged round, hallowed, within which special rules obtain."[18] Because play is set apart from normal, practical ways of thinking, it helps to use physical space as a marker for a different mental space. This can be done with a designated room. We don't have to use bean bags and colorful furniture. There are many ways to mark the space as different: the lighting could be dimmer, there could be shelves of interesting books, the space might have no electronics in it. However the space is delineated physically, the threshold works when it is reflected in social norms. The leaders within the group have the most influence in establishing such norms.[19] Thus, while our play itself is not serious, we should take the threshold seriously: entering the room, we should practice signaling the shift to a different mental state, one free from goals and open to improvisation and imagination.

Start with the Personal

Whether we're in a designated space or not, it can be hard to find a trigger that kicks off play. For a hint, we can look to the Greek word for play, *paidiá*, which is derived from *paîs*, the word for child. Children have a key lesson to teach us here: when they play, they allow their personal, spontaneous feelings to guide what they say and do. As adults, this is usually more of a challenge. Much of corporate work is impersonal: there is a rational way to proceed; we start with the problem or the logical beginning. In play, the starting point is personal: we must bring *our* impulses and imaginations to the engagement. Rather than thinking what is best or right to say, we must ask ourselves, "What do I really feel?"—even if the answer is unusual. That is, a good way to kick off play is to say something

---

18 Huizinga, J. *Homo Ludens: A Study of the Play-Element in Culture*, 1950, Martino Publishing, p. 10.
19 Hogg, Michael A., and Scott A. Reid. "Social identity, self-categorization, and the communication of group norms." Communication theory 16.1 (2006): 7–30.

spontaneous and idiosyncratic. We can lead by example here but also embed this practice in shared working norms, eliciting people's genuinely personal reactions and feelings, moving interactions temporarily from the rational to the impulsive.

Have Patience with Play

Play involves unpredictable, improvised moves from one thought to another and multiple divergent imaginations. Progress is unclear—you wander around for a bit, follow interesting things. At the end of one burst of play, there may be no outcome, or it might not be obvious. Perhaps next time you will stumble on a great connection; perhaps something half came to light that will become clearer later. These dynamics don't sit well with a push to assess the outcomes of each hour of work. But the value of play is in the long run. Play may not show returns on every occasion, but will bear fruit over time, as a generator of ideas and inspiration and as a forum for practicing important mental skills. To build a more playful corporation, we first need to see and convince others that play is a long-term commitment.

Play often seems marginal to work, because work is based mainly on goal-directed action and efficiency. But play is not the opposite of work—that's leisure. Play is rightfully seen as part of productive work. Doubling down on efficiency without a commitment to play risks creating institutions less able to unlock much-needed human capacities, like the ability to improvise, to imagine, to inspire others. We should take play seriously—with a sense of irony—as part of intelligent business strategy.

Part 3.3: **Link to Value Drivers of the Business**

Rich Hutchinson, Vinay Shandal, Judith Wallenstein, Mark Wiseman, David Young, and Kilian Berz

17 Six Steps to Sustainability Transformation

If you think the disruption caused by digital has been far-reaching, just wait. That impact will pale in comparison to the changes coming as companies wrestle with how to transform their businesses to become truly sustainable.

Sustainability, a company's ability to create positive environmental and societal impact, is rapidly reshaping competitive advantage. It is remaking whole industries, blurring and in some cases obliterating boundaries between industries, and generating new waves of growth. The scale of the disruption that will play out over the next few decades, along with the opportunity it creates, will be staggering. Just the push to limit global temperature increases to 1.5 °C—the central sustainability challenge of our time—will drive a massive transformation of the global economy and require investments totaling an estimated $100 trillion to $150 trillion by 2050.[1]

But while the opportunity is clear, the way to drive a successful sustainability transformation is less obvious. To succeed and create a competitive advantage, companies must simultaneously integrate an environmental, social, and governance (ESG) lens into every element of the business and capture the value that this transformation creates.

On the basis of our extensive experience working with companies and investors to drive sustainability transformations, we have identified six actions that distinguish leaders from the rest of the pack:

- Develop a sustainability strategy anchored in purpose.
- Capture business value.
- Build new sustainable businesses.
- Make the core sustainable.
- Build capabilities.
- Own the narrative, and engage investors and stakeholders.

Companies that fail to take up the challenge, and instead continue to view sustainability through a compliance or ESG reporting lens, will miss the opportunity to tap into lucrative new markets and create new, winning business models. They will also see their space for creating shareholder value narrow dramatically. On

---

1 https://www.bcg.com/capabilities/climate-change-sustainability/sustainable-investing.

https://doi.org/10.1515/9783111295268-018

the other hand, companies that execute effectively in all six areas will truly transform their business and turn sustainability into a competitive advantage.

Develop a Sustainability Strategy Anchored in Purpose

Companies must devise a strategy that takes as its starting point the principle that sustainability is a source of durable competitive advantage. The strategy must clearly connect to the company's purpose,[2] focus on long-term value creation, and be driven from the top, including the CEO and board.

To outline a clear strategy, companies should step back and look at their performance in all material environmental, social, and governance (ESG) areas. Then they should focus on the areas that matter the most to all stakeholders—not just to investors—today and in the future, and where outperformance can contribute most significantly to long-term business success. That prioritization is critical to helping companies avoid the all-too-common pitfall of creating a profusion of siloed initiatives that ultimately have little impact.

At the same time, companies can reassess their existing business model with the objective of understanding its degree of sustainability. This assessment will likely reveal opportunities to enhance the environmental and societal benefits that the company generates, but it will also strengthen the company's competitiveness by improving the resilience of its business model.

Capture Business Value

Companies that lead in sustainability, as reflected in ESG performance, can also outperform their rivals financially. But capturing the value that sustainability efforts create can be challenging.

That's why companies must be intentional and systematic about capturing this value. To start, they must develop a robust business case that accesses all sources of value that their sustainability efforts create. These sources are numerous and varied:

---

2 https://www.bcg.com/capabilities/climate-change-sustainability/sustainable-finance-and-investing.

- enhanced brand equity and loyalty
- price premiums
- fresh growth in the form of share expansion, penetration of new markets, or new businesses
- operational cost savings
- advantages in sourcing, including reliable supplies of scarce inputs
- improved access to or reduced cost of capital
- reduced risk
- valuation premiums

Once they have clearly articulated those business cases, companies should ensure that key areas of the business—including marketing, sales, product development, and finance—have the capabilities not only to capture the value created, but also to track and measure it accurately.

Companies can move quickly to test and scale changes and initiatives in areas where value capture is straightforward and likely to yield immediate financial results. Such efforts will validate the power of the overall sustainability transformation and can be the source of revenues or cost savings to fund other aspects of the journey.

Take, for example, decarbonization for auto OEMs. According to BCG analysis, eliminating 60% of scope 1 and 2 carbon emissions during an initial phase of decarbonization will generate significant annual savings, and those cost reductions can help fund the costs of eliminating the remaining 40%. Even in cases where manufacturing a sustainable product leads to higher costs, the increase often proves to be marginal and more than offset by the enhanced value perceived by customers. For instance, the increased cost associated with a smartphone with a net zero supply chain is less than 1%[3] for a $400 smartphone, according to BCG analysis.

Build New Sustainable Businesses

Companies have a major opportunity to unlock new sources of growth, particularly in relation to the trillions of dollars that the public and private sectors will be investing every year to drive the global economy to Net-Zero carbon emissions. They should look for places in those new markets where they have unique advantages, and create new offerings and business models to leverage those advantages.

---

3 https://media-publications.bcg.com/BCG-Executive-Perspectives-Time-for-Climate-Action.pdf.

Digital tools and technology will be critical in building new businesses and helping companies create solutions that fulfill customer needs in new ways. For example, Norwegian mobile operator Telenor partnered with microfinance bank Tameer (with additional support from the Bill & Melinda Gates Foundation, the International Finance Corporation, and the Consultative Group to Assist the Poor) to launch a mobile-based financial services platform for unbanked and under-banked consumers in Pakistan. By the end of 2019, the operation had become the largest branchless banking service in Pakistan, with approximately 6.4 million users. Companies also have an opportunity to invest in deep-tech innovation,[4] including in artificial intelligence (AI), synthetic biology, nanotechnologies, and quantum computing—to generate and commercialize breakthroughs in areas such as decarbonization.[5]

In addition, companies that embrace sustainable business model innovation[6] can help transform entire value chains and ecosystems. They can, for example, introduce new circular business models to reshape the whole product usage cycle. And they can create new business models or make investments in ventures that address the looming scarcity of critical sustainability inputs.[7] Consider recycled plastic. Some 45% of demand for recycled polyethylene terephthalate will be unmet by 2025, according to BCG analysis. Already, a number of companies are investing in innovation to address the gap, including through investments in R&D and recycling infrastructure.

Make the Core Sustainable

Companies that aim to become sustainability leaders must assess and enhance the sustainability of their existing portfolio and operations.

In supply chains,[8] for example, they have an opportunity to create end-to-end transparency, from sourcing through distribution. New tools and technologies are critical in this area. AI can help companies monitor, predict, and reduce their carbon emissions.[9] At the same time, companies can engage suppliers to impose

---

4 https://www.bcg.com/publications/2021/deep-tech-innovation.

5 https://www.bcg.com/publications/2021/next-generation-climate-innovation.

6 https://www.bcg.com/publications/2021/four-strategies-for-sustainable-business-model-innovation.

7 https://hbr.org/2021/07/the-green-economy-has-a-resource-scarcity-problem#:~:text=By%20anticipating%20bottlenecks%20in%20the,effectively%20evolve%20their%20business%20models.

8 https://www.bcg.com/publications/2020/supply-chain-needs-sustainability-strategy.

9 https://www.bcg.com/publications/2021/ai-to-reduce-carbon-emissions.

standards, track and improve their performance, and push the ecosystem in which they operate toward greater sustainability. Companies should also re-engineer product designs to make existing products sustainable. This may involve reformulating products with more sustainable ingredients, reducing packaging, and developing refillable products or concentrated versions that reduce weight (and therefore carbon emissions tied to transportation), water consumption, and packaging. Beyond Meat, for example, leveraged plant-based proteins[10] to re-engineer one of the world's most famous dishes—the burger. That innovation not only launched a popular new alternative to meat, but also helped fuel one of the most successful Intellectual Property Offices (IPOs) of 2019.

Build Capabilities

Companies that want to drive a sustainability transformation must ensure they have the right capabilities and foundation in place to succeed.

First, they must design robust governance of sustainability efforts, both at the board level and within the company itself, including accountability and incentives linked to ESG targets. Second, they need to develop strong, granular data capabilities and robust ESG reporting processes to enable the business to direct and adjust efforts on the basis of real-time performance data and to meet increasingly stringent regulatory reporting standards. Third, they should build new partnerships that allow them to pool resources, combine expertise, co-invest in ways that minimize risks associated with high-fixed-cost investments, and deliver sustainable outcomes at scale more quickly. Fourth, they must embed sustainable business model innovation in the organization.

This last element is particularly critical. Companies will need to continue to adapt their operations, product portfolio, and business models as the bar for sustainability inevitably rises over time. What qualifies as leading performance in carbon footprint or equitable business practices today, for example, will likely be table stakes in the future. As a result, companies must embrace an "always-on" mentality toward innovating in sustainability. The process of driving sustainable business model innovation will be central to that mentality, allowing companies to assess the degree to which their current business models create positive environmental and societal impacts and to improve that performance over time.

---

10 https://www.bcg.com/publications/2021/the-benefits-of-plant-based-meats.

Own the Narrative, and Engage Investors and Stakeholders

Leading companies must create a compelling and distinctive narrative around their sustainability strategy—one that connects and amplifies their purpose. At the same time, they can own their sustainability story in the public markets and share that story in a way that resonates with investors, rather than letting ratings agencies and investors tell their story for them. This means going beyond sharing the relevant information with rating agencies, and instead going directly to investors with an effective narrative that includes four key elements:

- a well-defined point of view about what is most material to the business
- a clear connection to purpose and an overall sustainability strategy
- targets, milestones, and initiatives to get there
- robust measurement and disclosure of ESG performance

The measurement and disclosure component is particularly critical, as it will provide evidence to investors that the business is hardwiring the narrative into the organization. Companies should go beyond the annual or biannual reporting cycle and instead provide real-time ESG measurement and reporting mechanisms that increase investors' confidence in the company's ability to monitor progress and correct course. Companies can also use ESG measurement to establish clear incentives and accountability mechanisms for employees and leaders.

As companies share their narrative with investors, they should proactively engage with shareholders, and they should do so not just during the release of quarterly earnings. In particular, they should maintain a strong dialogue with active investors who, unlike ETF or index investors, may move in and out of the stock over time. They should also share the narrative with other critical stakeholders, including customers, employees, and members of communities in which they operate. The buy-in of these stakeholders is ultimately what drives value creation.

Driving a successful sustainability transformation requires a fundamental shift in mindset. Company leaders should view the push toward sustainability not as a compliance exercise or a cost of doing business, but rather as an opportunity to create new value. Companies that do so will expand their competitive advantage and develop the muscle to continue to rethink and remake their business as expectations about sustainability inexorably rise in the years ahead.

David Young and Simon Beck
18 The Strategic Race to Sustainability

To get beyond the starting line, CEOs need to approach the challenges of sustainability from a strategic and value-creation perspective in terms of both the questions they ask and the answers they seek.

Rarely in business history have CEOs had more significant opportunities to capture advantages, reset industries, and anchor their legacies than at this moment in the global race to sustainability.[1] These opportunities span industries and regions, and they extend beyond current Net-Zero ambitions and environmental, social, and governance (ESG) targets. CEOs should formulate strategies that create and capture long-term competitive advantage from the transition to Net-Zero and sustainability.

This is a race—one that has already begun and is quickly accelerating. Capital markets have seen tremendous growth in ESG-related assets under management, and they are projected to rise from $35 trillion in 2021 to $50 trillion globally by 2025. Sustainability-linked loans and financing exceeded $1.6 trillion in 2021, up by a factor of three since 2019.[2] Banks are starting to engage their business customers to drive down financed emissions. And governments are seeking to drive sustainability through green public-procurement initiatives, which will provide an estimated $6 trillion boost to global gross domestic product (GDP) and create 3 million net new jobs by 2050[3] In addition, the number of companies committed to science-based targets more than doubled in 2021, and their most common goal is in line with keeping the global temperature rise to less than 1.5 °C.

And yet, most companies are still making their way to the starting line of the race to sustainability and have not addressed it in a strategic manner. This isn't surprising: when confronted with long-term endeavors, many CEOs struggle to balance the imperative of meeting quarterly expectations with the need to grapple with the many uncertainties of transforming their businesses. When it comes to sustainability, more than a few CEOs are attempting to walk this line by pointing to ambitious Net-Zero statements and ESG targets as evidence that their companies are front-runners in the race to sustainability. These are good moves, but

---

1 https://www.bcg.com/capabilities/climate-change-sustainability/overview.

2 Saijel Kishan, "ESG by the Numbers: Sustainable Investing Set Records in 2021," Bloomberg, February 3, 2022.

3 "Green Public Procurement: Catalysing the Net-Zero Economy," World Economic Forum, January 2022.

https://doi.org/10.1515/9783111295268-019

they are quickly becoming de rigueur for well-managed companies, and they are insufficient to seize competitive advantage.

If public commitments and ESG targets are no longer considered evidence of being a front-runner, what is?

The Leaders in Sustainability Strategy

Assessing the relative scope, scale, and speed of a company's business transformation can reveal whether it is a leader in sustainability strategy. Specifically, a company should have some degree of scale in *all* the following indicators:

- a morphing corporate portfolio, business boundary, and asset base that enable sustainability transformations in a company's operations, its customers' operations, and industry infrastructure
- an evolving product portfolio with a growing share of revenues and higher margins from the sustainability segments in the company's markets
- restructured supply chains that are designed to improve business resilience and lower emissions via more sustainable suppliers, capabilities, and content
- an innovation portfolio and supporting ecosystems that accelerate investment in sustainability technologies, infrastructure, products, and services
- new customer value propositions that are differentiated and priced according to their sustainability benefits
- a portfolio of commercial arrangements, investments, and ventures that mitigate and exploit sustainability scarcities in the value chain
- the creation of new business ecosystems that enable sustainability solutions and markets
- strategies aimed at resetting the basis of advantage for the industry that prompt commensurate competitor reactions and industry disruption

We examined more than 500 sustainability initiatives[4] from companies around the world, and we found that only one in five initiatives showed any meaningful connection to drivers of business value and advantage, and only one in fifteen was changing the basis of industry competition and the boundaries of the company's business model.

To get beyond the starting line of this race, CEOs need to approach the challenges of sustainability from a strategic and value-creation perspective in terms of

---

4 https://www.bcg.com/publications/2021/keys-to-being-a-leader-in-sustainable-business-model-innovation.

both the questions they ask and the answers they seek. This approach will not only ensure that their company will act on sustainability imperatives in an aligned and rigorous way but also assure their boards, investors, and other stakeholders that the company is properly prepared to enter the race to sustainability. Developing a strategic perspective involves answering four questions (see Figure 18.1).

– What is the lay of the land?
– Where does the company need to go and how fast?
– What will it take to get there?
– How must the company be rewired to act now?

What is the Lay of the Land?

Leaders typically begin a strategy-making exercise by understanding the near- and long-term challenges facing their company, customers, competitors, stakeholders, and value chains—and identifying the opportunities embedded in those challenges. Leaders should do the same to create advantage in an era of sustainability. In many companies, this will require adjusting the aperture through which the leadership team views sustainability and the team's strategic time horizon.

Too often, we see leaders viewing sustainability through the narrow aperture of operations. They tackle scope 1 or 2 emissions as an end in itself, for example, rather than using the effort to drive business growth. Reducing emissions is not inconsequential, but neither is it strategic in nature unless engineered to be so. At a time when the context for business is forcing leaders to deal with climate and sustainability challenges that extend far beyond the company's borders and planning horizons, leaders should become adept at viewing the challenges and opportunities in their company, industry, and business ecosystems through this wider strategic lens.

Once a wider aperture is set, companies can bring deep stakeholder discovery and rigorous scenario assessment to bear on sustainability. Stakeholder discovery is aimed at thoroughly understanding material stakeholders, their current expectations and priorities, and how they are likely to change. Shifts in consumer behaviors, procurement priorities, supply chain capacities, regulations, investment flows, new climate abatement technologies, and climate impacts on business resilience are just a few of the changes that could affect a strategic direction.

Scenario assessments explore the changing stakeholder expectations by region (including regulations) and what they may mean to the future performance of the business. Such assessments enable leaders to test how robust the business

What is the lay of the land?
- Understand the challenges for all ecosystem players
- Determine stakeholders' expectations and priorities
- Identify the risks and opportunities
- Pinpoint where competitive advantage will be found

Where does the company need to go and how fast?
- State an ambition
- Set bold targets and value-creation goals
- Choose which opportunities to pursue
- Proceed quickly to win the race

What will it take to get there?
- Restructure the corporate and product portfolios and business units
- Capture the value of sustainability
- Ensure the availability of sustainability resources
- Restructure stranded assets

How must the company be rewired to act now?
- Create an accountable sustainability-oriented culture
- Reset the innovation agenda
- Restructure the supply chain
- Shape the ecosystem for sustainability
- Communicate to stakeholders and investors

Source: BCG analysis

Figure 18.1: Leaders should take a strategic approach to the challenges of sustainability.

is likely to be given changing environments, stakeholder dynamics, and various constraints. For instance: how will the business perform under different carbon tax regimes? If the business is manufacturing, how will it fare when faced with regulations that extend the company's responsibilities for the social costs of its products? If the business sells consumer goods, how will it perform if behaviors shift and consumers expect and reward higher levels of proven sustainability in the content of products?

Understanding the lay of the land also includes identifying other potential risks and opportunities. These could emerge from shortages in resources (such as key materials needed to manufacture a more sustainable product). They could come from productive assets that become unsustainable (such as high-emission production equipment, data centers in water-scarce regions, or significantly diminished farmland owing to soil degradation). And risks and opportunities could result from changing labor demographics or norms and regulations that demand a living wage throughout a company's supply base. In essence, understanding the lay of the land entails identifying new risks and new spaces for growth that might arise from the push for sustainability.

All risks and opportunities need to be explored over short-term and midterm timelines. Already, evidence suggests that the prevailing forecasts for the adoption and penetration of electric vehicles and various devices powered by renewable energy have consistently missed the mark, with change happening faster than predicted. Leaders need to anticipate these and other possibilities if they are going to win the race to sustainability.

The goal of all this work is for leaders to come away with a conviction about where the competitive advantages associated with sustainability lie, how they may shift, and what the company can do to capture them.

To understand how sustainability trends could impact its profit and loss (P&L), Brussels-based Solvay, a global chemical company founded in 1863, uses a sustainable portfolio management (SPM) tool that informs capital allocation across all research and innovation projects, all capital expenditure decisions that exceed $10 million, and all mergers and acquisitions (M&A) deals. The SPM tool provides management with a fact-based dashboard that helps steer decisions in two ways: it assesses the company's products' environmental manufacturing footprint and operational vulnerabilities (across 19 sustainability indicators). It also provides a forward-looking view of market signals driven by sustainability benefits and challenges (qualitatively assessed by asking 60 questions). For example, for Paramove, a product that controls parasitic diseases in farmed salmon and enhances yields, the SPM tool revealed a very low operations risk when comparing the potential costs of externalities to revenue potential, and it uncovered no environmental risk (the product breaks down to water and oxygen). This assessment, combined with a potential growth in annual sales in excess of 10% annually, helped Paramove earn a star rating in Solvay's portfolio.

Solvay reports that the SPM tool has been applied to 80% of its product portfolio. In 2020, the company expected 77% of its research and innovation revenues and 52% of its global revenues to derive from sustainability solutions on the basis of its SPM assessments.

Where Does the Company Need to Go and How Fast?

Once leaders understand sustainability's risks and opportunities, they can state an ambition, set bold targets, and choose which opportunities to pursue. Selecting opportunities requires knowing how they will reinforce the company's advantage, differentiate its brands, and drive profitable growth. Leaders need to be able to win support for their decisions from the board of directors, employees, and investors—whose help will be required to deliver results, especially when broad business transformations are required.

CEOs also need to set bold value-creation goals to win the race to sustainability, to catalyze innovation, and to guide business model transformation. These goals should be connected to its core business and make a material contribution to its long-term performance. Companies on the leading edge of sustainability pursue it in a manner that leads to growth and enhanced business resilience, thereby leading to a virtuous cycle of greater sustainability and enhanced performance.

How quickly a company needs to act depends on its understanding of the competitive opportunity and risks. We find too many companies fail to analyze the risk of not acting. They compare investments in sustainability transitions to the current performance baseline of their business and do not recognize or consider the growing risks and disruption potential inherent to the current business model. Furthermore, as their competitors begin sustainability transitions, certain resources and infrastructure necessary to transition will become scarce and more expensive. Moving with the pack risks being competitively disadvantaged.

The pace at which green technologies are evolving and the rate at which their associated costs are falling have been consistently underestimated. For example, according to the World Economic Forum, projections of solar photovoltaic capacity in 2030 increased by a factor of 36 from 2002 through 2020, while projected unit costs dropped by a factor of three. And forecasts have underestimated the pace of societal change. The adoption of electric vehicles (EVs) is a good example: from 2016 through 2018, Exxon Mobil updated its estimate of the number of EVs on the road by 2040 three times, increasing it by more than 150%.[5] Leaders should recognize that the pace of the race is accelerating, and they should set their ambition and targets accordingly.

Hitachi, the Japanese conglomerate whose business segments include heavy construction equipment, electronics, mobility,[6] and technology, has put up the

---

5 "Electric Vehicle Outlook 2021," Bloomberg NEF.
6 https://www.bcg.com/industries/public-sector/mobility.

table stakes of sustainability. The company has made a public commitment to achieve carbon neutrality (scopes 1 and 2) by 2030 and to reach neutrality across its value chain by 2050. Hitachi substantiated its commitment with detailed near- to mid-term milestones and underpinned it with a robust decarbonization plan. But the company also has reframed its strategic vision around sustainability, and it launched a social innovation business unit that seeks to create social, environmental, and economic value across a number of realms, including manufacturing, energy, transportation, and urban development.

Hitachi's Lumada is a digital ecosystem platform that provides the underlying data infrastructure needed to work with clients and ecosystem alliance partners to cocreate sustainability solutions and define new value pools that leverage clients' assets and data. Working with Kashiwa-no-ha Smart City, for instance, Hitachi used Lumada to develop an area energy management system. The Advanced Energy Management System (AEMS) connects offices, shopping centers, residences, and public facilities with energy sources, such as solar power and batteries, through independent transmission lines and information networks. It also includes one of Japan's largest industrial lithium-ion storage battery systems and peak shift-and-cut controls to minimize the need for high-emission energy sources across regional borders in real time.

Hitachi's ambition is to grow group operating income to 1 trillion yen ($8.7 billion) by FY 2025 (up from 495 billion yen in FY 2020), with 50% of the gain derived from Lumada. In FY 2021, Hitachi businesses using the Lumada platform were expected to reach 1.6 trillion yen in sales.

What Will it Take to Get There?

Once leaders understand where they can generate significant value from sustainability, they can begin the work of reshaping the company. For most companies, this will be a necessity, because it is unlikely that the current strategy, business models, and corporate and product portfolios were designed with sustainability in mind.

As leaders begin their work, they should address four challenges: restructuring the corporate and product portfolios and business units—a necessary task to achieve a sustainability advantage; capturing the value of sustainability, including its impact on the cost of capital; ensuring the availability of sustainable resources needed to execute the strategy; and restructuring stranded assets.

Restructuring the corporate and product portfolios and business units. Companies seeking a long-lasting competitive advantage from sustainability will need customer offerings that deliver a step change in sustainability performance that can be differentiated in the market. Identifying such offerings usually requires the assembly of a new portfolio of sustainable businesses and products, with all the implications for the corporate development agenda and business boundaries that infers. Bolting sustainability onto existing businesses probably won't be enough: a few green product lines may offer incremental sustainability enhancements and buy some time, but they will not create lasting competitive advantage.

Paris-based Saint-Gobain, a manufacturer of construction and other high-performance materials, re-envisioned and reshaped its portfolio as a one-stop shop for sustainability solutions. The company assembled a unique combination of 117 brands that offer customers holistic sustainability solutions. For example, it has 33 products and services that when used together can improve the energy efficiency of a home by 70%. The new portfolio supports the company's mission to become the worldwide leader in light and sustainable construction and, in 2021, that portfolio was responsible for producing 72% of the company's sales.

Capturing the value of sustainability. Leaders need to develop a comprehensive understanding of how their company will create market value from their sustainability advantage (see Figure 18.2). Knowing where value can be captured requires deeply understanding the best mix and sequencing of abatement technologies, the trajectory of customers' sustainability needs, which market segments will evolve faster and offer a green premium, and the ESG dimensions that capital providers consider most material for preferred financing.

Swedish steel manufacturer SSAB, which is operating in one of the hardest-to-abate sectors, aspires to bring fossil-free steel to the market across its product portfolio, a critical enabler of its ambition to reach Net-Zero by 2030. SSAB sees fossil-free steel as an opportunity to expand its premium-products segment and capture value through a pricing premium in a less competitive space, while seeing operational improvements that provide greater volume flexibility and lower maintenance costs and capital expenditures. In 2021, SSAB delivered its first fossil-free steel to Volvo, and the company is already seeing a strong appetite for the product among its customers. It is working with Faurecia (a tier one supplier of automotive technology), Mercedes-Benz, and Volvo to create prototypes of components.

Investors are another important source of sustainability value. They are awarding higher values to companies that are well positioned to meet sustainability challenges, resulting in lower costs of capital. In addition, we have found evidence that some investors are willing to trade earnings today for reduced emissions and improved sustainability tomorrow. For example, a BCG analysis found that market valuations in the materials sector indicated that investors valued the elimination of a ton of recurring carbon at $45 in current earnings. In essence, it was a no-regret move for a company in that sector to pursue abatement investments up to $45 per ton. When companies understand where investors' marginal indifference point is

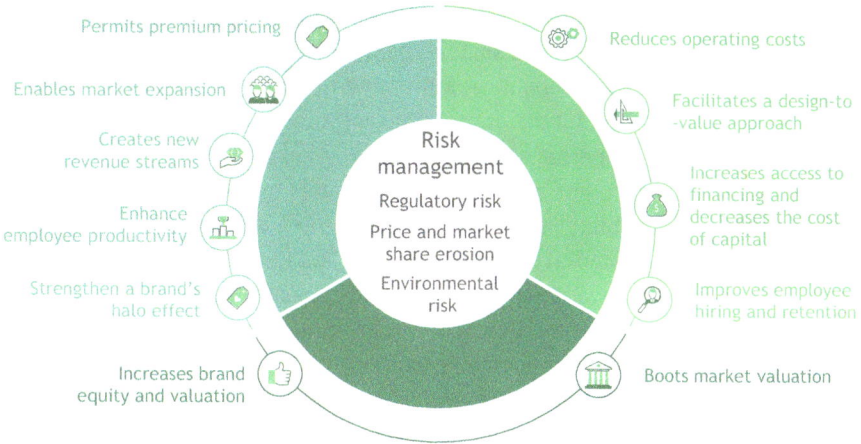

Permits premium pricing

Enables market expansion

Creates new
revenue streams

Enhance
employee productivity

Strengthen a brand's
halo effect

Increases brand
equity and valuation

Reduces operating costs

Facilitates a design-to
-value approach

Increases access to
financing and
decreases the cost
of capital

Improves employee
hiring and retention

Boots market valuation

**Risk
management**

Regulatory risk

Price and market
share erosion

Environmental
risk

Source: BCG analysis
Note: When customers have a positive experience with a product and, as a result, view the company's
other products favorably, the company's brand experiences a so-called halo effect

Figure 18.2: Having a sustainability advantage creates value for companies in many ways.

positioned—what percentage of earnings they can invest today to reduce emissions tomorrow—companies can invest more aggressively in business transitions and gain the advantage over their peers.

Ensuring the availability of sustainability resources. As more and more of the world's largest businesses develop new products and processes and redesign existing ones to reach sustainability targets, bottlenecks and scarcities are highly likely to emerge for critical inputs. To avoid being locked out, leaders need to identify where sustainability scarcities may emerge in their ecosystems and develop a robust set of portfolio responses to mitigate them. (See Figure 18.3.)

When Belgian recycler Umicore recognized that there were likely to be scarcities in key metals (including lithium and cobalt) as the global energy transition progressed, it created a closed-looped business model that aims to turn waste into feedstock for its customers and its own clean mobility production. The company also signed long-term contracts to obtain sustainable lithium supplies from two vendors to further secure inputs for its battery cathode products.

Restructuring stranded assets. As leaders transform a business in pursuit of the sustainability advantage, parts of its asset base will no longer be fit for purpose. This is especially true in high-emitting industries with long-life capital assets. In the oil and gas sector alone, the associated risks of stranded assets are estimated to reach \$1.4 trillion of cumulative net present value by 2036.[7] To reduce the significant risk of less sustainable assets becoming stranded, leaders need to identify at-risk assets, determine how to invest to transform them or wind them down, and set up the appropriate corporate and financial structure to facilitate the transition, perhaps with financial partners.

Identifying at-risk assets necessitates that leaders evaluate the company's assets against a sustainability scenarios matrix and then segment the assets by the actions required for disposal and the timing. In many cases, the investment demands for achieving the sustainability advantage in existing assets will rise above historical levels, sometimes by multiples. To meet this demand, leaders should encourage innovation across corporate structures, financial engineering, and capital mix. For instance, companies may need to tap new transition-financing instruments, sustainability linked bonds, or public–private financing, or all three.

In 2008, when Dong Energy embarked on the black-to-green transformation that would eventually lead to its 2016 IPO as Ørsted, it was producing 85% of its heat and power from fossil fuels, and it was responsible for one-third of Denmark's carbon emissions.[8] To meet its ambition to turn its portfolio on its head and generate 85% of its production from green sources, the company took multiple steps to wind down and transition stranded assets, including closing 40% of its generators, converting coal generators to biogas, making divestitures, and, in some cases, abandoning projects.

How must the Company be Rewired to Act Now?

Most companies will need to reshape their organization structure and culture to capture the sustainability advantage. Often, reshaping will require refreshed incentive and decision-making frameworks that can drive an accountable, sustainability oriented culture. It will also require a reorientation of a company's innovation agenda, supply chain, and ecosystem to support the quest to capture new value streams. And, as always, reshaping will require a compelling, integrated investor narrative that articulates a differentiated approach to sustainability that is aligned with the corporate purpose and anchored in competitive advantage.

---

7 G. Semieniuk, et al., "Stranded Fossil-Fuel Assets Translate into Major Losses for Investors in Advanced Economies," Political Economy Research Institute, October 7, 2021.

8 E. Reguly, "A Tale of Transformation: The Danish Company That Went from Black to Green Energy," Corporate Knights, April 16, 2019.

Secure supply
Strategically select and contract with suppliers of critical inputs that are likely to become scarce.
These steps will not only mitigate a shortage but also make the supply chain more resilient

Acquire the originators
Acquire suppliers or companies developing new sources for supplies that are likely to become scarce
These steps participate broadly in the upside as scarcity pricing premiums emerge across multiple suppliers

Target alternatives
Turn supply constrains into opportunities and resolve scarcity bottlenecks by redesigning goods
And services to reduce or eliminate the need for resources that are likely to be in short supply

Seed the market
Develop a broad portfolio of venture investments in early-stage technologies and new companies that aim to resolve
Critical sustainability scarcities. Consider investing particularly when many competing alternatives could exist

Arbitrage the options
Simultaneously purchase and sell critical inputs in order to benefit from various supply and pricing
Dynamics in different regions.

Broaden the market
Take steps to limit the impact of potentially scarce inputs by advocating for public policy and transition
Finance that enable technology innovation, expand the supply, or incentivize the use of alternatives

Act collectively
When it is in the company's strategic interests, catalyze or participate in industry and cross-sector
Coalitions to address supply constraints Coalitions should include governments and NGO members.

Exploit the value
Capture the value of sustainability by charging a premium price and gaining greater market share for products
That rely on sustainable materials. Or, build out entirely new business that provide sustainable inputs

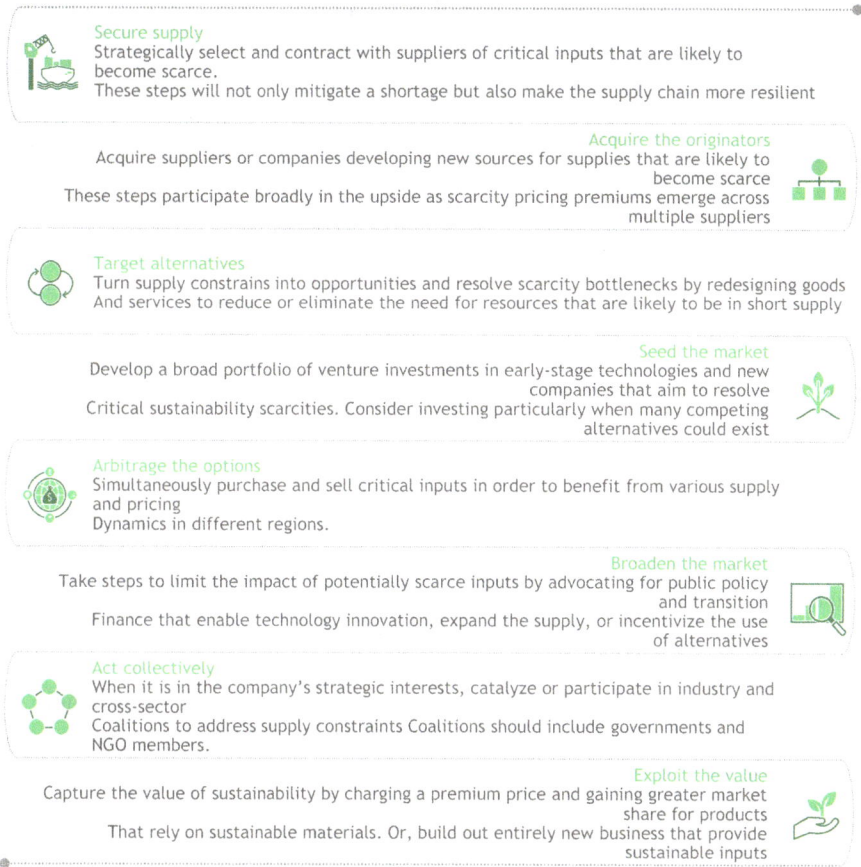

Source:BCG analysis
Note: NGO -nongovernmental organization

Figure 18.3: Companies should develop portfolio responses to potential sustainability scarcities.

Create an accountable sustainability-oriented culture. To drive the growth of a company, sustainability needs to be explicitly embedded in leadership and decision-making frameworks, capital allocation and governance practices, and incentives. Otherwise, the ability to practice sustainability as an advantage can run into resistance as it confronts mindsets and corporate DNA that have been developed and reinforced by decades of functional and operational optimization focused on shareholder value and quarterly earnings.

The race for sustainability requires new muscles and the courage to run off-trail. Thus, it isn't entirely surprising that our analysis of corporate sustainability initiatives found that more than 90% of the initiatives that created the most robust and resilient business models with the most significant environmental and societal benefits featured an internal vision and purpose that helped to energize an accountable sustainability culture. In this regard, CEOs must be convincing and clear and continually assure stakeholders that this race will be worth running—and that it will be run.

Tying the compensation, retention, and promotion of individual leaders to sustainability is essential, of course, but it takes more to activate a culture and an organizational mindset that embeds sustainability into every facet of the business and applies it as the lens through which decisions are made. It requires rethinking capital allocation tools (for example, new discount rates and payback periods), finding mechanisms that internalize the costs of externalities (such as carbon, water, and waste), creating governance structures (for example, carbon budgets), and re-equipping leaders, functions, and businesses with the necessary skills (such as those required for systems dynamic mapping).

Most industrial companies have analogous experience in embedding a safety-first culture. They have reset employees' safety mindset by continually making changes on the shop floor, integrating indicators on dashboards, reworking capital investment templates, and including performance measures in senior executives' compensation. Years later in such companies, many employees say, "Safety is just how we do things." We expect sustainability to follow a similar journey.

Reset the innovation agenda. Winning a sustainability advantage requires the creation of new technologies, business models, ecosystems, and markets. Accordingly, R&D and innovation investments need to be redirected.

An innovation agenda aimed at a sustainability advantage should be anchored by the company's R&D portfolio, enlist external strategic partners, and reflect emerging technologies in the rapidly expanding startup space. In addition, senior leaders need to be clear as to how that agenda will deliver on the company's strategic priorities and bolster its product and business portfolios.

Dow, a US-based chemicals and plastics manufacturer, redirected its innovation agenda toward sustainability by identifying and focusing its investments on three priority areas: climate protection, the circular economy, and safer materials. In 2020, the company invested approximately $770 million in R&D, with 80% of its R&D projects focused on those areas. Dow also linked its Sustainable Chemistry Index, a tool that assesses the sustainability attributes of its businesses and products, to its innovation agenda.

Restructure the supply chain. Fully implementing sustainability innovations at scale will require fundamental rewiring of a company's supply chain. Many innovations will be able to deliver their full sustainability and business potential only if the underlying supply chain is shifted to ensure that sustainability is measured and optimized at each step of the production process.

There are five actions that companies can take across their value chain to bolster sustainability and resiliency.[9] They can improve the sustainability of inputs, redesign products and packaging, increase resources within the chain for resilience, optimize the networks considering both efficiency and resilience, and pursue circularity.

We see examples of companies taking some of these actions, but few are doing all five in a way that will fully transform the supply chain. Consider McCormick & Company. Its sustainable sourcing standard "Grown for Good" focuses on safe and ethical supply chains, regenerative production systems, and resilient communities. The standard is certified by third-party verification and goes beyond industry standards by including criteria for women's empowerment and farmer resilience. It has been a driving force for reshaping the company's supply chains for sustainability beyond carbon, and it is the first standard to cover spices and herbs specifically.

Shape the ecosystem for sustainability. Sustainable companies need a sustainable ecosystem, and they should shape it in ways that benefit their strategic goals through bilateral partnerships, sustainability business ecosystems,[10] and corporate-led sustainability alliance.[11] For example, a beverage manufacturer may aspire to have sustainable packaging but be limited by the recycling capacity in key markets. The manufacturer should pinpoint the short-term and long-term recycling constraints and then determine when and where to collaborate with others to overcome those constraints.

An ecosystem for sustainability can encompass supply partnerships, solution partnerships, or alliances aimed at shaping standards and influencing public policy. For instance, in 2021, Texas-based Hyliion, a maker of low-carbon, electrified powertrain solutions for the heavy transportation market, formed an ecosystem named the Hypertruck Innovation Council to advance electrification solutions for commercial transportation. The council is a group of leading companies focused on removing barriers to sustainability, while creating unique sources of advantage. The companies—including Agility Logistics, American Natural Gas, NFI Industries, and Ryder System—collectively represent 100,000 Class 8 commercial trucks globally and represent some of the world's largest private fleets. Hyllion is

9 https://www.bcg.com/publications/2020/supply-chain-needs-sustainability-strategy.

10 https://www.bcg.com/publications/2022/how-to-build-sustainability-alliance.

11 https://www.bcg.com/publications/2021/ecosystems-could-help-with-sustainability-challenges.

working with the innovation council to pilot Hypertruck ERX™, a net-carbon-negative commercial transport.

Communicate to stakeholders and investors. Capturing the competitive advantage of sustainability requires engaging stakeholders and investors in the company's sustainability ambition and initiatives. The table stakes here include reporting ESG performance (compared with the converging standards), applying better disciplines in target setting (such as using science-based emissions-reduction targets), and being transparent about material ESG issues. But standing out means, at a minimum, clearly demonstrating, particularly to investors, the links between the company's sustainability agenda and the quality, competitiveness, purpose, and resiliency of the business.

This higher standard means infusing the company's sustainability ambition into brand and corporate narratives. The goal is to activate employees and strengthen their affinity because they know they are part of a company that is changing the world for the better. It also means strengthening the loyalty of customers and suppliers because they benefit from the value that the company brings to their journey to sustainability.

A decade ago, the luxury fashion retailer Kering started to develop an interactive tool that presents the environmental impact of its activities in order to demonstrate transparency to its stakeholders. Its online environmental profit-and-loss statement deconstructs the monetary impact of the company's environmental externalities across business units, processes, value chain players, and raw material inputs. This approach enables Kering to report its environmental performance in each area, maintain a running tally on its progress, and communicate clear targets for the overall environmental impact of the business.

A Call to Action

We are on the cusp of a remarkably broad and deep business transformation[12] propelled by corporate and infrastructure investments estimated at more than $3.5 trillion per year through 2050. This transformation offers enormous growth opportunities for the companies that understand how to pursue sustainability for advantage. Investors wielding trillions of dollars are on the hunt for companies that can deliver this sustainability advantage, and they are increasingly willing to penalize the laggards. Emboldened by hardening public opinion,

---

12 https://www.bcg.com/capabilities/business-transformation/overview.

governments are putting in place increasingly ambitious sustainability targets and backing them up with spending. But most companies are not moving with the bold foresight, ambition, and speed needed to secure sustainability as competitive advantage and reset the basis of competition. Companies must up their game to win what may well turn out to be the most important race of this business era.

Ron Soonieus, David Young, Wendy Woods, and Sonia Tatar

19 Directors Can Up Their Game on Environmental, Social, and Governance Issues

Board members at companies across geographies and industries understand that competitive advantage increasingly demands sustainability. And that is rapidly pushing environmental, social, and governance (ESG) issues higher on board agendas.

How well are boards positioned to provide oversight of ESG? BCG and the INSEAD Corporate Governance Centre have teamed up on a multiyear initiative, including regular pulse check surveys and interviews, to help answer that question. We will assess how boards are engaging with ESG issues today and to what extent existing board practices can deal with these complex and systemic challenges. For this inaugural report, we have interviewed more than 50 directors who have at least ten years' experience as a board member and who serve on more than 150 corporate boards combined. Our survey captured insights from 122 respondents who have an average of seven years of experience as a board member and who are affiliated with two boards on average.

Our initial survey and interviews reveal a number of insights:
– Roughly 70% of directors reported that they are only moderately or not at all effective at integrating ESG into company strategy and governance.
– Although directors think their boards should devote more time to strategic reflection when it comes to ESG issues, more than half (53%) said they are not effective at doing that.
– Boards clearly see addressing climate change as a top priority; still, among companies with a net-zero commitment, only 55% of directors reported that their organizations have prepared and published a plan for hitting that target.
– A full 43% of directors cited the ability of their companies to execute as one of the biggest threats to delivering on ESG goals.

https://www.bcg.com/about/net-zero.
https://www.bcg.com/capabilities/climate-change-sustainability/overview.

https://doi.org/10.1515/9783111295268-020

Certainly, there is no simple solution for boards when it comes to understanding, overseeing, and engaging with management on ESG issues. The topics that are material will vary by industry and are themselves dynamic by nature.[1] And a board's actions will also depend in part on the company's maturity level with respect to ESG management.

But there is no question that directors must up their game in this area. The capacity and effectiveness of the board when it comes to ESG is vitally important for companies aiming to improve the sustainability of their operations. After all, while corporate management is under constant pressure to deliver strong financial performance over the short and medium term, board members play a critical role in steering companies over the long term. And the ESG issues confronting companies today—including climate, income inequality, diversity, equity, and inclusion,[2] and geopolitical tensions, most recently the war in Ukraine—will require sustained, long-term action. Consequently, such matters sit squarely in the purview of the board.

To fully meet the new demands stemming from ESG, boards must pay attention to three critical areas:

– **Board approach to ESG governance.** Boards must make critical decisions about how to structure the ESG work and oversight they do. The most common approach (31%) for anchoring ESG into board governance is assigning oversight of these issues to the full board. In such cases, ESG issues can be discussed or worked on within committees, but the decisions related to these matters are made by the full board. Although this approach is prevalent, the risk is that ESG issues do not get sufficient time and attention given all the demands on the full board. The second most common structure (20%) is to have the issues governed by a dedicated ESG committee of the board, while the third most common approach (15%) is to have one member of the board —with no separate committee—lead on ESG issues. The right structure will depend on factors such as the composition and ESG knowledge base of the board, its existing governance practices, and the maturity of both the company and the board when it comes to addressing ESG topics.
– **Board knowledge.** Adding ESG education as part of regular board trainings can help establish a solid baseline of understanding among directors. However, boards should push for greater competency, systematically assessing what expertise they need in order to be effective at oversight of ESG issues. Certainly,

---

1 https://www.bcg.com/publications/2020/future-esg-environmental-social-governance-opportunities.
2 https://www.bcg.com/capabilities/diversity-inclusion/overview.

the list of potential ESG topics is long and the materiality of such issues can change over time, making it impossible for boards to have experts on every relevant topic among their current directors. Consequently, boards must determine whether they need an expert on a specific ESG topic to be on the board—or if they should instead solve the knowledge gap by leveraging other experts.

– **Board agendas.** Our survey revealed that 91% of directors believe that when it comes to aligning the company's long-term business strategy with ESG challenges, the board should focus more on improving strategic reflection than on monitoring operations. However, less than half of that 91% think they are effective at driving that strategic reflection. But how do boards ensure they have insight on the forces—including those related to ESG—that will be shaping the world in the years and decades ahead? Scenario planning can be a powerful tool in gaining that requisite foresight, enabling the board to identify complex, long-term risks.

Boards that take thoughtful action in all three areas can expand and enhance their focus on ESG. In doing so, they ultimately help the companies they oversee build sustainable business models—and sustained value creation.

Veronica Chau, Vinay Shandal, Douglas Beal,
Maria Leonore Tauber, Wendy Woods, and David Young

20 Unlocking Tomorrow's ESG Opportunities

Evidence is mounting that company performance regarding environmental, social, and governance (ESG) factors contributes to business success, and the speed at which those factors become material to any given business is increasing. Consider, for example, how quickly the COVID-19 crisis translated from a health crisis into one of the worst economic crises in recent history.

A number of drivers lie behind this increase in speed. They include greater availability of data and the related demands for transparency, society's changing expectations as public awareness of social and environmental challenges increases, and the growing influence of investors as they integrate ESG factors into mainstream investment processes.

Because not every ESG factor will be material to all businesses and sectors, it is essential for both companies and investors to be able to identify and manage those that are. That said, what is financially material will change over time—and with rapidly increasing speed. This requires the ability to understand what makes ESG issues become financially material over time and to adapt to the changes. In a new age of materiality, investors must proactively work to understand ESG factors and incorporate these trends into investment decision making in a more agile way.

Dynamic Materiality Demands Foresight

Pressure for disclosure is mounting, and among those calling for ESG disclosure is the world's largest fund manager. In his annual letter to CEOs in January 2020, BlackRock CEO Larry Fink said that the firm would be expecting disclosures in line with guidelines set by the Sustainability Accounting Standards Board and the Task Force on Climate-Related Financial Disclosures. Meanwhile, work is underway to streamline the reporting demands placed on companies. For example, the World Economic Forum's International Business Council is developing a method-

Note: *This article summarizes a report published by the World Economic Forum in collaboration with BCG* (https://www3.weforum.org/docs/WEF_Embracing_the_New_Age_of_Materiality_2020.pdf. *in March 2020).*

https://doi.org/10.1515/9783111295268-021

ology for ESG principles—including approaches to target and track climate emissions—that will complement standard financial metrics.

The launch of such initiatives does not mean that companies need to report less. If anything, the amount of data they need to disclose will increase, particularly as technological advances—such as satellite imaging that provides asset-level carbon emissions data—yield more and more information about the operations and impact of business. As a result, investors must enhance their research and analytical capabilities so that they can sift through the rapidly growing volume of data to identify the key trends influencing financial materiality.

Intensifying the pressure for transparency are such stakeholders as nongovernmental organizations (NGOs), activists, and civil society groups, which are increasingly targeting investors as a strategy for achieving broad-based change. These groups are now better equipped to track companies' social and environmental impact and, through the actions they take in response, influence corporate behavior. At a time when information is disseminated widely and immediately, movements such as #MeToo can achieve scale rapidly, creating legal, branding, recruiting, and other challenges for companies whose practices fail to meet stakeholder expectations. Investors need to anticipate these challenges and identify how they will affect a business and its performance.

Investors are factoring company performance on material environmental and societal factors into their value-creation plans and investor stewardship. The next step for investors is to engage with management teams on initiatives that can improve performance with regard to the ESG factors that are likely to become material in the future.

Four Trends Driving ESG Materiality

While the time frame in which individual ESG factors become financially material varies, they all do so with a dynamism that is driven by four trends: hypertransparency, stakeholder activism, societal expectations, and investor emphasis on ESG.

Hypertransparency. Mounting scientific evidence is driving the speed at which ESG issues become material to business. In several European countries, for example, studies on the damage to health caused by air pollution have provoked public and regulatory debates on whether to ban internal combustion vehicles. Similarly, academic research linking gender-diverse boards to improved financial performance is prompting debate on workforce gender diversity among policymakers and investors. Meanwhile, such technologies as artificial intelligence, blockchain, and virtual reality are creating unprecedented levels of transparency, enabling investors and other stakeholders to look beyond publicly reported ESG data.

Stakeholder activism. Key influencers—such as the media, public figures, or NGOs—can increase the materiality of a sustainability issue to business when they disseminate evidence and create narratives that change societal expectations or prompt action by regulators or investors. Social media greatly magnifies these voices, as seen by activist Greta Thunberg's ability to create the #FridaysForFuture youth movement on climate change, which led to global protests that attracted more than 6 million participants in September 2019.

Campaigns are becoming increasingly sophisticated. For example, within 20 days of the 2019 UN climate change conference in Madrid, the Polluters Out campaign had established a website, issued a video and a press release in multiple languages, and delivered a list of demands. Active in more than 40 countries, the group uses such online tools as Slack, Zoom, and Google Drive to organize collective action and engage others, including climate scientists. Large funders and the public are increasing their support to such groups. For example, the European Climate Foundation is financing several environmental NGOs and initiatives and contributing to the financial support of foundations. Investors must pay more attention to these efforts because, in the long term, they could lead to regulatory shifts that have sector-level impacts on asset values.

Societal expectations. The evolution of materiality also comes through the influence of key decision makers. Whether they are policymakers shaping legislation, consumers making purchasing choices, or employees deciding to work for certain companies, these influencers can have a direct impact on a company's profitability. And we see an uptick in the responsiveness of these three groups.

Policymakers are increasingly ready to take action. In Germany, for example, the government recently decided to phase out coal power by 2038. And in China, where public pressure to tackle air pollution is intense, the government has adopted a three-year action plan that includes ambitious targets for clean air and emissions in 2020.

Consumer attitudes are also shifting: demand for sustainable products and services is on the rise. According to a recent BCG analysis, 72% of consumers in Europe prefer products in environmentally friendly packaging, and 46% of consumers worldwide say that they would choose ecofriendly products over a preferred brand. In the consumer packaged goods industry, for example, a recent survey by the Corporate Eco Forum found that sustainable products were responsible for 50% of market growth from 2013 to 2018 and accounted for a dollar market share of 16.6% during that period.

We also see a shift in behavior among employees. BCG research[1] revealed that 67% of millennials expect the companies they work for to be purpose-driven and their jobs to have societal impact. Employees are also more willing to publicly criticize their employers' climate policies, and many are forming advocacy groups or submitting shareholder proposals.

Investor emphasis on ESG. Investors can influence the process by which issues become material. For example, they can evaluate companies from an ESG perspective and use the results to inform portfolio construction. And an influential investor that raises public awareness of a certain issue can cause management teams to pay attention.

This is something activist investor JANA Partners has done through its impact fund. Citing research on the psychological risks that excessive screen time poses for children, the firm pressured Apple to develop solutions. At the time, no major regulatory or societal pressure to curb youth screen time existed. But JANA Partners' pressure on a key market player made screen time for children financially material.

Investors also shape the market by pushing for greater transparency. Following the Brumadinho dam disaster, for example, the Investor Mining and Tailings Safety Initiative (investors representing $13 trillion in assets) called on more than 700 extractive companies to disclose information on their tailings storage facilities, prompting the creation of the first global database of tailings dams.

We are seeing more of this kind of ESG investor activism. In the United States, shareholder resolutions that focused on environmental and social issues—as varied as climate change, diversity, and human rights—made up half the total in 2017, up from 33% from 2006 to 2010.

Implications for Investors

To thrive in this new age, investors need to complement their sustainable investing capabilities with the ability to foresee and react to shifts in materiality more rapidly, dynamically, and flexibly. An always-on approach to materiality must be embedded into the investment process and applied with the same level of rigor given to the pursuit of an investment strategy's commercial elements. This means implementing the following practices:

---

1 https://www.bcg.com/publications/2019/organizing-future-tech-talent-purpose.

- predicting how the financial materiality of ESG issues will evolve by sector and industry, by maintaining a systems perspective on industry sectors and their stakeholder dynamics
- continually updating those predictions by applying new information and data that go beyond corporate reporting and ESG scores
- using the predictions to inform security selection and portfolio construction
- engaging with management teams on their strategies for improving performance on future material issues
- contributing to broader efforts to understand the dynamism of materiality through transparent reporting and disclosure about portfolios

A Win for All Stakeholders

Strong performance with regard to such ESG factors as carbon reduction and greater gender equality can unlock significant positive impact for investors, companies, and society. Similarly, integrating forward-looking ESG considerations into strategy and practice can lead to long-term corporate resilience and improved allocation of capital.

Consumers, activists, and employees all play a role in determining which ESG issues become material to business, but companies and investors can also become key influencers of the materiality process. Adopting an always-on approach to materiality allows investors to gain competitive advantage by optimizing performance with regard to current and future material ESG issues.

Robert G. Eccles, Vinay Shandal, David Young,
and Benedicte Montgomery

21 Private Equity Should Take the Lead in Sustainability

Despite their reputation in the 1980s as corporate raiders, most private-equity firms attempt to improve the performance of their portfolio companies through better corporate governance. Historically their business model has been to create value by sharpening the focus and oversight of largely ignored business units inside conglomerates or poorly managed private companies, such as dysfunctional family-run businesses. But although the G in "environmental, social, and governance" has been important in the PE industry from the outset, the E and the S have been virtually nonexistent. The industry has been content to seek returns with little concern for the long-term sustainability of portfolio companies or their wider impact on society.

A huge opportunity for private equity—and for society—now exists. PE has moved far beyond its Wall Street niche to become a major player in the global economy. In 2021 the industry had $6.3 trillion in assets under management (compared with about $90 trillion for public equities) and close to $2 trillion in "dry powder" (funds raised but not yet invested). Those assets are projected to exceed $11 trillion by 2026. Roughly 10,000 PE firms worldwide oversee more than 20 million employees at about 40,000 portfolio companies. Some of the largest PE firms—Apollo, Blackstone, Carlyle, EQT Partners, KKR, and TPG—are now publicly listed themselves and therefore subject to the same pressures that all public companies face.

Because the industry is now so large, society won't be able to tackle climate change and other major challenges without the active participation of private-equity firms and their portfolio companies. And unless those challenges are addressed, the PE industry, along with all other economic activity, will fail to thrive.

To better understand ESG's impact on PE and the opportunities and challenges facing the industry, we interviewed 100 people across the globe. They included industry experts and individuals from 22 limited partners (LPs)—the pension funds, insurance companies, sovereign wealth funds, endowments, and wealthy families and individuals whose money firms use to make investments—and from 39 general partners (GPs), which manage and invest money for LPs. (Disclosures: one of us, Robert, serves as the chair of KKR's Sustainability Expert

Note: "Private Equity Should Take the Lead in Sustainability" was first published in the *Harvard Business Review*, July 2022. Reprinted with permission. Copyright 2022 by Harvard Business Publishing; all rights reserved.

https://doi.org/10.1515/9783111295268-022

Advisory Council. Vinay, David, and Benedicte are consultants to the industry, including to several firms at which we conducted interviews for this article.)

We found that members of the industry have been slow to realize the importance of ESG for its future relevance, profitability, and even license to operate. The immediate challenges that PE faces are numerous and substantial: job losses at portfolio companies, the location of funds in tax havens, investments in private prisons and other controversial industries, the purchase of oil and gas assets from publicly listed companies (especially without a credible plan to improve their sustainability performance), donations to far-right organizations, and substantial payouts—sometimes hundreds of millions of dollars—for senior partners and other employees at a time when income inequality is a major societal challenge. But we also learned why the industry is well-placed to take the lead in sustainable investing—and how it can accelerate an adoption of ESG principles.

Why PE Now

Private equity's business model gives it clear advantages over investors in public equities when it comes to implementing a sustainability agenda. A PE firm has virtual control of its portfolio companies from an ownership and governance perspective, even when it doesn't own 100% of a company: it has one or more representatives on the board and a strong influence on who else serves. It has access to any information it wants about both financial and sustainability performance—whereas investors in public companies see only what the company reports. Finally, the firm determines executive compensation and can fire a CEO who is not delivering. "Our investment model—whereby we are often in control ownership positions and have a long-term perspective—and our expertise can help our portfolio companies advance their ESG journeys," says Elizabeth Lewis, the deputy head of ESG at Blackstone.

PE-owned companies operate on a longer time horizon than publicly traded companies do, further facilitating a focus on ESG. The average holding period for portfolio companies has increased from about two years in the industry's early days to about five today, which gives a GP and its handpicked CEOs ample time to make investments without the glare of quarterly earnings calls.

Of course, private-equity firms aren't likely to integrate ESG into their management unless they feel it's in the interest of long-term profitability—which is why they've largely ignored it until recently. But signs suggest that this mindset is quickly changing. Principles for Responsible Investment (PRI) reports that the number of PE and venture capital managers among signatories to the network has quadrupled over the past five years, for a total of 1,090 today. Nine of the top 10 GPs globally are now members of PRI. Of the world's 100 largest PE firms, 70 are based in the United States. Twenty-eight of those are PRI signatories, and 13 have signed on in the past two years—evidence of how quickly the industry is evolving.

Three forces are pushing ESG in the industry. First, ESG is becoming more important to limited partners and their beneficiaries. The largest asset owners— among them pension and sovereign wealth funds—are increasingly concerned about the system-level effects of climate change and inequality. A recent survey[1] of LPs by INSEAD's Global Private Equity Initiative found that 90% of them factor ESG into their investment decisions and 77% use it as a criterion in selecting general partners. Many LPs are developing more sophisticated approaches to evaluating the ESG capabilities of their GPs, and some are helping them improve their ESG capabilities.

For example, the Dutch pension investor APG has about $36 billion invested with 75 GPs across the globe. Starting in 2016, APG put processes in place to draw greater attention to sustainability from its GPs. Every year it scores each GP on a scale of 0 to 100 using a framework of 30 questions. No minimum score is required of a new GP, but all must report annually on what they are doing and show progress. Failure to do so will put future fund allocations at risk, however attractive a GP's financial returns may be. APG also gets yearly reports on the key performance indicators for ESG issues that are material to each of the GP's portfolio companies.

Another Dutch pension fund, PGGM, publishes an annual report on PE responsible investment. It uses a 1-to-5 scale to evaluate GPs. The fund won't allocate capital to those getting a 1 rating but will do so for those getting a 2 if it has reason to think they'll improve. Throughout the year PGGM monitors the approaches of its GPs and engages with them on ESG issues. The distribution of scores vividly illustrates how PGGM's general partners have improved on ESG: in 2016, 13% were rated very low or low, and 16% were rated high. In 2020 those percentages were 3% and 37%, respectively.

The rise of coinvesting, whereby an LP makes a direct investment in a portfolio company alongside the GP, is increasing pressure on GPs to focus on ESG. Coinvesting gives the LP direct access to the ESG performance data of portfolio companies.

---

1 https://www.insead.edu/sites/default/files/assets/dept/centres/gpei/docs/green-shoots-can-pri vate-equity-firms-meet-the-responsible-investing-expectations-of-their-investors.pdf.

The Institutional Limited Partners Association has published an ESG assessment framework[2] to help LPs evaluate and build the capabilities of their GPs.

The second force pushing ESG in the industry derives from the belief of many LPs and GPs that it will be essential if private equity is to continue delivering its historically high returns. The work of Harvard Business School's George Serafeim and others has shown that attention to ESG can lead to outperformance in public markets. LPs such as CalPERS, the largest U.S. pension fund, and Nuveen, a subsidiary of TIAA, believe that ESG is as relevant to private equity as it is to public equities. "ESG is important for all asset classes," says Amy O'Brien, the global head of responsible investing at Nuveen. "ESG is agnostic to ownership structure."

The third force is portfolio companies' increasing recognition of the importance of ESG issues. The reasons are unsurprising: a changing zeitgeist reflected in the preferences of employees and customers; growing awareness of the significance of climate change; social expectations regarding diversity, equity, and inclusion; pressure from large public companies to which the portfolio companies are suppliers; awareness of the sustainability focus in publicly listed companies; opportunities to boost their own value through sustainability; and increasing regulation.

The confluence of those three forces has had a powerful, albeit somewhat counterintuitive, effect. Many of the GP representatives we talked to, especially those who were sophisticated about ESG, said that a commitment to sustainability was a selling point and a differentiator in their negotiations with potential portfolio companies that are being targeted by multiple GPs.

What Distinguishes the Leaders in ESG?

Until recently, ESG in private equity was a box-ticking exercise at best. LPs would give GPs a form—called an ESG due-diligence questionnaire—to fill out when a new fund was being raised. The form was unique to each GP and often long, and it rarely had any effect on whether the LP invested in the fund. It was simply filed away, and everyone got on with the business of investing and making money.

This approach still exists among less-sophisticated GPs and LPs. But according to Giovanni Orsi, the head managing director of relationships and partnerships and private equity at the Canadian pension fund PSP Investments, "Five years ago there were clear leaders, with laggards significantly behind. Today the gap is narrowing."

---

2 https://ilpa.org/esg_framework/.

What are the leaders in ESG doing differently? They are becoming more so-phisticated in three ways: (1) integrating ESG factors in due diligence, onboarding, holding periods, and exit strategies; (2) increasing transparency in the reporting of sustainability performance; and (3) assessing and improving the ESG capabili-ties of portfolio companies.

Integrating ESG

Each target or portfolio company's performance is assessed on the critical ESG issues that will affect value creation. That means moving from a short "risk and compliance" checklist in the due diligence phase (to screen out any obvious prob-lems that could have financial consequences) to a sophisticated analysis of how well a portfolio company understands and is managing the ESG issues material to its business. That analysis is followed by collaboration with the company's board (on which the GP always has a seat) and with management to improve its perfor-mance (often with substantial help from the GP).

Leading GPs are continually improving the integration of ESG considerations into portfolio-company management. For example, in addition to monitoring and managing ESG risks during the holding period, Apollo Global Management is ex-perimenting with a post-exit analysis of investments to determine how ESG issues affected performance and how the firm might apply that knowledge to future in-vestments. "We are developing a template to help us assess ESG performance over the lifetime of an investment, and we will continue to evolve our approach," says Laurie Medley, Apollo's global head of ESG.

Until recently the separation in PE between those making investment decisions, those overseeing an asset once the deal was done, and those responsible for sustain-ability was clear. At some firms it is becoming less pronounced as deal teams un-dertake training in ESG. For example, Investindustrial, a firm with $12 billion in assets under management, sends its deal teams and portfolio-company managers to a sustainability certification course at New York University. They are supported by in-house experts in environmental and social issues. Apollo, Ares Capital, Bain Capi-tal, Carlyle, EQT, Generation Investment Management, IG4 Capital, Investindustrial, KKR, PAI Partners, TowerBrook, and Verdane all told us that they are creating a process to make deal teams more knowledgeable about ESG.

Increasing Transparency

With the growing recognition that ESG performance contributes to financial performance, GPs have become much more disciplined about gathering ESG data. They often collect a standard set of key performance indicators (KPIs) from their portfolio companies on an annual or even a quarterly basis. In some cases the number of KPIs ranges from 50 to 100. KPI reporting now almost always includes the ESG issues that are material to a company's financial performance. (For example, water usage is more relevant to a food and beverage company than to a bank or a tech company.) Triton, with $15.6 billion in assets under management, has since 2014 had a reporting system based on "three Ps": *policy* (what it is doing on the ESG front), *program* (its plan to implement the policy), and *performance* (how well the program is being implemented at the portfolio-company level). It uses various resources, including the Sustainability Accounting Standards Board, to identify material ESG issues when screening for investments and when managing them.

Transparency between GPs and their LPs is also increasing. Apollo has been reporting on ESG to LPs for 12 years, and in recent years its annual ESG report has been publicly available on its website—a practice some other GPs have now adopted. Some LPs are requesting ESG data, such as for carbon, at the portfolio-company level.

Improving ESG Performance

The private-equity business model puts general partners in a good position to help portfolio companies improve their ESG integration and reporting practices in a number of ways. These include identifying relevant issues and best practices for dealing with them, providing measurement and reporting tools, benchmarking against other portfolio companies, offering access to internal and external experts, and monitoring regulatory developments.

Some GPs have developed methodologies for assessing the degree of ESG sophistication in potential portfolio companies and helping them improve practice. Carlyle's process for evaluating targets starts with risk (basic compliance on environmental, safety, and health issues), moves to value (captured from the company's current business model and capabilities), and ends with growth (how to enter new areas). Its resources can enable portfolio companies to improve on sustainability faster than they could on their own.

Graeme Ardus, the head of ESG at Triton, told us that "deal teams and portfolio companies can see how each business is doing in comparison to the 'Triton benchmark.'" The firm holds monthly calls to share good practices with its portfolio companies and hosts events where CEOs and other senior executives present what they are doing on ESG. Triton also has a formal annual ESG gathering at which companies can network with and learn from one another.

Another leader where we interviewed is Nuveen, which acts as both a GP and an LP. In its role as an LP, it has a framework for doing an ESG assessment of every general partner and every fund in which it invests. Nuveen also gathers ESG data at both the fund and the portfolio-company level, including carbon footprint and alignment of each investment with the UN's Sustainable Development Goals—among them ending poverty and promoting responsible consumption and production. It then uses those capabilities in its engagements with private companies. "The challenge for many private companies," O'Brien says, "is the lack of capacity and resources to work on ESG integration and reporting. We are almost like consultants for the company."

To spur learning, Investindustrial has for five years held an annual sustainability meeting with its portfolio companies. Attendance is a good indicator of how interest in sustainability has grown in the PE sector. "In the first year the company typically sent only one person—whoever was most closely associated with sustainability," says Serge Younes, Investindustrial's head of sustainability. "At our last virtual meeting we had more than 200 people from 25 portfolio companies, including many members of senior management such as the CEO [chief executive officer] and the CFO [chief financial officer]."

What Comes Next?

Although our interviews revealed that the private-equity industry is taking (long overdue) steps to adopt a sustainability agenda, considerable room for improvement remains. Here are four initiatives that can be helpful.

Standardize ESG Reporting

Firms can adopt a mechanism for simplifying and harmonizing ESG data reported by their portfolio companies to GPs and by GPs to LPs. Every general partner where we interviewed had a bespoke set of KPIs and a methodology for collecting, analyzing, and reporting data, and all agreed that some degree of standardization would be useful. Portfolio companies with multiple GPs face multiple data requests. Similarly, GPs receive wide-ranging and differing data requests from their LPs.

Solid progress is already being made on this front, starting with the ESG Data Convergence Project,[3] led by CalPERS and Carlyle (and to which BCG was an adviser). They brought together a group of leading LPs and GPs to agree on six ESG issues—Scopes 1 and 2 greenhouse gas emissions, renewable energy, board diversity, work-related injuries, net new hires, and employee engagement—and the key performance indicators for each, all based on existing standards and frameworks. GPs participating in the project agree to collect data from their portfolio companies and make it available to their LPs. The data will then be anonymized and put into a database for benchmarking purposes. As of this writing, the project includes a group of 100 global GPs and LPs representing $8.7 trillion in assets under management and 1,400 portfolio companies.

The project's leaders anticipated that getting agreement between GPs and LPs would be extremely difficult, because people have unique data needs, and no regulations currently exist to enforce standards. But the rapid uptake of the ESG Data Convergence Project indicates that the industry is ready to meet this challenge in a more aligned way. (That said, nothing prevents a GP or an LP from requesting additional data.) Other groups are working on a similar idea, including PRI, the Ceres Investor Network, the Institutional Investors Group on Climate Change, and the Initiative Climat International (iCI). The Institutional Limited Partners Association is working to ensure alignment rather than competition among these initiatives.

Make Net-Zero Commitments

Given the size of this asset class, the PE industry needs to make the kind of commitment to "Net-Zero by 2050" that all financial institutions under the umbrella of the Glasgow Financial Alliance for Net Zero[4] are making. Important work for private equity is being done by the iCI, which was launched in 2015 by five French PE firms to help achieve the objectives of the Paris Agreement on Climate Change. Thanks in large part to support from PRI, the iCI now includes more than 164 general partners representing more than $2 trillion in assets under management. In March 2022 Elizabeth Seeger, the managing director of sustainable investing at KKR, was named chair of the North American chapter. The iCI's members commit to reducing carbon emissions in their portfolio companies and seek to ensure long-term sustainable financial performance by managing the risks and opportu-

---

3 https://www.carlyle.com/media-room/news-release-archive/private-equity-industry-establishes-first-ever-lp-and-gp-partnership-standardize-esg-reporting.

4 https://unfccc.int/news/new-financial-alliance-for-net-zero-emissions-launches.

nities presented by climate change. However, there is a major difference between reducing emissions in a portfolio (where a GP may simply ditch dirty companies) and reducing emissions in a portfolio company (which a GP may help go green).

Improve Diversity

The industry needs to improve its track record with DEI. Today private equity is still predominantly white and male, particularly on deal teams. Evidence continues to mount that a more diverse workforce leads to better performance. Diversity is also important in the war for talent. Hence it has become a top issue for limited partners in managing their investments (and themselves), and they are putting pressure on their GPs. Encouragingly, some GPs already recognize the importance of DEI. EQT, for example, is committed to creating truly diverse, gender-balanced (at least 40% female) investment-professional teams. To demonstrate the seriousness of its commitment, EQT has issued a credit instrument whereby its interest rate will ratchet up if EQT fails to meet the short-term target of 28% female by 2026. Other firms should follow its lead.

DEI standards must apply to portfolio companies as well. Sherrie Trecker, the sustainability officer at the Washington State Investment Board, says, "GPs have the ability to change board structures quickly. This is impactful, and I think we will see rapid change here, especially compared with public equities." Kara Helander, the chief diversity, equity, and inclusion (DEI) officer at Carlyle, says, "Ten years ago there was less focus on this, but today DEI is a business priority for our portfolio companies." Carlyle has a goal of at least 30% diverse board membership for its controlled portfolio companies. Since many of those board members are Carlyle employees, the firm understands its obligation to improve its own diversity. Carlyle's CEO, Kewsong Lee, leads the DEI initiative and, along with other Carlyle executives, sets the tone from the top by holding all Carlyle colleagues accountable through DEI objective setting and by hosting discussions on mitigating unconscious bias.

Spread the Wealth

The PE industry needs to directly confront the fact that the tremendous wealth it has created has been unevenly distributed. LPs, GPs, and the top executives of portfolio companies have benefited to a much greater degree than other employees of those companies. Shared ownership, whereby *all* company employees participate in the value created during the holding period, is important. Take TowerBrook's

2020 investment in CarTrawler, a company providing technology solutions to the global travel industry. All 400 or so employees have received shares that will allow them to garner proceeds when they depart. Similarly, in a number of its investments KKR offers substantial ownership to employees outside the C-suite and provides them with basic financial education.

Demonstrating a broader industry commitment to spreading the wealth, 19 PE firms have mobilized a group of asset managers, financial services firms, foundations, and nonprofits to launch the nonprofit Ownership Works. Its mission is "to increase prosperity through shared ownership at work." It has set an ambitious target of generating at least $20 billion by 2030 for hundreds of thousands of new employee-owners—among them lower-income workers and people of color who have been excluded from this wealth-building opportunity for generations. According to Anna-Lisa Miller, the executive director, "This movement is about working in concert to create a future . . . where employers and employees can win together."

To be sure, shared ownership doesn't work for all companies. In the retail sector, for example, where turnover is high, it would be an ineffective way to incentivize and reward employee performance.

Important elements—including social pressure, LP pressure, and shareholder pressure on publicly listed PE firms—are pushing private equity to take the lead in ESG integration. But will that be enough? PE firms must commit to moving their involvement in ESG from box-ticking to the center of their reason for being. Despite the best of intentions, it is all too easy for the industry to get lost in the weeds of the ESG agenda and forget that its social license to operate is not guaranteed.

To be successful in the future, PE leaders must speak openly and often about the importance of sustainable value creation. They must recruit people who care about it in the broadest sense and aren't joining the industry just because it can be very lucrative. We foresee three consequences if the industry fails to fully embrace ESG: its social legitimacy will increasingly come under attack; it will no longer be able to deliver its historically high returns; it will fail to fulfill its potential to help solve, rather than exacerbate, environmental, social, and governance problems.

Part 3.4: **Enable Systems Level Strategy**

David Young and Simon Beck
22 How Companies Shape Ecosystems to Achieve Sustainability and Advantage

Companies are increasingly embracing sustainable business model innovation (SBM-I) to simultaneously address environmental and societal challenges and create competitive advantage. But those efforts often run into significant constraints stemming from the underlying structure, resource and capability bottlenecks, and other limitations of the broad socio-economic ecosystem in which companies operate.

Overcoming these constraints to develop scaled, sustainable solutions often requires coordination, collaboration, and co-designing of solutions by multiple actors in the ecosystem, including suppliers, customers, employees, and governments. For example, when Unilever first committed to use only cage-free eggs for their Hellmann's mayonnaise in North America by 2020, there simply were not enough cage-free hens in the United States to meet their demand. As a sustainability pioneer, they had to rebuild their supply chain working with independent third-party verifiers to improve supplier practices, ultimately achieving their commitment three years ahead of schedule. Today, we see companies like Tesla actively reshaping their ecosystem to ensure greater sustainability and competitive advantage.

But how can companies reshape the dynamics of their socio-economic ecosystem? As we've previously outlined[1], companies should start by systematically mapping their ecosystems to determine where there are meaningful constraints to SBM-I. Our research of more than 100 in-depth case studies identified nine ways in which companies can then remake their ecosystems to unlock those sustainability constraints (see Figure 22.1).

Some companies, it turns out, are already putting these approaches into action. More than 90% of SBM-Is we studied are reshaping the dynamics of their ecosystem in at least one way. Meanwhile, sustainability front-runners[2] use combinations of four or more of these modes to alter ecosystem dynamics. In particu-

1 https://www.bcg.com/publications/2021/four-strategies-for-sustainable-business-model-innovation.
2 https://www.bcg.com/en-ca/publications/2021/keys-to-being-a-leader-in-sustainable-business-model-innovation.

https://doi.org/10.1515/9783111295268-023

Shape customer demand/preferences - Educate customers, raise their expectations and deliver value proposition with superior environmental and/or societal benefits

Expand distribution channels - Share value to incentive collaboration to expand or create new distribution channels, train distribution or salesforce, or create take-back programs to scale SBM-I and impact

Improve supplier practice - Implement or enable adoption of more sustainable practices in supply chain to build advantage with superior/guaranteed sustainability inputs

Increase transparency in ecosystem - Generate information to create the underlying data layer that can be leveraged by the ecosystem to create transparency about practices and shape ecosystem dynamics

Raise/set new industry standards - Adopt and deliver superior practices and/or products and establish these as new norm in Strategically select and contract with suppliers of critical inputs that are likely to become scarce. These steps will not only mitigate a shortage but also make the supply chain more resilient

Establish position as dominant platform/ infrastructure - Establish your SBM-I as dominant solution on a particular sustainability issue in order to achieve scale and lock-in effect

Attract/catalyze funding for innovation in ecosystem - Set up financing vehicles or deploy capital to enable, accelerate and grow the potential for SBM-I in the ecosystem

Collective action for joint R&D across the ecosystem - Set up vehicles for collaborative and coordinated R&D across value chains, sectors, etc. to enable solutions at-scale (particularly where technical breakthrough is needed to achieve sustainability targets

Influence/shape regulations, gain government support - Lobby to define SMB-I as new regulatory standard or get SBM-I incentivized or subsidized by government; create greater certainty in regulatory/policy environment to create potential for SBM-I

Source: BCG analysis of 115 SBM-I case studies based on public data (March 2020 -July 2021)

Figure 22.1: 9 ways companies act to reshape ecosystems dynamics to unlock greater competitive advantage through SBM-I.

lar, front-runners are far more likely to seek to establish themselves as the dominant platform or infrastructure than other SBM-Is.

The Nine Modes we Observed

Shape customer demand and preferences. Companies can educate customers and raise their expectations to demand products and services that generate superior environmental/societal (E/S) benefits. For example, Docomony, founded in Sweden in 2018, has created the "DO" mobile banking platform to track and offset consumers' CO_2 emissions, and also offers its "DO Black" credit card that limits spending when a carbon threshold is reached. With these two products, Docomony educates and incentivizes customers to significantly change their spending habits and demands, for example by buying from more sustainable merchants.

Expand distribution channels. Companies can expand or create new channels to distribute products or recycle products at their end of life by sharing value to incentivize collaboration. This can include training new salesforces to distribute products in rural environments or creating take-back programs to scale recycling programs. Interface, the world's largest manufacturer of modular flooring, is now offering the world's first "carbon negative" flooring products that are made from recycled contents and bio-based materials and store carbon—preventing its release into the atmosphere. The company has expanded its supply of recycled materials, including by working with coastal communities to collect and recycle fishing nets into yarn and establishing programs to recycle vinyl-back carpet tiles.

Improve supplier practices. Companies can work with suppliers further up the supply chain to adopt more sustainable practices. For many SBM-Is this creates advantage through guaranteeing a supply of more sustainable inputs. For example, Primark partners with the NGO CottonCollect to train women smallholder farmers in India to adopt sustainable farming practices that boost yields while reducing the use of chemical pesticides, fertilizer, and water intensity. This effort has helped the company expand their supply of sustainable, organic cotton used in its "Primary Cares" line.

Increase ecosystem transparency. Trust within an ecosystem is critical to creating the right incentives and verifying the inputs used in sustainable products. Companies can generate data and analytics that create transparency about sustainable production practices (for example, child-free labor); environmental and societal impact (for example, the carbon content of inputs); and certifiable origins of sustainable products (for example, sustainable fisheries). In Singapore, Sembcorp developed a blockchain Renewable Energy Certificate (REC) platform that aggregates RECs and allows companies to purchase them to offset their carbon footprint. The platform boosts transparency, integrity, and competitiveness in the renewable energy market.

Raise or set new industry standards. Companies can adopt more sustainable practices and/or deliver more sustainable products—and then advocate and catalyze alignment around these solutions to establish them as new norms in the industry. This also includes working collaboratively to set new industry standards among players across the value chain. Finnish oil and gas company Neste, for example, has become a leading player in renewable fuels and chemicals and currently chairs the Roundtable on Sustainable Biomaterials (RSB). In that position, the company has participated in the establishment of RSB's globally recognized industry standards and certifications for sustainable biofuels.

Establish position as dominant platform or infrastructure. Companies that can make their platform or infrastructure the primary means for solving a specific sustainability issue can enable sustainable solutions to achieve scale while locking in their competitive advantage. Consider TEESS, a 50–50 joint venture of Total and Envision. TEESS combines Total's robust experience in energy production and commercial operations with Envision's AIoT Operating System (EnOS), the world's largest IoT energy platform, to develop on-site, distributed generation, solar projects for B2B customers in China.

Attract or catalyze funding for ecosystem innovation. Companies can set up joint-financing vehicles and/or mobilize and deploy capital to enable, accelerate, and grow sustainability innovations within the ecosystem. For example, BNP Paribas has pioneered Sustainability-Linked Loans (SLLs), which allow companies to lower their cost of funding based on the achievement of certain sustainability targets and KPIs.

Collective action for joint R&D across the ecosystem. Companies can establish vehicles for collaborative and coordinated research and development of scalable solutions, efforts requiring alignment across many players within the ecosystem. Often this R&D focuses on fundamental components of underlying industry infrastructure that must be re-invented to enable greater sustainability for all parts of the value chain. Collaborators contribute financial resources, complementary capabilities, and expertise talent, for example, established in 2020, the *Mærsk Mc-Kinney Møller* Center for *Zero Carbon Shipping* to conduct joint R&D on priority areas that are needed to decarbonize the maritime industry.

Influence or shape regulations, gain government support. Companies can work with regulators and policymakers to establish new regulatory standards or make policy changes to directly subsidize, incentivize, and de-risk sustainable business models and sustainable innovation. For example, in the run-up to COP26 many corporate-led sustainability alliances have begun to call for clear government policy on carbon pricing. Recently, the CEO Climate Dialogue, a corporate sustainability alliance that includes oil and gas super majors, utilities, and chemicals companies called for significantly reduced emissions and for market-based policy approaches that assign a cost to greenhouse gas emissions.

In order to maximize the advantage found in sustainability, companies must quickly establish where and how they need to reshape their ecosystem for advantage. Depending on the constraints at issue, they can then adopt one or more of the nine modes outlined above to alter ecosystem dynamics. The best approach to executing each mode may differ. For example, companies that want to reshape an ecosystem by changing supplier practices may decide to build partnerships on their own with NGOs or may decide to take collective action through a sustainability alliance, working with their competitors to influence supplier practices. In other instances—for example, companies aiming to attract funding for ecosystem innovation—it may be necessary to build an entirely new "business ecosystem"[3]—a specific form of collective action wherein a dynamic group of independent businesses create products or services that together constitute a coherent solution to a marketplace or consumer need.

There is no doubt that driving ecosystem-level change is a complex undertaking. But companies that understand how their broad ecosystem needs to evolve— and know the right means to drive that change—will emerge as winners in the race for SBM-I.

---

3 https://bcghendersoninstitute.com/how-to-benefit-from-business-ecosystems-if-you-are-not-the-orchestrator/.

David Young, Ulrich Pidun, Balázs Zoletnik, and Simon Beck

23 When a Business Ecosystem is the Answer to Sustainability Challenges

The success of ecosystems is a hot topic these days—and rightly so. Apple, for example, has built a powerful business ecosystem of app developers and software players around its iOS operating system. Amazon has similarly built a robust business ecosystem including brick-and-mortar and online retailers. And Visa has built a robust business ecosystem around its payment platform. But what if the power of business ecosystems could be taken a bit further? What if business ecosystems could be leveraged to help save the planet?

That's not as far-fetched as it may sound. As companies around the world remake their business models to advance their sustainability and boost their business advantage,[1] many are finding that they need to drive change beyond the boundaries of their business. Creating changes in the wider system in which a company operates demands collective action. In some cases, that change is best driven through the creation of a business ecosystem—a specific form of business collective action wherein a dynamic group of independent businesses creates products or services that together constitute a coherent solution[2] to a marketplace or consumer need.

Business ecosystems are complex and often more difficult to develop[3] than alternative approaches to collective action, including partnerships or joint ventures, as well as broad-based corporate-led sustainability alliances. So how do companies determine when a business ecosystem is the best option for a specific sustainability challenge? On the basis of BCG Henderson Institute's continuing research into sustainable business model innovation (SBM-I) and business ecosystems, we have identified six barriers that often inhibit a company's ability to address a sustainability challenge, either in their own operations or for their customers, and where business ecosystems could provide a solution:

- fragmented demand
- fragmented supply
- matching challenge
- lack of trust

---

1 https://www.bcg.com/publications/2021/keys-to-being-a-leader-in-sustainable-business-model-innovation.

2 https://www.bcg.com/publications/2019/do-you-need-business-ecosystem.

3 https://www.bcg.com/publications/2020/why-do-most-business-ecosystems-fail.

https://doi.org/10.1515/9783111295268-024

- insufficient co-innovation
- lack of close coordination across industries

Companies looking to tackle sustainability challenges that exhibit at least one of these barriers should consider creating a business ecosystem to drive collective action toward an ecosystem with enhanced sustainability performance.

The Sustainability Imperative

Our research on more than 115 sustainable business model innovations[4] finds that companies on their own frequently run into constraints within the wider system. That, in turn, limits their ability to achieve greater environmental or societal benefits in a way that is economically or operationally feasible for the business.

Consider the challenge of reducing plastic waste, for example. Major consumer-facing brands are making significant commitments to reduce the use of virgin polyethylene terephthalate (PET), in part by using recycled PET (rPET). But companies looking to switch to rPET face yet another challenge: by 2025, according to BCG estimates, roughly 45% of demand for rPET will be unmet due to limited supply. Filling that gap will require a portfolio of ecosystem interventions that include R&D into such alternatives as biodegradables, the scaling of emerging solutions, and coordinated approaches to expand recycling infrastructure.

This is where collective action can be particularly helpful in removing the constraints that limit the adoption of more sustainable business practices. There are three primary methods for engaging in collective action to remove system sustainability constraints:

- **Sustainability partnerships or joint ventures.** These arrangements involve formalized agreements among organizations to advance a specific sustainability-related product, service, or initiative. Royal DSM, for example, has partnered with several public, private, and social-sector players—including the government of Rwanda, international development banks, and NGOs—to set up Africa Improved Foods, which will increase access to affordable and nutritious foods. Such partnerships tend to be built by and around a single core business and its own value chain to deliver an SBM-I.
- **Broad-based, corporate-led sustainability alliances.** These alliances are a form of collective action that involves more than two entities with a focus on establishing joint standards, policies, or approaches that advance sustainabil-

---

4 https://www.bcg.com/capabilities/innovation-strategy-delivery/business-model-innovation.

ity. Corporate-led sustainability alliances operating today include One Planet Business for Biodiversity, which focuses on cultivating and restoring biodiversity; the Global Platform for Sustainable Natural Rubber, which aims to make the natural rubber value chain fair, equitable, and environmentally sound; and the Consumer Goods Forum, which focuses on addressing such issues as environmental sustainability and the opportunity to develop products that contribute to global health and well-being.

- **Sustainability business ecosystems.** This is a very specific type of collective action that is often highly focused on addressing a particular market need—and is more than just a kind of loose affiliation, which the word "ecosystem" often evokes. (See "Understanding business ecosystems.") And the approach has been gaining traction. Too Good To Go, for example, has built a business ecosystem to reduce food waste through a marketplace connecting customers with restaurants and stores that have surplus food.

Understanding Business Ecosystems

The term "ecosystem" is widely used in business but often carries a meaning that differs from the one we intend in this article. For example, some might describe London's financial center—with large investment banks, small financial players, and the network of companies and employees that support them—as an ecosystem. Silicon Valley—with its large network of established companies, startups, and leading research institutions—might also be labeled as such. But neither fits the bill of a business ecosystem under our definition.

That's because a true business ecosystem is not simply a means for connection or collaboration. Rather, it is a collection of independent businesses, orchestrated by a business at the center, that come together to address a specific need in the market. Most important, the solution that is developed by the business ecosystem creates value for every participant. And to make things a bit more complicated, business ecosystems can also incorporate the other two forms of collective action: partnerships and alliances.

Business ecosystems in general have grown more prevalent over the past decade, and they play an increasingly vital role in sustainability efforts. In our study of more than 115 SBM-Is, we found that roughly 30 of them built business ecosystems as a core part of their SBM-I. Notably, many were what we call sustainability front-runners: SBM-Is that most successfully push the boundaries of competition and reimagine their businesses in order to create more robust competitive advantage from sustainability.

In general, business ecosystems are the right choice to address a sustainability challenge that requires combining complementary solutions from different businesses in a highly coordinated fashion. To succeed, the business ecosystem must yield economic benefits for all players along with creating unique value to the end customer. While complex to build, business ecosystems offer the ability to easily access capabilities, scale fast, and achieve flexibility and resilience. In addition, business ecosystems can sometimes be a good interim solution to business sustainability challenges that stem from the absence of clear standards and universal regulation. For example, several players in the world of smart homes—including Samsung (SmartThings), Apple (HomeKit), and Amazon (Alexa)—are expanding their own connected ecosystems while, at the same time, setting up an alliance to work on establishing an industry-unifying, royalty-free connectivity standard called Matter.

Our research has found that sustainability business ecosystems tend to focus on addressing a few specific sustainability challenges and currently tend to be concentrated in a few industries, including financial services, education, and health care. However, business ecosystems remain a relatively untapped opportunity in many other industries.

When Business Ecosystems Make Sense

To determine whether a business ecosystem[5] model is the right solution to a sustainability challenge, companies should assess the nature of the problem they are trying to solve. We have identified six barriers to addressing sustainability challenges that indicate when a business ecosystem approach may offer a viable solution. These barriers are not mutually exclusive; in fact, most sustainability challenges where business ecosystems are successfully deployed exhibit several of them (see Figure 23.1).

Fragmented demand. Some sustainability challenges are difficult to address because of an inability to aggregate demand so that an SBM-I reaches sufficient scale. This is critical in situations where demand is highly fragmented (often across many small-scale customers), making the economics of serving those customers unattractive. Expanding financial inclusion or access to health or education for rural populations and underserved communities often requires addressing challenges with disaggregated subscale demand.

Consider insurance startup BIMA, for example. The company uses mobile technology to bring vital health and insurance products to more than 35 million customers in ten countries: seven in Asia and three in Africa. BIMA's platform integrates offerings from various companies (telco providers, mobile money providers, and insurance underwriters) and provides a seamless, user-friendly experience from registration to claims processing with no paperwork involved. To aggregate demand, BIMA employs 3,000 agents to educate and build trust among customers, three-

---

5 https://www.bcg.com/capabilities/digital-technology-data/digital-ecosystems.

Fragment Demand
Business ecosystem can quickly aggerate demand, including among small-scale customers, to make supply and innovation economically viable

Fragmented Supply
Business ecosystem can improve supplier practices and aggregate fragmented or small-scale distributed supply to support market depth and liquidity

Matching Challenge
Business ecosystem can help create markets with sufficient depth to ensure buyers can find and access sustainable products and sustainability services

Lack of Trust
Business ecosystem can reinforce the trust that a product is produced or sourced sustainably through verification, certification, and tracing

Insufficient Co-Innovation
Business ecosystem can incentivize and link the innovation activities of many players to create a sustainability solution, often targeting common infrastructure challenges

Lack of Close Coordination Across Industries
Business ecosystem can drive close coordination across players, value chains, and industries to provide customers with coherent solutions

Source: BCG Henderson Institute analysis

Figure 23.1: Business ecosystems can help address six sustainability barriers.

quarters of whom, typically, are accessing insurance services for the first time. Those agents then direct interested customers to BIMA's multiple channels—including an app, a call center, and social media—to make their purchase.

Fragmented supply. Supply of certain inputs to a sustainable offering, typically some sort of commodity, can also be a constraint—particularly when supply is highly fragmented (often across many small-scale suppliers). In such instances, transaction costs for customers are prohibitively high. As a result, supply needs to be aggregated before customers can find sufficient market depth to meet their demand or sufficient liquidity in the market exists to enable consistent transactions.

The need for aggregated sustainably produced supply is often an issue for companies that are aiming to improve the practices of small-scale producers throughout their supply chain, particularly in sustainable agriculture. Supply aggregation is also likely to be valuable in the renewable energy sector where energy generation need not only be done at utility scale.

For example, Singapore energy company Sembcorp launched its renewable energy certificate (REC) aggregator platform in 2020 to enable companies to purchase certified renewable energy (from Sembcorp and other suppliers) in lieu of paying government carbon taxes. The platform creates liquidity and flexibility by aggregating sources of RECs and will allow more large energy users to manage their energy portfolios across different sources and geographies and to achieve their renewable energy targets.

Matching challenge. Companies attempting to market new sustainable products or services can find that high search costs prevent them from transacting with potential customers. In such instances, the challenge is less about scaling supply or demand and more about creating transparency about the offering and consolidating distinct products or services to enable sufficient depth for matching to occur. Sustainability challenges with this barrier include those related to improving resource efficiency, such as increasing the utilization of shipping containers or car sharing, and to providing access to recruitment and job opportunities for underrepresented groups. This barrier can also often be found in challenges in the circular economy, where certain products—such as excess or imperfect foods and second-hand items—require little or no adaptation to make them valuable to other users.

Poshmark plays that market-making role in the fashion industry,[6] facilitating circularity and shopping for second-hand goods. The company—which went public in 2021 and now has more than 80 million registered users in Australia, Canada, India, and the United States—has developed a platform for buying and selling items, mainly clothing, in a variety of categories. The platform aims to combine the human connection of a physical shopping experience with the scale, reach, ease, and selection benefits of e-commerce, leveraging a variety of social tools and features designed to drive engagement, including sharing, liking, following, commenting, and real-time virtual-shopping events, such as "Posh Parties."

Lack of trust. In some cases, a lack of trust among parties is the major barrier for successful SBM-I, and a business ecosystem can help address this challenge. Trust can be created through verification, certification, and tracing applications. This is particularly important when what matters most to a buyer is how a product was made and what materials went into its production—so, for example, a buyer may choose a sustainably made product over an identical one that was made in a less environmentally friendly way. This could involve certifying that a certain amount of sustainable content (for example, the amount of nonvirgin PET in a bottle) or a product (for example, cotton) has been produced in a sustainable manner.

---

6 https://www.bcg.com/industries/retail/fashion-industry.

This is also critical in the carbon offset market, where concerns about the underlying quality of offsets have increased in recent years.

The sustainability action platform rePurpose Global, founded in 2016, takes aim at the trust challenge. The platform enables individuals and businesses to offset their plastic footprints through the purchase of so-called plastic credits. These credits are created through the verified removal of low-value plastics from the land and plastics from the ocean, along with investment in recycling facilities in underdeveloped areas and new innovations for plastic alternatives. The platform also provides advisory services to clients to address the root causes of plastic use. It removes roughly 11 million pounds of plastic waste each year and provides fair employment for more than 9,500 waste workers through partner organizations in Colombia, India, Indonesia, and Kenya.

Insufficient co-Innovation. Frequently, distributed players, in tandem, need to innovate their products or services in order for a coherent solution set for a sustainability challenge to emerge.

Business ecosystems can drive co-innovation among fragmented players, including those in different industries or parts of the value chain, to create a solution to a specific problem. The need for coordination in sustainability often relates to the underlying common infrastructure for a product or service for which clear operational standards are required. Consider the heavy transportation industry, for example. Battery-powered electric vehicles that require a long time to recharge are ill-suited to an industry in which an idle truck is a drag on profitability. Innovations that rely on natural gas, particularly renewable natural gas or blue and green hydrogen, are being developed to decarbonize the heavy transportation industry. But without coordination, truck manufacturers, fuel distributors, and logistics[7] companies are unlikely to adopt any kind of solution quickly.

Business ecosystems can also create the conditions for distributed innovation without a focus on a specific sustainability solution. Here, the business ecosystem provides the underlying platform that supports the exchange of ideas and data involving multiple players. Microsoft's AI for Good initiative, for example, offers an artificial intelligence (AI) platform for innovation ecosystems that includes cloud computing services, AI tools, and technical support as well as cash awards to facilitate collaboration among key public and private stakeholders to address sustainability challenges.

We believe that there are several SBM-Is that could explore creating a sustainability business ecosystem to address the need for distributed innovation.

---

7 https://www.bcg.com/industries/transportation-logistics/logistics.

Consider Salesforce's Sustainability Cloud platform, for example, which provides clients with data on their greenhouse gas emissions and energy usage. By opening its platform to external solution providers, Salesforce can offer them the opportunity to leverage the underlying data platform to create differentiated solutions for energy and emission management for Sustainability Cloud's clients across different industries.

Lack of close coordination across industries. Some sustainability challenges are difficult to address without continuous coordination among different types of stakeholders. Such coordination is especially required in situations where a coherent solution for customers is needed—such as in health care, where multiple care providers need to be coordinated for each patient. And coordination can be particularly important in circular economy solutions. That's because multiple players often have a role in a product's life cycle and therefore must make adaptations to their own products and processes to ensure that circularity can be achieved. Companies involved in the production, use, recycling, and second-life applications of plastic packaging, for example, must coordinate across the entire circular life cycle, including for the collection of waste products from often fragmented end users.

Cityblock Health, a 2017 spinout from Sidewalk Labs (an Alphabet company focused on urban innovation), has cultivated the development of a business ecosystem that addresses the need for close coordination in health care. Cityblock, working with ecosystem participants— including primary care providers, behavioral health specialists, social workers, and community partners that address social needs, such as transportation, housing, and food—provides health care to Medicaid and lower-income Medicare beneficiaries. Cityblock's proprietary care management platform, Commons, provides a 360-degree view of a patient's health, enabling care teams to make recommendations on the basis of a holistic understanding of the patient and support coordination among experts. This tech-enabled community care model has proven to be cost-effective, resulting in a 15% reduction in emergency room visits and a 20% reduction in inpatient hospital stays. Cityblock currently serves 90,000 members in Connecticut, Massachusetts, New York, North Carolina, and Washington, DC.

Business ecosystems are an emerging model for tackling sustainability issues confronting society. While such ecosystems add complexity, they also provide access to critical capabilities and resources and the ability to scale rapidly.

To understand if a business ecosystem is the right way to organize to address a sustainability issue, companies must start by identifying the core barrier limiting their progress. In instances where the sustainability challenge exhibits at least one of the barriers outlined above, the development of a business ecosystem may unlock critical constraints and help companies address daunting societal challenges while creating competitive advantage.

David Young, Simon Beck, and Konrad von Szczepanski
24 How to Build a High-Impact Sustainability Alliance

Companies are setting more ambitious climate and sustainability[1] goals than ever before—but many are finding that sustainability cannot be achieved singlehandedly. This is partly because, for many companies and products, 90% or more of greenhouse gas emissions are outside their direct control.

To achieve sustainability across the entire value chain, companies must act aggressively—and collectively—to transform their ecosystems. Three forms of collaboration can be used to achieve sustainability goals. Companies can forge partnerships to advance a specific sustainability-related product, service, or initiative. They can participate in or orchestrate a broader sustainability business ecosystem,[2] that is, a dynamic group of independent businesses that together constitute a coherent solution to address a specific sustainability need in the market. Or they can participate in a corporate-led sustainability alliance. (See "Three Models for Collaboration.")

Three Models for Collaboration

There are three primary methods for engaging in collective action to support sustainability targets: company-specific partnerships, business ecosystems, and corporate-led sustainability alliances.

Sustainability partnerships. Partnerships are contractual relationships typically established along a single company's value chain to deliver on its unique business and sustainability goals. This type of collaboration tends to be a one-to-many relationship, that is, a central company coordinates with a set of sustainability partners. For example, in 2020, organic cotton production represented only 1% of global cotton production. Primark, a fast fashion company, collaborated with CottonConnect to shift smallholder farmers to more sustainable practices and with Oritain to forensically trace and validate the cotton. These partnerships have enabled Primark to break the constraints of its ecosystem and access scarce supply for products merchandised under its "Primark Cares" label.

Sustainability business ecosystems. Business ecosystems are a form of collective action wherein a dynamic group of independent businesses creates products or services that together constitute a coherent solution to a marketplace or consumer need. Monetary value exchange is explicitly built into the design of the business ecosystem to align the incentives of actors, and while there may be an orchestrator, business ecosystems are rarely hierarchical. BIMA, a health and insurance provider, uses mobile technology to bring vital health and insurance products to more than 35 million customers in parts of Asia and Africa. BIMA's platform delivers societal

---

1 https://www.bcg.com/capabilities/climate-change-sustainability/overview.
2 https://www.bcg.com/publications/2021/ecosystems-could-help-with-sustainability-challenges.

https://doi.org/10.1515/9783111295268-025

value by integrating telco providers, mobile money providers, and insurance underwriters to provide a seamless, user-friendly experience for its users.

Corporate-led sustainability alliances (CSAs). These alliances are a form of multistakeholder collective action that focus on setting industry standards and increasing data transparency across value chains, influencing regulation, and shaping customer preferences, or supporting innovation through joint R&D and catalyzing capital. What distinguishes CSAs from other forms of sustainability alliances is that businesses and their priorities are the driving force behind the alliance, shaping the collective agenda to enable businesses to transition to more sustainable practices in a way that is economically viable. Corporate-led sustainability alliances operating today include One Planet Business for Biodiversity, which focuses on cultivating and restoring biodiversity; the Global Platform for Sustainable Natural Rubber, which aims to make the natural rubber value chain fair, equitable, and environmentally sound; and the Consumer Goods Forum, which focuses on addressing such issues as environmental sustainability and the opportunity to develop products that contribute to global health and well-being.

Although partnerships and business ecosystems are important collaboration models, they are too limited in scope for many industries' most deeply entrenched sustainability challenges, particularly those in hard-to-abate sectors. In many cases, what is needed is option number three: a corporate-led sustainability alliance (CSA): a multistakeholder, business-led coalition designed to advance the sustainability of its members and their industries for the common good.

Consider a typical mining company. More than 90% of its CO_2 emissions are so-called Scope 3 emissions, occurring downstream. Steel production from iron ore produces significantly more emissions than the mining process itself. To decarbonize steel making, therefore, mining companies, steel makers, technology providers, suppliers of novel raw materials (such as hydrogen), research institutes, and end users (such as automotive original equipment manufacturers) must work together to decarbonize the whole value chain.

How do companies build a high-impact corporate-led sustainability alliance? The BGC Henderson Institute studied more than 50 CSAs across multiple industries, geographies, and sustainability challenges to understand what makes some highly successful while others underperformed. The most effective alliances excelled in multiple ways: they understood whom to collaborate with, what was needed to accelerate progress, and how to mobilize collective action. Based on our research, we identified ten key success factors for building a high-impact corporate-led sustainability alliance.

The Alliance Advantage

Compared with partnerships and business ecosystems, corporate-led sustainability alliances can bring together a much broader range of stakeholders: not just businesses and suppliers, but also regulators, policymakers, the social sector, customers, competitors, academics, and researchers. Led by corporations, they galvanize stakeholders to address the most complex sustainability challenges—societal or environmental—that also have significant implications for their businesses. We see three primary motivations for companies engaging in collective action through alliances (see Figure 24.1).

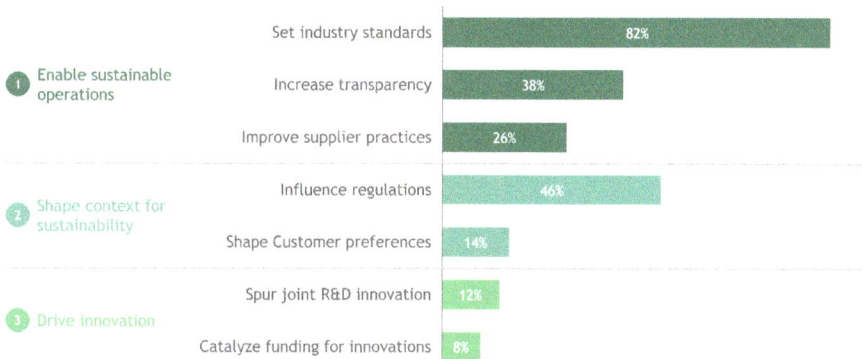

Source: BHI analysis
Note: N = 50.

Figure 24.1: Three motivations for collective action through alliances.

– Alliances enable more sustainable operations by setting industry standards, increasing data transparency across value chains, and improving supplier practices.
– They allow companies to shape the sustainability landscape by collectively influencing regulation and shaping customer preferences.
– They drive innovation by spurring joint research and development and mobilizing capital investments around emerging solutions to shared sustainability challenges.

To build a high-impact alliance, companies must collaborate with the right stakeholders, drive the process forward effectively, and mobilize action that delivers meaningful benefits by targeting root causes of the environmental or societal issue. The frontrunners are doing just that by taking ten crucial actions.

Ten Factors for Success

Whether companies are carefully constructing a portfolio of alliances to achieve sustainability goals, or they're already engaging in existing alliances, it's critical that they maximize their return on investment.

In our study of more than 50 corporate-led sustainability alliances, approximately 30% were able to address root causes to deliver at-scale social and environmental benefits. The remaining 70% were either focused on mitigating negative societal and environmental impacts without addressing root causes or targeting root causes but not yet able to scale their initiatives. And of those alliances that have a real impact, half are more than 15 years old—demonstrating that it takes time for an alliance to become a truly effective vehicle for collective action.

Our analysis of CSA leaders versus the laggards pointed to ten key actions that helped them outperform their peers—and that we group under three umbrellas: who, what, and how (see Figure 24.2).

Think Strategically About Who You Collaborate With

It's important for companies to think carefully about the types of organizations that should be included in the alliance and what value they bring. While a corporate-led sustainability alliance will always be led by business priorities, it should include a variety of stakeholders, including suppliers, regulators, policymakers, nongovernmental organizations (NGOs), customers, competitors, academics, and independent experts. Specifically, high-impact alliances adhere to the following actions.

Start with highly committed market leaders as champions. Corporate-led sustainability alliances founded by a group of market leaders (at least two members of the Fortune Global 500) were 1.7 times more likely to achieve impact at scale. Market leaders have sufficient scale and market power to credibly signal to the broader ecosystem the level of commitment to change and materially shift the incentives of stakeholders outside the alliance. This is particularly important for alliances focused on sustainability issues that span multiple industries, such as ending deforestation.

In 2002, Danone, Nestlé, and Unilever created what would become the Sustainable Agriculture Initiative Platform as a precompetitive space for collaboration and knowledge sharing in the food and drink industry. Today it has more than 150 mem-

WHO you collaborate with

1. Start with highly-committed market leaders as champions
2. Actively engage members across the chain
3. Enlist external experts with deep capabilities and knowledge

WHAT you do

4. Establish industry norms and principles, supported by operating standards and metrics
5. Create data transparency across value chains
6. Drive innovative solutions
7. Take a proactive stance toward business diplomacy

HOW you mobilize

8. Build trust among members and partners
9. Invest in a dedicated secretariat
10. Measure and report progress against

Percentage (%) of CSA's achieving scaled impact on root causes

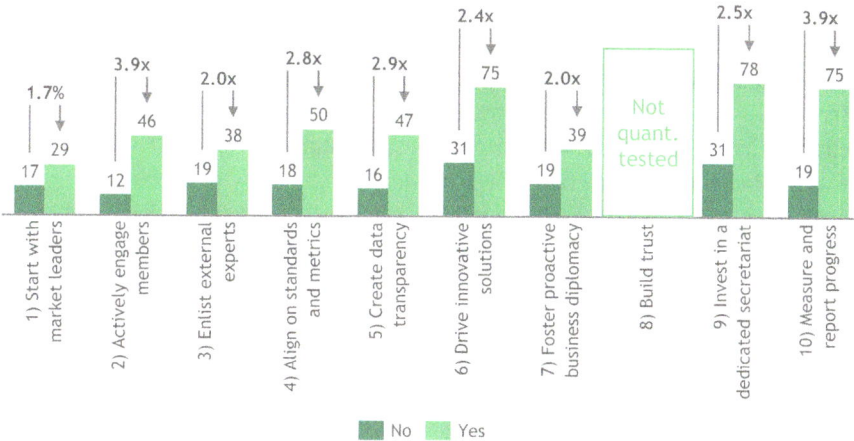

Source: BHI analysis.

Figure 24.2: Ten success factors for high-impact corporate collective action. that make achieving scaled impact significantly more likely.

bers, including farmer co-ops, manufacturers, processors, and retailers, working together to advance sustainable agriculture[3] practices and pilot innovative projects.

Actively engage members across the value chain. Corporate-led sustainability alliances that include a broad set of value chain participants—and that ensure members across the value chain are represented and engaged in decision-making

---

3 https://www.bcg.com/capabilities/social-impact/food-systems-food-security.

forums, such as boards and executive committees—are four times more likely to achieve impact at scale. Inclusive and engaged membership ensures greater buy-in to the alliance's activities, which is particularly important for alliances that need to change standard ways of operating up and down the industry's value chain. It's important to prioritize the value chain segments that have the greatest role to play in addressing shared sustainability challenges.

For example, the Initiative for Responsible Mining Assurance (IRMA) set a comprehensive global standard that covers all mined materials (except energy fuels) for industrial mines around the world. It is governed equitably by a wide variety of stakeholders, including the mining industry,[4] downstream purchasers, finance and investors, NGOs, affected communities, and organized labor—all of which have equal board representation and equal decision-making authority (so that the interests of any one given stakeholder group cannot override IRMA's members' collective interests). This was critical given IRMA's primary focus on creating a global standard that required buy-in from across the value chain to ensure adoption and drive critical mass. As an example of the growing impact of IRMA's "Standard for Responsible Mining," several leading auto companies, including Mercedes-Benz,[5] committed their intention to source lithium and cobalt for battery cells only from IRMA-audited mining sites in the future.

Enlist external expertise. Corporate-led sustainability alliances that engage cross-sector partners with deep expertise, such as academic researchers and third-party certification organizations, to support key activities of the alliance were two times more likely to create impact at scale. These experts serve as accountability partners and provide external legitimacy. This is particularly important for alliances that undertake joint research projects, ensure verification of supply chain programs, or enable data sharing.

The Tire Industry Project (TIP), which covers more than 60% of the world's tire manufacturing capacity, is a global forum for the tire industry on sustainability issues. TIP coordinates a global team of industry experts and scientists to ensure its projects maintain a high level of scientific integrity, quality, and accountability. This research group, led by an industry board—with guidance from an assurance group of independent scientists—helps objectively focus the alliance's research agenda toward the highest impact topic areas in the industry and helps build greater alignment across members.

---

4 https://www.bcg.com/industries/industrial-goods/metals-mining.
5 https://group-media.mercedes-benz.com/marsMediaSite/en/instance/ko/Mercedes-Benz-will-in-future-only-source-battery-cells-with-cobalt–lithium-from-certified-mining-sites-while-signifi cantly-reducing-cobalt.xhtml?oid=48096119.

Focus Alliance on Activities that Drive Impact

BCG Henderson Institute research found that high-impact corporate-led sustainability alliances are action-oriented, transparent with data, focused on innovative solutions, and willing to engage with regulators and government leaders to shape the sustainability agenda. Specifically:

Establish industry norms and principles. Alliances that create alignment around robust operating standards, supported by detailed metrics and reporting protocols, are 2.7 times more likely to create impact at scale. It's not enough to establish high-level guiding principles; they must be translated into clear product or operating standards, supported by measurement methodologies and regular progress reports.

The Poseidon Principles, an initiative of the Global Maritime Forum, established a common, global framework to quantitatively assess and disclose whether signatory financial institutions' marine lending portfolios are aligned with UN climate goals. This framework translates high-level principles into a clear accountability mechanism to ensure lending decisions promote international shipping's decarbonization.

Create data transparency. Alliances that create data transparency for members, as well as external stakeholders, are three times more likely to create impact at scale. Data transparency allows alliance members to monitor their progress toward sustainability targets and build a culture of accountability. This involves fostering alignment on the most important metrics, establishing strict data definitions, and developing tools and platforms to seamlessly collect data from stakeholders.

The Sustainable Apparel Coalition, a global, multistakeholder alliance for the fashion industry, collaborated with more than 250 global members and stakeholders to develop and launch the Higg Index—a core suite of tools to measure and assess sustainability performance in a standardized way. The Higg Index allows companies to assess the social and environmental performance of their value chain and publicly disclose the environmental impacts of their products to consumers in a comprehensive and credible way. The user base includes more than 21,000 organizations across 119 countries, with membership covering approximately 40% of the apparel, footwear, and home textiles industry.

Drive innovative solutions. Corporate-led sustainability alliances that drive innovation by participating in collaborative R&D and directing capital towards sustainability solutions are 2.5 times more likely to have significant potential to create impact at scale. This is especially important for alliances in hard-to-abate sectors since they typically require substantial technical innovation to achieve climate goals. Alliances should take a portfolio approach to ensure innovation focuses on near-term and long-term sustainability solutions. From the outset, the organization will need to rigorously ensure members' intellectual property is appropriately protected. When mobilizing capital, alliances should seek out broader support beyond just financial contributions to leverage members' capabilities, such as mentorship, expert advisors, access to labs and facilities, and pilot opportunities.

The Oil & Gas Climate Initiative (OGCI) launched a $1 billion innovation fund investing in technologies and projects that accelerate decarbonization across the energy, industrial, commercial buildings, and transport sectors. OGCI members support commercial adoption by launching pilots and investing in promising new technologies. OGCI Climate Investments has made 24 climate investments to reduce methane emissions, reduce carbon dioxide emissions, and support carbon capture, utilization, and storage solutions.

Take a proactive stance toward business diplomacy. Corporate-led sustainability alliances that proactively shape the regulatory and policy environment for greater sustainability and business advantage are 2.1 times more likely to create impact at scale. This is particularly true when members can't reach their climate goals without public sector investment and greater regulatory certainty.

In 2021, the Global Maritime Forum called on governments to establish the necessary policies and investments to decarbonize international shipping by 2050. More than 230 signatories urged governments to support industrial-scale, zero-emissions shipping projects and deliver policy measures that will make zero-emissions shipping the default choice by 2030.

Understand How to Mobilize Collective Action

The most successful corporate-led sustainability alliances put the right elements in place to foster collaboration and get results. They build a culture of trust, dedicate resources to a secretariat, and continually monitor progress against their impact strategy. Specifically:

Build trust. High-impact alliances spend meaningful time up front establishing a culture of trust[6] among members, as well as with external partners. This can best be achieved by developing a set of shared values, finding ways to create mutual benefit for all participants, and ensuring that leaders of the alliance proactively address any emerging issues. The most influential members of the alliance must demonstrate early on that they are clearly aligned and fully committed to the mission. As trust continues to rise over time, the alliance requires lower

---

6 https://www.bcg.com/publications/2021/building-trust-in-business-ecosystems.

levels of orchestration. Each participant influences and is affected by the others, creating an increasingly strong alliance that can sustain itself in the long run.

Create a dedicated secretariat. Corporate-led sustainability alliances led by dedicated secretariats staffed by professional teams with the strategic capabilities to deliver are 2.5 times more likely to achieve impact at scale. The secretariat should facilitate the alliance's activities and will require specialized skills, particularly with regard to driving innovation, establishing industry standards, and improving suppliers' sustainability practices.

The Roundtable on Sustainable Biomaterials (RSB) has a lean secretariat with staff who oversee the development, promotion, and implementation of the RSB standard. Staff members are aligned to specific sectors across aviation, energy, ground transport, chemicals and polymers, and textiles and fibers, with deep expertise in their specific sectors.

Measure and report progress against a clear impact strategy. Corporate-led sustainability alliances that have a comprehensive impact strategy (also known as a theory of change) and continually track progress toward achieving long-term outcomes are four times more likely to create impact at scale. An impact strategy allows alliances to align members on key priorities, routinely test and measure progress toward goals, and demonstrate value to members and external stakeholders.

The Roundtable on Responsible Soy is developing a detailed impact strategy around six long-term objectives, accompanied by short-term and mid-term compliance indicators for soy companies. The indicators focus on core environmental and social issues, such as soil conservation, biodiversity, work safety, and human rights, allowing the alliance to track impact and report progress to members and external stakeholders.

Today's sustainability challenges require collective action to bring about system-level change. Corporate-led sustainability alliances are becoming increasingly common, particularly in hard-to-abate sectors, as companies recognize that there's a limit to how much progress they can make within the walls of their own organization.

As companies embark on their sustainability transformation,[7] they need to understand how to get the most out of existing alliances—and recognize when it's time to join or create new alliances. By applying the ten success factors we've just described, companies can engage collective action to improve the common good and unlock new sources of competitive advantage.

---

7 https://www.bcg.com/publications/2021/steps-to-a-sustainability-transformation.

Part 4: **Conclusion**

Martin Reeves and David Young
25 Winning Through the Great Climate Upheaval

Societal and economic progress is not evenly paced. For long periods of time, the configuration of economic relations doesn't change much, and progress comprises incremental innovation and piecemeal change. But every few generations, the economy fundamentally reconfigures due to a deep social, geopolitical, or technological disruption. The great technology revolutions are good examples of this, where the pattern of production and consumption were successively changed beyond recognition by the advent of first steam power, then electricity, electronics, and most recently the Internet. But such events are not exclusively technological. Other system-wide dislocations occurred as the result of political or societal changes, such as the Enlightenment or the Renaissance.

At such times, there is pervasive and deep change that creates disadvantage for many enterprises and advantage for some. Take, for example, the Internet revolution, which started with the "mother of all demonstration"[1] in 1968 and triggered the proliferation of new technology companies, the rethinking of business models across sectors, a wave of brutal competitive disruption, and a complete reshaping of the league table of businesses. The big banks and oil companies were replaced within a decade by technology platform businesses. The turnover of winners and losers becomes much harsher at such times.

We are now at such an inflection point driven by climate change. This is a different type of change, not driven primarily by a new technology or a social change, although these will certainly be evident too, but rather by impending ecological limits. The impacts and responses from companies and investors are already beginning to be felt across industries and geographies, within value chains and on store shelves. The massive consequences of insufficient action and their imminence create a huge driving force for change. Products and entire companies risk obsolescence driven by displacement from end products no longer necessary.

If we imagine any version of an economy that had halted or reversed climate change, it would be profoundly different in almost every respect. From energy, through housing, the design of cities, transportation, distribution, materials and infrastructure to taxation and accounting. We are already seeing smart money and entrepreneurs pouring into climate technologies. In virtually every sector there is a race to discover new business models that deliver climate-wise products

---

1 https://www.youtube.com/watch?v=B6rKUf9DWRI&t=1s.

https://doi.org/10.1515/9783111295268-026

and services, that profit from less energy, fewer virgin inputs and higher circularity and are informed by a new sense of what is ethical or desirable. We already see fortunes being made by pioneers like Tesla, dislocating incumbents and creating massive new market value at a surprising pace.

For companies to avoid becoming a victim of creative destruction and to survive and flourish, they need to adopt a mentality and ways of innovating and operating very different from the ones that dominate in more stable times. They need to behave more like pioneer species in a disturbed forest ecosystem, quickly filling gaps, growing rapidly to avoid being shaded out by other plants, and adopting a so-called r-type reproductive strategy, creating many seeds and dispersing them widely, even though few will succeed in becoming established.

For companies to survive and thrive through these ecosystem disturbances and resets, there are six practices that improve the odds.

Adopting an Opportunity Mindset

Every constraint for an incumbent player becomes an opportunity to a pioneer. COVID provides an instructive example of this,[2] albeit on a smaller scale of change. COVID reshaped not just the level but also the pattern of demand in even the hardest hit sectors. In each sector there were clear winners and losers, and winners were consistently focused on opportunities for differential growth by exploiting these new opportunities rather than only on mitigating short-term health, logistical and financial constraints.

Relaxing Boundaries

Traditionally the units of analysis for business are the company and the industry. Bruce Henderson, BCG's founder, proposed the rule of 3 and 4, observing that in each industry three volume players make money and their market shares usually approximated to the ratios of 4:2:1. The trick he observed was in determining the natural boundaries of competition. Pervasive disruptions reshape boundaries, disadvantaging those companies that have a fixed idea about the structure and scope of their industry. The last pervasive disruption of the Internet did much to

---

2 https://bcghendersoninstitute.com/how-resilient-businesses-created-advantage-in-adversity-during-covid-19/.

blur the boundaries between industries and even companies, with the rise of horizontal digital ecosystems. We expect the great climate upheaval to have the same effect.

Embracing Urgency

Forecasted adoption rates from renewables to electric vehicles significantly underestimated the actual rates at which these technologies have penetrated the market and the compounding and cascading changes that followed. Using the same incremental processes of innovation and scaling that worked well in more stable times is unlikely to keep pace with the rapid pace of competitive change. To win requires comfort with rapid cycles of innovation, release, scaling, and learning.

Relaxing Assumptions About What is Possible

In stable times, companies are mainly focused on the factual and the evidenced. When disturbance requires that new to the world ideas are conceived and realized, data and prevailing wisdom about what is possible or most effective can impede this. Conventional wisdom dictated it takes five to ten years to develop and launch a vaccine, but the urgency of COVID pushed Pfizer to realize this within a year, as described in Albert Bourla's book *Moonshot*. As Nelson Mandela said, "It always seems impossible until it is done."

Rebalancing Performance With Future Option Value

In stable times companies relentlessly optimize their current business models. But in times of upheaval future option value becomes proportionally more important and incremental optimization is less likely to deliver long-term performance. Rather, a higher rate of experimentation and comfort in acting before everything is fully worked out become necessary. That requires comfort with rapid cycles of innovation, trial, and scaling—often reaching beyond the capacities inside the walls of today's businesses.

Focusing on Reimagining the Business for New Circumstances

A mental model of how a business or an industry works is a choice, not a fact. But this is hard to see, if a company's thoughts and actions are highly converged and grounded in an optimized, historically successful model. In addition, when new ideas are surfaced it can be hard to distinguish the novel but implausible from the merely unfamiliar. The success of pioneers is often grounded in a culture and practices that facilitate imagination.[3]

Imagination "games"[4] can help this process of reimagination. By creating opportunities to playfully recombine and explore ideas, the prison of conventional wisdom can be prized open. Play is necessary since the process needs to be curiosity driven, counter-factually based, and free from fear of being wrong. Here we exemplify two of the 16 games we describe in The Imagination Machine[5] for this purpose.

In the maverick game, participants attempt to see the world through the eyes of companies that are making a very different bet on the future from their own. First, the company's own bet on the future—the essence of their business model —is codified. Then based on this a list of mavericks is created, from within and beyond the industry and the essence of their bets codified. Then follows an exercise in elaborating the consequences of each maverick bet being the right one. Finally, participants stand back and articulate the implied opportunity from their expanded perspective.

In the friction game, participants generate ideas by focusing on the most logical places for disruptors to focus, even if no such disruptors are yet visible. These are the points of economic friction—places where misunderstanding, mismatching of needs, transaction costs, rework, and the like are significant. For the next upheaval, this can be narrowed to frictions resulting from climate change either intrinsic to the customer's own business model or constraints that your business model imposes on them. Then follows an exercise of roughly ranking these points of friction and for the biggest ones, ideating on how these could be preemptively reimagined if the company's future depended upon doing so.

Conversely, a poor strategy for developing advantage during upheaval is to be stuck in an incremental and status quo mindset, particularly easy now during the race to announce climate targets and demonstrate compliance to ESG metrics.

---

3 https://bcghendersoninstitute.com/competing-on-imagination/.
4 https://bcghendersoninstitute.com/the-playful-corporation/.
5 https://theimaginationmachine.org/.

Compliance will rapidly become a matter of hygiene not advantage. Advantage will involve creating what does not currently exist, not optimizing or constraining what does. It will not come from focusing energy on compliance with emissions reductions goals, but instead by reconceiving the business to surpass them. A deductive mindset can create a similar snare by reasoning towards well-founded solutions based upon what we know, rather than testing new ideas and questioning the very fundamentals underpinning today's business model.

Companies that follow these principles can individually survive and outcompete their rivals in times of upheaval. Unleashing the forces of creative disruption has a more subtle collective benefit too however, relative to the alternative of relying only on top down, monolithic mechanisms like economy wide regulations, norms, and best practices. Competing for the future involves innovation. One of the characteristics of the climate challenge is that we don't have all the answers we need. Generating new answers is an essential part of the solution. Furthermore, a variety of solutions compete for relevance, and competitive pressures speed this process up. The granularity of solutions using such a decentralized approach will also better fit the varied needs of a complex economy. Competition is also dynamic, with new solutions continually emerging from an ever-changing situation, as opposed to regulatory solutions that are inevitably more static in nature. Fundamentally, however, by focusing on benefits rather than on compliance and constraints we create the motive force for the system to perform and have a higher likelihood that the end state is not simply a more constrained or expensive version of the status quo but is actually better.

In summary, we are entering a period of deep and broad upheaval created by climate change, where the biggest winners and contributors will be determined by their ability to compete on imagination, rather than their ability to comply with constraints.

Martin Reeves, Madeleine Michael, and David Young

26 New Abundance: Resource Constraints as Strategic Opportunities

Since the Industrial Revolution, we've lived in an economic system predicated on high growth. For the past 20 years, that growth has relied on an abundance of capital and other external resources and has benefited from tailwinds like global economic integration. Today, however, that model is at risk—we can see the limits of resource abundance encroaching on multiple timescales. The acute constraints we've experienced since the COVID pandemic began, including supply chain disruption, declining workforce availability, and energy shortages, are slowing the rebound to normal rates of growth. Furthermore, slower rebound can be an early warning indicator[1] of deeper systemic change, in this case signaling an era of protracted scarcity of labor, capital, and natural resources that will make growth harder and require new strategies.

This new scarcity could threaten the successful business models of today's large companies, which are built on virtually unlimited access to resources such as labor, raw materials, and energy.

But threats to current business models need not threaten business itself, so long as firms embrace new constraints, leverage them to advantage, and perhaps, in the process, uncover new sources of abundance. Recall Michael Porter's "The Competitive Advantage of Nations" in *Harvard Business Review,*[2] which argues that a nation's competitive advantages sometimes stem precisely from those areas with the tightest bounds. Japan, for example, pioneered lean production techniques in part because it was a mountainous island nation with very little excess land. Singapore is another example of a prosperous but highly resource-constrained economy.

These constraint-related advantages may include more integrated approaches to sustainability, new types of resource efficiency, and innovation around new inputs. They may also include more radical approaches such as de-materialization or an emphasis on well-being over physical production and consumption. Ultimately, the ability to navigate this environment can be a significant competitive differentiator, giving rise to a new set of models for thriving in a new context.

---

1 https://www.nature.com/articles/nature08227.
2 https://hbr.org/1990/03/the-competitive-advantage-of-nations.

https://doi.org/10.1515/9783111295268-027

The End of Abundance?

Three major global trends are driving resource scarcity for businesses:

– First, capital is becoming less abundant as interest rates rise, ending a two-decade streak of nearly free capital. In the medium term, interest rates are projected to settle well above the near-zero levels of the past 20 years.[3] Also, the tailwind of global economic integration has played out.

– Second, pandemic-induced labor shortages are merely a prelude to more widespread and persistent labor scarcity. Compounding pandemic-related shortages, the WEF estimates that, by 2025, half of all workers globally will need to reskill to meet changing labor demands.[4] And the long-term challenge of population aging and decline will take hold in the coming years; the UN reports that two-thirds of the global population already live in countries with births below the replacement rate.[5] Migration[6] into those countries is likely the only way to prevent population decline.

– Third, the supply chain woes of recent months are also merely harbingers of more persistent resource depletion, scarcity, or price increases. Resource scarcity is already apparent for some inputs like water, which the WWF says will be insufficient for two-thirds of the world's population by 2025.[7] Depletion of other inputs, including many chemical elements, may occur within the century, including 12 chemical elements.[8] Further, as planetary challenges push countries to begin pricing in externalities like climate change, current business models will likely come under pressure even before depletion is fully apparent.

For businesses, it will become harder and harder to find easy growth by relying on traditional notions of abundance. Instead, businesses will need to innovate to create new types of abundance, whether that comprises novel sources of talent or new types of input to create offerings with fewer harmful externalities.

---

3 https://fred.stlouisfed.org/graph/?id=TB3MS.

4 https://www.weforum.org/reports/the-future-of-jobs-report-2020/digest.

5 https://www.un.org/development/desa/pd/sites/www.un.org.development.desa.pd/files/wpp2022_summary_of_results.pdf.

6 https://www.weforum.org/agenda/2022/11/5-key-predictions-for-the-future-of-talent-migration/.

7 https://www.worldwildlife.org/threats/water-scarcity.

8 https://www.weforum.org/agenda/2022/09/endangered-elements-at-risk/.

Prosperity Without Easy Growth

Farsighted leaders will counter the global boundary-tightening trends by rethinking business models to navigate and even exploit scarcity in the short term and to find new abundance in the long. This will require leaders to take various strategic actions on different time horizons.

Today, adapt your market positioning and your stance on innovation to mitigate and exploit scarcity to your advantage. These actions will be familiar to most companies from other contexts. The challenge will be to take sufficient action, with sufficient speed.

– **Reposition for growth.** In each economic crisis, demand patterns shift, and winning formulae for growth change. Even in times of low aggregate growth within a sector or an entire economy, there is always growth somewhere, so reposition into product and market segments that are growing. The 2008 financial crisis significantly shifted demand patterns. So did COVID-19, which significantly increased consumer appetite for digital shopping and consumption. Dell had done big business selling desktop computers to companies. But when the pandemic hit and work-from-home materialized, companies no longer wanted desktops; instead, they had an increased need for laptops for their employees. Dell was able to capitalize on the shift[9] and is now better positioned to support enduring changes in the pattern of work. Now, an impending crisis of scarcity is priming consumers to shift their demands toward sustainable and long-lasting products, as well as to experience and entertainment services.

– **Expand talent access.** Adapt your talent strategy for advantage today and tomorrow. Create a "bionic organization" by focusing human talent where it is needed most, in areas requiring imagination, empathy, or ethics, and leveraging AI where it is especially adept. Further, broaden your talent search, in order to find the best talent and the freshest perspectives. Expand the search at home by developing upskilling or reskilling capabilities[10] to support evolving talent needs and reach underrepresented populations. For example, Amazon must rely on nontraditional IT and tech workers to staff its rural data centers, so they train talent by partnering with local community colleges to create purpose-built vocational programs.[11]

---

9 https://bcghendersoninstitute.com/how-resilient-businesses-created-advantage-in-adversity-during-covid-19/.
10 https://hbr.org/2022/04/6-strategies-to-upskill-your-workforce.
11 https://www.aboutamazon.com/news/aws/in-rural-oregon-aws-data-centers-change-lives.

Expand supply by making your talent search global, and by creating a culture and a structure that support borderless collaboration. Africa and South America will have the most population growth in the next century and will therefore be potential sources of labor. Start building an international culture in your company now. Rakuten,[12] a Japan-based e-commerce firm, made the transition early and mandated in 2010 that the company become English-first, in order to become globally relevant. The transition took two years, but the company reaped the rewards, growing revenues from $3.9 billion in 2010 to $15.3 billion in 2021.

– **Build resilient supply systems.** We know from physics that there are often early warning signs of critical phase transitions (such as collapses) in complex systems. The signs include increased variance and a slowing down of the return to normal after disturbance. We have seen both occur in supply systems during the COVID pandemic, requiring a more holistic approach to enterprise resilience. For example, Totino's faced a rotating list of ingredient shortages for its frozen snack, so the company developed a modular set of 25 recipes[13] that allowed it to continue producing despite such shortages. Diversity (in this case of recipes) is one of the six principles that form the pillars of system resilience.

Adaptability, another pillar of resilience, can be very valuable in adjusting production capacity in volatile markets. This is relevant in all businesses—even in aluminum smelting, with its notoriously inflexible manufacturing systems. For example, TRIMET, a German aluminum producer, invested in new technology to allow its smelters to vary energy consumption and aluminum production by up to 25%[14] in either direction (compared with the usual range of 5 percent). This allows TRIMET to adjust consumption to produce at off-peak hours, saving money and energy. In the new volatile and resource-constrained context, companies will have even more reason to tap into each of the six biological principles for creating resilient systems:[15] diversity and adaptability, discussed above, as well as redundancy, modularity, prudence, and embeddedness.

In the medium term, find new abundance through innovation and by making environmental sustainability a durable competitive advantage. It's a challenging task—currently, only 20% of businesses even claim to be able to accomplish it—but it has the power to create true differentiation.[16]

---

12 bcg-when-innovation-has-no-borders-culture-is-key-jun-2022-r2.pdf.

13 https://www.nytimes.com/2022/08/31/business/totinos-pizza-rolls-ingredients.html.

14 https://www.bcg.com/publications/2021/benefits-of-becoming-electricity-trader.

15 https://hbr.org/2020/07/a-guide-to-building-a-more-resilient-business.

16 https://www.bcg.com/publications/2021/keys-to-being-a-leader-in-sustainable-business-model-innovation.

– **Innovate for growth.** A stagnating industry or economy is not a death sentence for an individual company. If you can't find growth passively, make it happen. To that end, innovate to defy the industry average growth rate. In scarcity-constrained, low-growth environments, innovation becomes more important as companies compete more viciously for limited resources. By creating offerings using new inputs and business models, innovators can find reprieve and new abundance.

– **Practice disciplined innovation.** Continued evolution in technology, shifting economics of input resources, and demands for more sustainable business models require innovation at the very same time that an elevated cost of capital makes it more expensive. A new, more disciplined approach to innovation is therefore necessary. One such approach would be the adoption of "co-ambidexterity,"[17] wherein the assumed tradeoff between exploration and exploitation is broken. Customer interactions are mined more effectively to identify and shape emerging preferences with shorter learning cycles and more targeted innovation.

– **Leverage "sustainability scarcity."** When many companies simultaneously attempt to shift to environmentally sustainable and renewable materials, a new (more temporary) scarcity takes hold in the market for sustainable goods.[18] Build advantage by getting one step ahead of such cascading shortages; embrace the bottleneck, and then work to help solve it for yourself and your industry. Do this either by securing your own supply of sustainable materials, as both Coca-Cola and Pepsi have done through investments in recycled plastic R&D and infrastructure, or by contributing to the formation of sustainable resource markets by advocating for advantageous policy, investing in early innovation, or forming coalitions to address supply chain constraints.

– **Build sustainable business models.** Business leaders must reinvent business models so that companies can thrive even as consumers and governments become more concerned with preventing degradation to the planetary systems that support life. We find that the most successful sustainable business model innovators have reimagined their core business models[19] around new environmental, societal, and financial priorities, rather than simply adding sustainability as a separate consideration. There are many archetypal strategic moves that businesses can make to transform current business models into sustainable ones, including own-

---

17 https://bcghendersoninstitute.com/co-ambidexterity-a-framework-for-winning-in-a-new-era-of-competition/.
18 https://www.bcg.com/publications/2021/how-to-tackle-resource-scarcity.
19 https://www.bcg.com/publications/2021/four-strategies-for-sustainable-business-model-innovation.

ing the origins, owning the whole cycle, expanding societal value, expanding value chains, innovating in ecosystems, relocalizing or regionalizing, energizing the brand, and building bridges across sectors.

For example, Cotopaxi made a name for itself in the outdoor gear market with its colorful bags and clothing by expanding societal value, energizing the brand, and expanding value chains. The zany, mismatched fabric combinations come from the company philosophy of using fabric scraps from other, bigger bags. The company made sustainability and waste reduction synonymous with its brand, and in doing so found market success with a model that minimizes the raw inputs required.

In the long term, prepare for a world where material growth may be severely constrained in aggregate. The growth hockey stick, which began with the Industrial Revolution and created modern business and society, cannot continue indefinitely for reasons of both simple arithmetic and ecological sustainability. We currently have few answers as to how continued prosperity can be reconciled with these escalating constraints. But we can reasonably suppose that the path forward will involve both reducing the material intensity of production and consumption and realigning economic value with what we as humans will value in a resource-constrained future.

– **Stop relying on material growth.** Dematerialize your product offering by taking "reduce, reuse, recycle" to the next level; embracing the service and experience underpinning product offerings; or innovating in the digital realm. Selfridges, the British department store, set a goal of having half of its customer transactions based on resale, repair, rentals, or reuse by 2030.[20] This benefits customers, who will have more options for engagement with the brand, and Selfridges, which will create durable business lines with lower material intensity. Importantly, it will also benefit Earth.

When it comes to experience, luxury clothing brands are also pioneers. The luxury sneaker brand Golden Goose differentiates itself in a crowded space by promising the highest level of shoe repair.[21] It fits the company's brand of quality shoes that are built to last and creates an immaterial business arm and differentiator. Another tack that luxury fashion brands could lead is expansion into the metaverse; Morgan Stanley projected in 2021 that luxury fashion in the

---

20 https://www.theguardian.com/business/2022/sep/02/selfridges-wants-half-of-transactions-to-be-resale-repair-rental-or-refills-by-2030.
21 https://www.nytimes.com/2022/07/09/style/golden-goose-sneaker-repair.html.

metaverse could be a $50 billion industry by 2030.[22] Whatever method a business takes to dematerialize, the result is both lower cost and a decoupling of revenue from scarcity-induced instability.

– **Change your metric for success.** Become a company that experiments with its metrics for success. Daniel Leventhal, a leading thinker in corporate strategy, posits that leaders might reimagine corporate exploration as experimentation with new metrics of performance.[23] As we value more and more our shared context, it is logical that we will measure and manage it with new metrics that reflect this. The proliferation of ESG and impact investing firms resulted in an abundance of success metrics from which to choose, though at the highest level the goal of a company must of course be dictated by its values. At the level of a nation or society, we could also change our goals. We could, for example, adopt inclusive well-being as an umbrella goal. Or we could adopt inclusive wealth, which is a macroeconomic concept that includes natural capital and human capital, in addition to the more familiar production capital. The United States plans to start publishing inclusive wealth metrics, alongside GDP, within the next few years.[24] Such a development would naturally have implications for how companies are taxed and regulated, and therefore how they ought to measure success. Some companies are already experimenting with different ways of measuring value. Everytable, a fast-casual food chain and delivery service, uses economies of scale and central kitchens to beat competitor prices for healthy meals. The company also uses a variable pricing model to reach disadvantaged neighborhoods, capturing customers in more areas precisely because it prioritizes fighting food insecurity as part of the business model.

Ultimately, it will be the companies that use these new cascading constraints to their advantage that will succeed by creating new abundance.

---

22 https://www.reuters.com/technology/metaverse-50-bln-revenue-opportunity-luxury-ms-2021-11-16/.

23 https://academic.oup.com/book/42112/chapter-abstract/356126842?redirectedFrom=fulltext&login=false.

24 https://www.economist.com/united-states/2022/09/15/the-biden-administration-aims-to-quantify-the-costs-of-ecological-decay.

List of Figures

https://doi.org/10.1515/9783111295268-028

Index

https://doi.org/10.1515/9783111295268-029